FRACTURE AND FRAGMENTATION IN BRITISH ROMANTICISM

What associates fragmentation with Romanticism? In this book, Alexander Regier explains how fracture and fragmentation form a lens through which some central concerns of Romanticism can be analysed in a particularly effective way. These categories also supply a critical framework for a discussion of fundamental issues concerning language and thought in the period. Over the course of the volume, Regier discusses fracture and fragmentation thematically and structurally, offering new readings of Wordsworth, Kant, Burke, Keats, and De Quincey, as well as analysing central intellectual presuppositions of the period. He also highlights Romanticism's importance for contemporary scholarship, especially in the writings of Benjamin and de Man. More generally, Regier's discussion of fragmentation exposes a philosophical problem that lies behind the definition of Romanticism.

ALEXANDER REGIER is Assistant Professor of English at Rice University.

CAMBRIDGE STUDIES IN ROMANTICISM

Founding editor
PROFESSOR MARILYN BUTLER, *University of Oxford*

General editor
PROFESSOR JAMES CHANDLER, *University of Chicago*

Editorial Board
JOHN BARRELL, *University of York*
PAUL HAMILTON, *University of London*
MARY JACOBUS, *University of Cambridge*
CLAUDIA JOHNSON, *Princeton University*
ALAN LIU, *University of California, Santa Barbara*
JEROME MCGANN, *University of Virginia*
SUSAN MANNING, *University of Edinburgh*
DAVID SIMPSON, *University of California, Davis*

This series aims to foster the best new work in one of the most challenging fields within English literary studies. From the early 1780s to the early 1830s a formidable array of talented men and women took to literary composition, not just in poetry, which some of them famously transformed, but in many modes of writing. The expansion of publishing created new opportunities for writers, and the political stakes of what they wrote were raised again by what Wordsworth called those 'great national events' that were 'almost daily taking place': the French Revolution, the Napoleonic and American wars, urbanisation, industrialisation, religious revival, an expanded empire abroad and the reform movement at home. This was an enormous ambition, even when it pretended otherwise. The relations between science, philosophy, religion and literature were reworked in texts such as *Frankenstein* and *Biographia Literaria*; gender relations in *A Vindication of the Rights of Woman* and *Don Juan*; journalism by Cobbett and Hazlitt; poetic form, content and style by the Lake School and the Cockney School. Outside Shakespeare studies, probably no body of writing has produced such a wealth of comment or done so much to shape the responses of modern criticism. This indeed is the period that saw the emergence of those notions of 'literature' and of literary history, especially national literary history, on which modern scholarship in English has been founded.

The categories produced by Romanticism have also been challenged by recent historicist arguments. The task of the series is to engage both with a challenging corpus of Romantic writings and with the changing field of criticism they have helped to shape. As with other literary series published by Cambridge, this one will represent the work of both younger and more established scholars, on either side of the Atlantic and elsewhere.

For a complete list of titles published see end of book.

FRACTURE AND FRAGMENTATION IN BRITISH ROMANTICISM

ALEXANDER REGIER

CAMBRIDGE UNIVERSITY PRESS
Cambridge, New York, Melbourne, Madrid, Cape Town, Singapore,
São Paulo, Delhi, Dubai, Tokyo

Cambridge University Press
The Edinburgh Building, Cambridge CB2 8RU, UK

Published in the United States of America by Cambridge University Press, New York

www.cambridge.org
Information on this title: www.cambridge.org/9780521509671

© Alexander Regier 2010

First published 2010

Printed in the United Kingdom at the University Press, Cambridge

A catalogue record for this publication is available from the British Library

ISBN 978-0-521-50967-1 Hardback

Contents

v

Acknowledgements

This book wants to begin by giving thanks to individuals, groups, and institutions without whose support it would have been impossible to write it. The work on this project has gone through several stages, many marked by moments of deep confusion. Luckily, I found a great number of people who were, and still are, willing to discuss, fight over, and share the insights that living such moments can give us. Some of these people I want to mention individually here. Mary Jacobus, a truly generous thinker, has been both the most critical and the most supportive reader of the following pages. I am immensely grateful to her for sharing her insights and helpful advice. Peter de Bolla has been a deeply inspiring presence for me, especially as an uncompromising colleague and friend: his ability to ask questions kept the wider ambitions of this project alive. Paul Hamilton is unsurpassed in his most intelligent and unassuming knowingness: I flatter myself when I think of him as a fellow Romantic. Marjorie Levinson is a truly amazing colleague; her sharpness, precision, and generosity have made her more important than she would ever like to admit. Simon Jarvis's clarity and exactness of criticism are exemplary; he always makes me think harder about my own assumptions – and prevented me from committing terrible philological blunders. Stephen Heath, Nigel Leask, and Christopher Prendergast read parts of this book critically and attentively, and I thank them all for their helpful suggestions.

This is also the place to acknowledge a certain number of institutions that provided the contexts in which this project grew, developed, and was completed. My deep gratitude goes to the Provost, Fellows, and students of King's College, Cambridge. I feel lucky to have been a student and a Fellow at such a wonderful place for so many years. Many warm thanks also to the members of the Department of English at Rice University for placing confidence in me, and creating an environment of immense intellectual generosity. I also want to thank James Chandler, as well as Linda Bree, Maartje Scheltens, Elizabeth Hanlon, and the two anonymous readers at

Cambridge University Press, for guiding the manuscript through its different stages. Parts of this book have appeared in similar form in print. I acknowledge the editors of *European Romantic Review, FMLS* and Duke University Press. Many thanks also to the Metropolitan Museum in New York for permission to reproduce Paul Klee's *Winterreise* on the cover, and to Rowan Boyson for preparing the index.

The most personal and intimate gratitude goes to my friends and family. Their closeness, respect, grace, and laughter provide the intellectual and emotional exchanges that weave a wonderful fabric of intellectual rigour, daring thought, and frivolity. They have accompanied me in England, the United States, and Australia, and I want to thank them all deeply for the hours they have given me. I am thinking particularly of Ericka Beckman, Laura Ceia, Kevin Donnelly, Sharon Doyle, Rebecca Edwards, Jonathan Hall, Jason Hawkes, Gabriel Heaton, Vanessa Hodgkinson, Hallvard Lillehammer, Jo Maybin, Matteo Mameli, Duncan O'Connor, Kyle Rand, Carla Stang, Stefan H. Uhlig, Anna Whitelock, and Ross Wilson. Separate and very special thanks go to Sarah Dunstall, the intrepid lagartija. Back in Germany, Spain, Colombia, and Argentina, my family's support has been unwavering. Lastly, I want to thank Clara and Christian, to whom I dedicate this book. My debt to them remains my dearest treasure.

Abbreviations

CJ	Immanuel Kant, *Critique of Judgment*, trans. Werner S. Pluhar (Indianapolis: Hackett, 1987).
DQ	Thomas De Quincey, *The Works of Thomas De Quincey*, ed. Grevel Lindop and others, The Pickering Masters, 21 vols. (London and Brookfield, VT: Pickering and Chatto, 2000–3).
Excursion	William Wordsworth, *The Excursion*, ed. Sally Bushell, James A. Butler, and Michael C. Jaye, with the assistance of David García (Ithaca: Cornell University Press, 2007).
Gauss	Paul de Man, *Romanticism and Contemporary Criticism: The Gauss Seminar and Other Papers*, ed. E. S. Burt, Kevin Newmark, and Andrzej Warminski (Baltimore: Johns Hopkins University Press, 1993).
GS	Walter Benjamin, *Gesammelte Schriften*, ed. Rolf Tiedemann, 7 vols. (Frankfurt am Main: Suhrkamp, 1991).
KC	*The Keats Circle*, ed. Hyder Edward Rollins, 2 vols. (Cambridge, MA: Harvard University Press, 1965).
L	John Keats, *The Letters of John Keats*, ed. Hyder Edward Rollins, 2 vols. (Cambridge: Cambridge University Press, 1958).
Life	*Life, Letters and Literary Remains of John Keats*, ed. Richard Monckton Milnes, 2 vols. (London: Edward Moxon, 1848).
OED	*Oxford English Dictionary*, second edition, prepared by J. A. Simpson and E. S. C. Weiner, 20 vols. (Oxford: Clarendon, 1989).
Prose	William Wordsworth, *The Prose Works of William Wordsworth*, ed. W. J. B. Owen and Jane Worthington Smyser, 3 vols. (Oxford: Clarendon, 1974).
RC	William Wordsworth, *'The Ruined Cottage' and 'The Pedlar'*, ed. James Butler (Ithaca: Cornell University Press, 1979).
RR	Paul de Man, *The Rhetoric of Romanticism* (New York: Columbia University Press, 1984).

RT   Paul de Man, *The Resistance to Theory* (Manchester:
            Manchester University Press, 1986).
1799   William Wordsworth, *'The Prelude', 1798–1799*, ed. Stephen
            Parrish (Ithaca: Cornell University Press, 1977).
1805   William Wordsworth, *The Thirteen-Book 'Prelude'*, ed. Mark
            L. Reed, 2 vols. (Ithaca: Cornell University Press, 1991).

Broken origins: an introduction

> To fill a Gap
> Insert the Thing that caused it –
> Block it up
> With Other – and 'twill yawn the more –
> You cannot solder an Abyss
> With Air – [1]

How do we fill gaps? Why do we want to fill them? What is the nature of fracture and fragmentation, in contrast to wholeness and plenitude, and our fascination with them? How can we get a grasp on our intrigue with the conceptual, historical, and material fissures that we use to account for ourselves? Emily Dickinson's concentrated lines, written in 1863, broach these questions of fracture and fragmentation effectively. Her poem thematises how an anxious desire to fill a 'Gap' only leads to replacing the fracture with its origin, which is 'the Thing that caused it'. Any attempt to 'Block it up' with another substance results in the gap 'yawn[ing] the more'. But whatever caused the fracture to begin with must repeat this break. To 'insert' the cause of a 'Gap' is endlessly to reproduce the fracture. The impossibility of 'filling' this gap either with itself or with emptiness – with 'air' – leaves the fracture unrepaired at the centre of the poem. The 'Gap' turns into an 'Abyss' that cannot be soldered, marked by the parenthesis and incompleted punctuation in the poem. The origin of our means to solder turns out to be broken. This book traces a number of strategies in Enlightenment and Romantic writing that articulate a dynamic, in both thought and language, that resembles Dickinson's 'Gap' and its broken origins.

One of the main arguments of this book is that fracture and fragmentation provide a lens through which some central concerns of Romanticism can be analysed in a manner that is particularly effective in telling us something not only about Romanticism but also about ourselves. By opening up the notions of fracture and fragmentation conceptually, the book provides an exposition of the different manners in which the dynamic at work in Dickinson's poem operates in Romantic writing. Such an approach implies a set of claims, two of which are especially relevant here. First stands the claim that fracture and fragmentation specifically are two conceptual categories that are particularly promising for exploring Romanticism. They, rather than others, allow us to understand an important aspect of Romanticism anew. Secondly, the study maintains that 'Romanticism' is a relevant term, description, and concept in contemporary literary studies. While each chapter of the book addresses both claims in relation to its respective focus, this introduction will discuss them briefly in a more general manner. It will thereby provide a background for my particular readings of William Wordsworth, John Keats, Immanuel Kant, Thomas De Quincey, and Paul de Man.

The brief reading of 'To Fill a Gap' suggests that fragmentation and fracture are terms that enable our thinking about more general aspects of aesthetic criticism, such as poetic form, history, and philosophy. Fracture and fragmentation turn out to be particularly fertile for certain forms of critical analysis. One of the central aims of this book is to understand and circumscribe how these two notions achieve such a productive status, both critically and historically – and, furthermore, why such an understanding is best developed in connection with Romanticism. Fragmentation and Romanticism have a special relationship, and we can understand both of them much better through comprehending their interrelation. As a result, we can reconfigure the way we think about a term such as 'Romanticism'.

In the most general terms of such a reconfiguration, this book concludes that it is precisely Romanticism that teaches us how to think about, and investigate critically, many of the central pillars and assumptions of our conceptual frameworks. Historically and conceptually, Romanticism provides a large number of the materials and methods that constitute our thinking about aesthetics, history, and criticism. Crucially, this not only is a claim about historical sources but also concerns our contemporary modes of thought. It is Romanticism that teaches us to think about 'Romanticism' as a category, even if the term designating the period only comes into existence much later. On a concrete level, the book explains why, and how, fragmentation is a particularly good example of understanding some unique qualities of Romanticism that help to shape our current way of thinking, especially about aesthetics. The focus on aesthetics at this particular moment does not result from a philosophical privileging of this sphere (although there are plenty of very good arguments for singling out aesthetics). Rather, it is the simpler reason that aesthetics and literary criticism form the main areas of my study. Although I want to gesture towards a continuous presence of Romanticism in a variety of disciplines, this book does not want to develop a universalising history. It focuses mainly on literature, criticism, and aesthetics. And although it is certainly comparative, it does not claim expertise in all of the disciplines that its fields of study connect with. Romanticism is central to us, and fragmentation is central to Romanticism. While this relation is not exhaustive, aesthetics certainly can indicate its relevance, and the richness and complexity of the terms involved in it.

The attractive power fragmentation holds for aesthetic criticism, and the reading of poetry in particular, has a history. This trajectory is part of the appeal that the link between fragmentation and Romanticism holds. And it is not surprising that one of the most important – and ultimately broken – origins of this history is to be found in works of the Romantic Period itself. Most readers will associate the importance of the fragment for literary criticism with the writings of early German Romanticism. Friedrich Schlegel and Novalis are two commonly cited figures, and their writing raises many questions that are invoked and cited by contemporary criticism. Some passages have become ubiquitous in certain contexts of literary and cultural criticism. A good example is Schlegel's memorable statement that 'A fragment must be, like a small work of art, wholly isolated from the surrounding world and in itself complete, like a hedgehog.'[2] Irrespective of whether this statement is derided or embraced, whether its influence is welcomed or repelled, its critical presence (alongside many other *Athenaeum* fragments) is remarkable. It is indicative of the power that authors such as Schlegel and Novalis, as well as their forms of writing, hold on many different parts of criticism today. In this aspect, *Fracture and Fragmentation* is no different. Much important work on the fragment, in several languages and periods, deeply informs the thinking of this study and its links to wider interpretative issues. However, while this book is happy to invoke such a powerful genealogy, it also wants to present something emphatically new. It aims to do so in relation both to specific scholarship on Romanticism, British and German, and to our wider thinking on fragmentation. In order to make these points clearer, the introduction will discuss below how scholarship has understood fragmentation in the past and what we can learn from it. Before this rather technical discussion, however, I will sketch briefly the versatility of fragmentation. My focus will lie on how fragmentation helps us to reconsider the way Romanticism shapes many of the frameworks that underlie our current self-understanding as critical subjects, including our understanding of the very category 'Romanticism'.

One aspect of the fragment that has ensured its continuous presence in the field of criticism is its status as an oxymoronic, yet critically self-replenishing and productive, concept. A genre or concept that fulfils its self-definition by being incomplete – fragmentary – has an evidently problematic representational status. Especially since it not only contains and performs this internal contradiction, but also becomes representative – typical – of Romanticism. As a result, the contradiction that the fragment harbours becomes essential both to itself and to a certain version of Romanticism. Criticism can react to such a conceptually irresolvable problematic, and its history, in two ways. It can understand it as an invitation to continue an investigation whose results will necessarily be shaded by that contradiction. Alternatively, it can abandon such an attempt owing to its necessary shortcomings. This book takes the first route. In fact, it considers that there are several reasons why a fresh and sustained reconsideration of fragmentation and Romanticism is not only welcome, but necessary. One of them is that fragmentation, as I have already indicated, helps us to define what is special about Romanticism. A second is that fragmentation, as it is understood here, emerges as a critical lens that concentrates the analysis of central philosophical, philological, and linguistic moments of Romanticism in a new way. It allows us to discover and read texts in a critically innovative and alert manner. Thirdly, fragmentation allows us to formulate a sophisticated philosophical question that leads us back into the period of Romanticism. It illustrates how we depend on that period for the formulation of our self-understanding, including the questions we deem to be critical. Simultaneously, however, it also insists on the relative brittleness of the sources it provides, avoiding an all-too-celebratory invocation of these roots.

Fracture and fragmentation strike us as tools and concepts of considerable import because we are still situated in a Romantic framework that allows us to recognise them as such. In many ways, this book is an explanation why such a situatedness within Romanticism is, contrary to the received opinions of many current scholars, something to be embraced. The book makes clear why this is not simply a naive or retrograde claim. It will show how fragmentation highlights that Romanticism includes and performs on itself the analytical apparatus that makes its own critique possible. Therefore we do well in returning to a close analysis of the thought, language, and concepts which prove so foundational for our contemporary approaches. The reader will have to judge whether these sources do indeed exhibit a meta-critical character. Either way, it is worth insisting that the initial interest we take in them, irrespective of whether we ultimately judge them to be critical, objectionable, or ideologically suspect, is often shaped by their own self-formulation in a much more significant manner than we assume.

Fragmentation, by definition, resists totalisation. Yet it remains a continuously important subject in philosophy and literature, especially in relation to Romanticism. The analysis of both fragmentation and Romanticism repeatedly suggests that they are unable to provide an exhaustive account of one another. Nevertheless, we are continuously drawn back to this conjunction of Romanticism and fragmentation. This seems, at least on the face of it, puzzling, since we know historically the conjunction to be limited in its ability to provide a satisfactory answer. Fragmentation seems to reveal its oxymoronic dynamic to be part of its categorisation as typically Romantic. It would seem appropriate, then, to discard it as an analytical tool, if we are interested in giving a seamless account of either fragmentation or Romanticism. Especially because, although fragmentation, or indeed the fragment, might resist totalisation, this does not necessarily imply that they resist explanation. The inquiry and the object of inquiry are logically distinct. Nevertheless, the case of fragmentation is peculiar in this regard. The fragment, because of its contradictory nature, invades the form of inquiry that it is subject to. That does not mean that they are equivalent, or that I want simply to repeat the Romantic discourse (imagined or real) that identifies them. Nevertheless, this book believes that any attempt to explain fragmentation exhaustively is bound to fail. But it also maintains that this is not a sufficient reason to abandon our inquiry. The continuation of a necessarily failing discourse is not simply a repetition or mimicry of previous analyses. Nor is it a confusion between the mode and the object of inquiry. It is, however, an acknowledgement that the historical and conceptual parameters of this book are, despite its explanatory ambitions, limited by the subject of its analysis. And that these limitations, both historical and conceptual, need to be embraced in order to maximise the book's potential. In the case of fragmentation this is particularly pertinent. As will become clear, an explanatory attempt of fragmentation that incorporates an awareness of its own necessary failing is ultimately more convincing than a discussion of it which does not believe that its subject of inquiry sets unsurpassable limits.

At least since the Romantic Period, criticism keeps returning to fragmentation as a source of explanation and discussion. Moreover, it seems that the resulting accounts often profit, rather than suffer, from the unsuccessful but felicitous conjunction between fragmentation and Romanticism. Both these categories accommodate layers of critical investment that allow and demand a constant return to their deep tensions and contradictions in the knowledge that they cannot be resolved. Even though we know that neither fragmentation nor Romanticism is completely successful in its explanatory function, we continue to find them helpful – maybe for that very reason – in defining one another. Thus, the seemingly simple question why, as present-day Romanticists, we still find the interplay between fragmentation and Romanticism intriguing betrays a commitment to the terms and history in which that question is posed. Both the terms and the history reveal that we always fail in our attempt to account for fragmentation and Romanticism. But they also insist that we nevertheless continue to return to, rather than discard, their discussion. One of the objectives of this book is to illustrate how this dynamic reveals the critical depth of fracture and fragmentation rather than their limitation.

There has been a historically robust interest in issues of fragmentation and ruin, which remains present today. Naturally, it is important to attend to how the chronological and geographical specificities of this interest develop. It is also crucial, however, to recognise that these terms are present in many of Romanticism's self-definitions. They play a major role in describing relevant aspects of the defining literary and aesthetic categories of the period. This presence singles them out as promising candidates in refining our account of Romanticism. However, there is not only a historical precedent. I also want to claim that the notions of fracture and fragmentation are helpful in ways of reading specific texts. They invoke considerations of a conceptual and thematic kind in relation to works or arguments as well as draw our attention to formal aspects of textual breaks and fissures. And these, in turn, allow me to uncover the specifically Romantic aspect of these texts. My readings can thereby show how fracture and fragmentation are pervasive in many aspects of writings which we normally do not consider under these headings. For instance, sometimes we might find a thematic concern with fragmentation in a seemingly coherent and cohesive text. Thus my championing of fracture and fragmentation as critical notions is motivated historically as well as hermeneutically. As a result, the book discusses many texts that are not often considered in relation to fragmentation.

Of the two terms that form the interpretative axes of my explanations, fragmentation is the more commonly used in Romantic studies. However, the category of 'fracture' here does not only figure as distinguishing a particular kind of fragmentation. Although the two notions are very closely connected, there is a difference between them which determines how they are employed in the readings. Fracture describes a break that is located on a structural level. It is not a process, and does not encompass a temporal element in that sense. It might be historically or genealogically located, but that is not its deciding feature. Rather, it is a rupture of a structural and logical kind, a break that acts as an unbridgeable division between two spheres. One example of such a break is the division between nature and human which is often presented as an unbridgeable gap. Another instance of fracture is the deployment of a citation or a sign of punctuation (such as a parenthesis) to break a text. Fragmentation, differently from fracture, is a process. Even though it can be final, it is defined by a series of changes. It is the unfolding of a break that happens either once or over and over again. Examples of such a process include the Tower of Babel as an image for the fragmentation of language, or an epistolary correspondence as forming a fragmented body of writing. Fragmentation might be final in the sense that there is no way back or forward, but it involves movement to begin with. Thus, fracture can be likened to a condition, part of a structure; fragmentation more to a process, an unfolding. While the two can overlap, and often do in my analysis, it is important to remain aware of this distinction.

The seven chapters of this book comprise readings and critical discussions of seven instances in which fracture or fragmentation stand in a relevant relation to central literary or philosophical texts. Each chapter will illustrate differently why these notions offer particularly illuminating ways of approaching the material at hand. We will see how fracture and fragmentation become conceptual categories as well as heuristic tools, helping us to understand how certain writers construct the Romanticism we take them to represent. Each chapter illustrates how various 'openings' of ideas of fracture and fragmentation – thematic, figural, rhetorical – change the emphasis and objective of the analysis, without losing the overall focus. Depending on the text in question, I will present fracture or fragmentation as a theme, foreground the fragmentation of structures, or explore the use of the figure of fracture as a critical tool with a rhetorical dimension. The power of each individual case, as well as its successful role in a larger argument, illustrates that the multifaceted nature of fracture and fragmentation is a symptom of flexible strength rather than of loose definition. Such a sketch, stressing the heterogeneity of its subject matter, as well as of its forms of discussion, indicates the suppleness of Romanticism. It also brings me to the second implicit claim, mentioned in the opening pages, namely, the relevance of the category of Romanticism to our contemporary modes of inquiry.

On a very direct level, this book explores how we might understand Romanticism, what Romanticism 'is', both conceptually and historically. This is evidently a large and complex field with a long and distinguished history of inquiry. It will be useful to provide a very brief and partial genealogy of the relevant critical context here. This will serve as a platform to sketch my own methodological heritage, as well as indicate how my approach differs from that of other scholars. Hopefully, it will thereby illustrate how this book contributes to the critical debate from which it has grown. One version of Romanticism that emerges out of my readings, which I believe is philologically and philosophically present in Romanticism historically, is a Socratic or meta-critical endeavour in the Hamannian sense. It is characterised by irony, humility, and a particularly developed understanding or practice of meta-critical reflection. It enjoys a constitutive scepticism regarding its own procedure that does not blunt its critical edge. The present book attempts to pursue this line and thereby attend to the possibilities of what Paul Hamilton calls a 'reworking of the immanence of romantic self-critique'.[3] One aspect of this reworking that is especially relevant, both in Romanticism and in its reading, is its focus and attention to the role of language and its connection to thought. It has been a classic contention that language plays a major role in Romanticism and the way we understand it. I will show how such a focus need not entail, as has been suggested, a conceptually weaker or historically less critical understanding of either Romantic thought or contemporary analysis. Focusing on language means, in Romanticism and here, focusing on thought. The widely discussed overlap between philosophy and literature is the most immediate illustration of this connection. Here literary language and philosophical insight can illuminate one another historically, negating mechanistic application of one to the other. Such a philological approach uncovers a Romanticism which stresses the importance of language to all forms of expression and thought, without making it out to be a simple forerunner of post-structuralism.[4]

This book presents a philosophical problem that lies behind the definition of, and our involvement in, Romanticism. The form of my discussion, an intertwining of philology, literature, and philosophy, already indicates how I suggest we can address this issue. Moreover, it explains why fracture and fragmentation help to focus and unravel this complex question in different forms. In this manner, I hope to explore further the fertile suggestion that 'Romantic self-consciousness, pushed to its limits, seeks to shatter the reflection or image of plenitude it has created.'[5] My intellectual allegiance here is not only with Hamilton, but, even more importantly, with his shattering sources. The fragmentation of plenitude, the uneasiness that goes with this destruction, including its compensatory fantasies of organic wholeness, are deeply Romantic moves that amount to a leitmotiv of this book. They present a complex yet ultimately enabling strategy that cannot be diagnosed simply as a set of self-deluding beliefs which have to be discarded or superseded.

My study often complements literary analysis with a reading of theoretical sources of Romanticism. It wants to address the philosophical dimensions of its central questions adequately. A familiarity with the most sophisticated thought of the period helps to strengthen our hold on Romantic texts without turning this grip into a clench. Some discussions in literary studies convey a sense of reluctance or trepidation when it comes to such an overlap of philosophy and literature. In contrast, this volume wants to display a determined confidence in comparative work. If a philosophical reading of Romanticism is intended, as it is here, it is more than advisable to include the relevant sources of that field in our analysis. Since German philosophy presents some of the most considerable thought of Romanticism, its central figures form part of some of my readings of British sources. I read these texts in conjunction with a view to the philological implications of the philosophical thought they present. The results illustrate why a comparative approach is both an intuitively and an analytically adequate method for our present concern. That is, the so-called crux of relating German philosophy and British writing here is not conceived of as a crux at all. It can be understood as an insurmountable barrier if the critical objective is to prove historical influence (or its absence). I do not want to deny the interest, and sometimes the crucial importance, of such source study. However, it is not the primary concern of this project (just as this introduction does not provide a comprehensive theoretical account of the book's own position). One larger methodological claim buried in such preferences is that a comparative approach can combine philological detail and historical specificity in a powerful analysis of Romantic texts. I hope my readings underwrite this approach successfully. The reading of *any* two texts in conjunction has to be performed with care, whatever the agenda of the critic. In fact, Romanticism does much to alert us to this demand. This project wants to rise to the challenge in an unabashedly cosmopolitan manner.

Highlighting the overlap and intersection between literature and philosophy here is not only an invocation of a particular version of the Romantic period or scholarship. It is also a positive assertion that we are still within Romanticism and, crucially, that there are far worse places to be. The book will attempt to show that this claim is less naive, or possibly reactionary, than it might appear to some. As we know, the question whether or not we remain in Romanticism is not new, and it remains one of the most difficult topics in current literary scholarship.[6] It is often related to a discussion about the nature of modernity – an even more contested term – which, depending on the account, is a continuation, a replacement, or an erasure of Romanticism. There are various helpful ways in which to frame the different positions within this debate, including their respective motivations and parameters. One recurring issue, which brings our difficulties into focus, concerns the theorisation of the relation between historical continuity and discontinuity. How do we understand the accessibility or inaccessibility of a period such as Romanticism? Does it matter that the term itself became currency only after the period it describes began? More fundamentally: are we barred from certain ways of historical understanding through insurmountable epistemic breaks? Can the account of a subject that claims to be always transcendentally self-present take sufficient care to recognise its own historical situation? Does chronological distance from a poem allow a reader to gain critical insights, which, while embedded within the text, no reader could possibly have had at the time of composition? The following readings demonstrate how seriously these questions ought to be taken.

The book starts with two common assumptions. First, that Romanticism is chronologically associated with the time between the mid-eighteenth and mid-nineteenth centuries. And, secondly, that Romanticism informs a wide array of notions central to our self-understanding. The relative vagueness of such a general time-span does not neglect historical specificity, especially when it comes to individual analysis of authorships, or the genesis of concepts, and I certainly want to claim more than a link of the fragment and Romanticism through their *Zeitgeist*. Recent decades have produced several powerful accounts which locate the emergence (and creation) of fundamental categories of our thinking (such as aesthetics, literature, or the subject) in the historical period between 1750 and 1850.[7] Just as Romantic auto-criticism does not entail lack of precise reflection, the analysis of its historicity can be specific without having to predetermine its exact chronological limits. Thus, this book does not provide a *Begriffsgeschichte* in Reinhart Koselleck's or Erich Rothaker's sense, a history of the concepts 'fracture' or 'fragmentation'.[8] Nevertheless, my approach takes its cue from a number of related discussions such as Peter de Bolla's *The Discourse of the Sublime* (1989) and David Simpson's *Romanticism, Nationalism, and the Revolt against Theory* (1993) that have illustrated how the emergence (and creation) of fundamental categories within our discourse, such as aesthetics or the subject, are historically tied in specific ways to the periods of the Enlightenment and Romanticism.[9] While both of these accounts stress the historical and conceptual contingency of their subjects, their genealogical method attains its power through emphasising a certain continuity (even when they argue for a radical shift). It elevates their status from conventional narrative history to a study of a phenomenon that implicates us as contemporary subjects. The birth of the subject or aesthetics, such as these critics describe it, is so pressing because it implicates *us* as those subjects.

The emphasis on continuity that this book displays includes the suggestion that some of the perceived resemblances or patterns over the last two centuries prove rather more welcome than expected. To claim powerfully (rather than admit guiltily) that we are still a part of Romanticism need not be encouragement for a new sentimentalism, naivety, or suspect allegiances. It is the result of carefully embracing the possibility, and desirability, of a position that does not believe itself to be theoretically more advanced or sophisticated by virtue of its contemporaneousness. It is precisely one of Romanticism's main intellectual contributions to show us how the automatic association between superiority and contemporaneity is analytically misguided as well as hermeneutically inattentive. In contrast, a criticism of exacting humility and irony allows us to reread our own sources in a more rewarding and insightful way. Again, this need not be uncritical or an exercise in veneration. It involves recognising the contemporary nature of Enlightenment and Romantic thought, and their power in shaping the present (including an understanding of how the conceptual shape of what we recognise as a 'problem' or 'Romanticism' comes about). Our position as present-day critics improves if we develop a sense for the importance of historical specificity as well as for its relation to analytical statements. This happens much more successfully if we do not suffer from an overdeveloped sense of independence from our sources. Romanticism provides us with enough condensed and sufficiently representative examples why such an attitude need not result in an *un*-critical view.

My book openly admits the historically contingent nature of its own account of Romanticism. This does not entail a lack of commitment to its explanatory power. The project does not proclaim a return to a theory of undecidabilty between different critical and theoretical narratives, nor a focus on modes of discourses, such as in the work of Ernesto Laclau and Friedrich Kittler.[10] Accepting the impossibility of *knowing* what Romanticism is does not mean it is not worthwhile attempting as exact a definition as possible. The present account has, like most explanatory models, a narrative element, a temporal structure. It also differentiates itself qualitatively from models that employ competing accounts or narratives. *Fracture and Fragmentation* tells a particular story, and it wants to do so strongly and convincingly with a versatile self-awareness. The project admits that its sources will inevitably influence the content and form of its argument. It maintains that to deny this would be to succumb to an idealism that borders on the presumptuous. The contingency of such a narrative, its possible substitution in the future, however, does not prevent me from championing its correctness, and defending its precision or value. This literary criticism is part of a genealogy that 'Ever tried. Ever Failed.'[11] However, it also concludes from this that 'No matter. Try again. Fail again. Fail better.'[12] As Samuel Beckett shows, loss of redemption is compatible with coherence of theology.

It is important to acknowledge a certain unease that some readers might feel regarding the potential circularity of this approach (or coherence). Ultimately, the power of such an objection relies on an alternative promise, namely, to develop a meta-description for a project such as this one. It seems to me that such a strategy is neither methodologically promising nor desirable. The reasons for holding such a position are varied, and many are developed throughout the book. One of the strongest turns on the way we cognitively and methodologically shape our interests, and how it is inextricably bound to the sources that form the object of our study. In the case of fragmentation, this is particularly important. Here, the object and method of inquiry not only are closely related, but also, as I have already pointed out, turn out to be subject to a set of inherent limitations that distinguish them from other categories. The claim about the type of conceptual framework, as well as the heuristic tools, that fragmentation allows me to develop here insists on its immediate connection with concrete case studies. The ultimate test for the arguments these particular instances present, then, does not lie in developing a supposedly unconnected meta-claim about them in this introduction. Thus, to point to the limitations and contingencies of this study here is not to admit circularity. Rather, it signals, firmly within the genre of an academic book, a particular knowingness regarding the power of its sources and how we might negotiate the necessary limitations that they impose upon us.

One of the symptoms and characteristics of the Romanticism uncovered here is that it continuously performs, thematises, and sometimes knowingly comments on, the hermeneutic problem of distance and self-representation. All of my readings reveal the extent to which some of the systematising categories we use to construct our understanding of 'the aesthetic' or of 'Romanticism' have at their centre a moment that undercuts their rationalising or aestheticising objectives. Correspondingly, the figure of fracture constantly threatens to disrupt the rhetorical system of which it is a part. The figure's conceptual implications often prevent it from being systematised coherently, thereby destabilising the framework that holds the figural in place. Despite their differences, these moments of destabilisation are structural features of the texts that I discuss. They are negotiated both in and through language. By extension, this dynamic becomes relevant in relation to broader categories such as the Romanticism to which these texts belong and of which they are representative.

The structure of the process enacted by the notion of fracture and fragmentation exhibits, in a variety of different ways, a contradictory force at its very centre. As the various chapters illustrate, this can occur in literary, rhetorical, or philosophical terms. These instances have in common that they all display and investigate their own broken origins. They are linguistic, conceptual, grammatical, or philosophical structures that are based on, or germinate in, a moment that is already fissured at its inception. Their origin, both conceptually and historically, is itself already broken. My overarching argument is that Romanticism is partly defined through its broken origins. Each chapter of this book illustrates one aspect of its brittle foundations. In their sum, they show many of Romanticism's self-examinations of these origins to be knowing. In many cases, though not all, they are meta-critical. Importantly, all of the texts show that the problems they expose, the broken origins they reveal, also relate to our own conceptual foundations. They are immediately relevant, and formulate questions and critical categories that we still consider central to an understanding of the present. Suddenly, the chronological distance between these texts and our contemporary situation, often perceived as remote, shrinks significantly.

Notoriously, the Romantic Period produces such a heterogeneous body of works that it is difficult to speak of 'representative' texts or genres. In a similar way there is no rule regarding the degree of self-critique any of these texts allows. Nevertheless, it is worth noting that many of them exhibit a meta-critical pattern in connection with fragmentation. While this is certainly not a seamless link, and the question of Romanticism's meta-criticism is a fraught issue, such difficulties should not stall an investigation along such lines; in fact, the level of reflection exhibited by many of the texts discussed here urges us on. Their sophistication and openly self-critical modes of introspection reinforce the argument that they often perform these moves knowingly, specifically as a result of considering the tools that allow them to reflect on their own status as literature, text, or aesthetic construct. They certainly encourage us to reconsider the confidence we often encounter in contemporary approaches that dismiss Romanticism as lacking in analytical self-examination and criticism. It turns out that one of the reasons we give meta-critique such an important status is not so much a reaction against but a continuation of Romanticism. This also accounts for our remaining fascination, and frustration, with a period that gives us the materials and methods to discover the broken origins of our own interests. It provides a bridge that connects eighteenth-century sources with their twenty-first-century counterparts.

One figure whose work helps me to theorise the relation between historical distance, philology, and literary text through fragmentation is Walter Benjamin. He is one of the main methodological and philosophical reference points throughout this study, and his work is explicitly discussed in three chapters. Benjamin, both openly and covertly, thinks about Romanticism as a historical phenomenon as well as conditioning part of his own writing. His early work on language in particular, considered in the first chapter, helps to frame some of the central ideas of this book along these lines. In hermeneutic and strategic terms, his characteristic tracing of a minute and seemingly irrelevant observation to its much wider significance permeates this study. However, at no point do I want to suggest, or, even worse, attempt to perform, a mechanistic application of Benjamin's thoughts and methods to literary material. On the contrary, this book feeds off a criticism of irony and humility that announces its own historical situatedness, also in relation to Benjamin. This seems a lesser, yet deeper, risk to take, compared to an 'application' of a methodological system or to an unshaking conviction in the importance of my own readings. This volume wants to produce a criticism that allows precise and confident inquiry without fears of being mistaken or suffering from a lack of playfulness. To view this as a direct result of its allegiance to Romanticism sets it apart from many other schools of thought which focus on the literature and culture of that period. I will broadly outline where some of these differences lie by indicating what this book tries to learn from, and where it disagrees with, New Historicism and deconstruction, the two fields that have defined much of Romantic Studies over the past few decades.[13]

Many studies of a New Historicist character have done much to encourage both a deep and a serious appreciation of Romanticism. This book attempts to continue some of the concerns to be found in such work. There is, however, one significant difference in my approach. For all its interest and investment in the literature and thought of the late eighteenth and early nineteenth centuries, New Historicism is confident not only that chronological distance allows for a deeper and more sophisticated insight when it comes to reading texts, but also that these texts themselves are incapable of generating meta-critical insight at the time of their production. The following chapters suggest that this position is not always completely convincing when faced with many philosophical and literary productions of the time. The study argues that the idealising force of Romantic projects proves repeatedly more productive and self-critical than their supposedly therapeutic counterparts, which diagnose these texts as suffering from 'Romantic Ideology'. Is it not the complexity of the texts in question, including their self-analysis and meta-critique, rather than the possible reduction of these complexities into deciphered versions of our contemporary anxieties, that generates our interest in the Romantic Period? In fact, might a commitment to the belief that an ameliorating analysis is possible, desirable, or necessary not have counter-productive results? Explaining this general suspicion in relation to the 'demystifying' aspect of Romantic Ideology will help to illustrate the positive methodological commitment and conceptual direction of my project.

It has been a commonplace for some time that certain versions of criticism whose aim is to detect ideological commitment often risk suffering from their own idealistic impulse. While this is an important observation, it is more fundamental to consider whether such 'demystificatory' criticism might be working with problematic notions of the supposed ideological status, coherence, and implications of the idealism it attempts to criticise.[14] What is striking about a work such as Jerome McGann's classic *The Romantic Ideology* (1983), for example, is that it seems to assume to have identified successfully both what 'Romantic' and 'Ideology' were and are, and that, at least in relation to the former, a diagnostic distance is possible and desirable, ultimately leading to a treatment that wants to believe in progress of a singular kind:

[T]he present work [*The Romantic Ideology*] proposes a new, *critical* view of Romanticism and its literary products. To realize this aim necessitates an initial critique of the scholarly and critical traditions which have delivered these subjects into our hands. The ground thesis of this study is that the scholarship and criticism of Romanticism and its work are dominated by a Romantic Ideology, by an uncritical absorption in Romanticism's own self-representations.[15]

While McGann's work has been modified, expanded, and updated in many fascinating ways (by himself and others), this general outlook rests on a set of methodological assumptions that is still pervasive. Quite apart from whether one agrees with his qualitative assessment of the critical tradition and its sources, McGann's organic or theological metaphor of delivery shows how he thinks of a Romanticism that is painless in its birth and genealogically relatively simple. Close textual analysis shows that neither the villains of McGann's account (Coleridge and Hegel) nor the hero (Heine) fit this picture. In contrast, the subjects that a Socratic Romanticism and its scholarship deliver are full of self-contradictory birth pangs, some of which this study will focus on. While it will do so with some clinical distance, it does not aim to chastise the origin for its interest in representing itself. Especially, and this is an important contention, if the self-representation is not in fact as naive as it is made out to be. Some readers might feel that such a criticism of *The Romantic Ideology* ignores its status as a polemic manifesto. However, manifestos are often revealing in what they take to be their good intentions. McGann sketches a version of both scholarship and Romanticism that has become very influential. It is precisely its foundational quality, and confidence therein, that makes McGann's account a representative target here.

Other work in a New Historicist vein has attempted to avoid the pitfalls of these objections. Not least in its careful incorporation of psychoanalysis, such scholarship has provided us with highly sophisticated accounts of the critical assumptions that are brought to bear on its readings. Marjorie Levinson, for instance, claims shrewdly that she sees her work as a 'criticism that seeks to take hold of the conditions of literary production in a profounder way than historical inquiry into manifest theme is capable of. It is a self-consciously belated criticism that sees in its own necessary ignorance – its expulsion from the heaven of Romantic sympathy – a critical advantage: the capacity to know a work neither as it, nor its original readers, nor its authors could know it.'[16] This is quite evidently a different proposition from *The Romantic Ideology*, and there is much that the present study has learned from it. I take Levinson to offer us an optimistic version of criticism (in both the general and the specific sense) without being crudely progressivist or charting a straightforward moral improvement. The argument is not, and here Levinson is more subtle than most, that we 'learn' something morally improving about the world in which, say, Wordsworth's text was produced. Neither is it an accusation that Wordsworth should have known better. In other words, Levinson's approach is far more than just a reminder about the pressure of ideological conditions upon the present (whether it be on a text, a thought, or an action). For much of this book, I hope to incorporate this alertness in directing my reading. However, there is a structural and methodological claim to Levinson's argument that I find hard to share. It is the claim that chronological distance is necessary to generate a reading in which the meta-critical insight of the text reveals itself.

That conviction reveals a dimension to this version of New Historicism about which this book is doubtful. It is uneasy about a certain Whiggish confidence in the tools of contemporary criticism and its retrospective insights (which also goes beyond the frequent Marxist inflection of New Historicism). Too many of the readings in this book discover a certain Romantic scepticism that makes it hard to adopt a confidence such as Levinson's, for all its subtlety and sophistication. To anticipate this difference in the vocabulary of her discussion: it seems to me that Romanticism already reflects on, and articulates, its own melancholy insight that the expulsion from heaven is part of the reason Romanticism can never think itself out of itself. Even today we cannot escape this Romantic agony; and while there is no promise of redemption either, this does not translate into an inability to articulate our own conditions meta-critically and poetically.

In relation to contemporary criticism, it seems that New Historicism's view involves two central ideas. First, that the gap between, say, 1829 and 2009 is sufficiently wide to allow for meta-critical insights. Secondly, that our contemporary analytical tools are different enough to detect, analyse, and articulate these insights. The experimental readings that follow leave us less confident on both accounts. They discover that to recover many of the texts on their own terms shows them to be knowingly thinking about the brittle foundations they are built on, and acting this insight out. They do this in a way that suggests the timely proximity of 1828 rather than its location in the distant past. This, then, leads to a set of aspects of the historical albeit staunchly anti-Whiggish element of my readings. They nurture the idea that, while we have to be historically precise, there is no historical progress, at least not in the sense that it is commonly understood. This results in a scepticism about the supposedly privileged power of temporal detachment – quite apart from doubting that the present-day analytical tools are so altogether different, and, if so, better, compared to the not-too-distant past of two hundred years ago. One alternative positive suggestion is that, rather than adopting a developed version of analytical texts originating in the period (such as twentieth-century Hegelianism, say), we return to these foundational texts themselves. Tentatively, we might even play with the possibility that it is not what we think of as analytical interventions which allow the most insightful analyses. Could we speak of Keats's letters, for instance, as providing us with such material? This is to suggest that resisting a contemporary, but by now orthodox, model of history and analysis in literature might make us reconsider whether we adopted too narrow a version of literary history to begin with. Put polemically, might reading Wordsworth allow us to see where Hegel (or what we have come to see as 'Hegel') has helped us to canonise Wordsworth, but also where he led us astray? Or yet in another way: do the meta-critical insights of Georg Hamann's *Aesthetica in Nuce* (1762) not include a convincing suggestion that their power depends less on our contemporary detached viewpoint than on our willingness to attempt to follow their force in ironising history?

Some accounts in the New Historicist vein specify which aspects of Romantic authorships can be retroactively approached and analysed. Many, however, claim that no textual construct can ever enact and fulfil its own meta-critical potential. Once again, I want to focus on the important – and contested – second claim. Often literary interpretations uncover aspects to poems that lie hidden within them, whether as formal decisions, historical accidents, or conceptual assumptions. To tease out these dimensions is both a meaningful and an important feature of scholarship. However, does it not seem odd how often such an uncovering is presented as the diagnosis of a lack on the poem's part? It is not immediately clear why an attentive reading should reveal an inherent lack, a shortcoming, or a mistake. It will do so if the analysis provides a framework in which such a shortcoming or blind spot does indeed reveal an undesirable aspect. It might be, but need not. Furthermore, it will only be negative if there is a preconceived idea of what the poem, or the analysis, is supposed to perform and represent. It seems that all too often we believe that poetry is under a peculiar obligation to provide a holistic view of the sphere it represents. Or at least that the specific choice of electing only to represent a portion of its surrounding context somehow bars it from meta-critical insight. Does this not stem from a restricted view of what poems try to do, and a lack of sympathy for what they try to do and try not to do? As critics we naturally emphasise the areas of analysis we think most important. That does not mean that failure to reach a meta-critical analysis in them taints the poems' ability to perform such insight in other areas. It is completely understandable if critics highlight certain arenas of particular interest to them that they find to be silently passed over by the poem. And it is not a matter of singling out the agenda of these critics because we might think their foci of attention are the wrong ones. As I have indicated, often they are insightful and productive. Rather, the question is whether it is possible to locate a different set of foci for which chronological distance is not a necessary part of generating an analytical or meta-critical insight.

It should be clear that this contextualisation, and the new proposition that goes with it, is not an attack on New Historicist practice per se (as far as there is such a thing). However, I hope it has become clear that this project has quite a different agenda, which defines itself not so much against as alongside current scholarship in that vein. The following readings uncover a Romanticism that is much more meta-critical and doubtful about itself than is often assumed. It is a Romanticism that repeatedly transpires to be more cautious than the supposedly advanced and detached criticism which diagnoses unwelcome ideological commitments. While this is not an all-encompassing quality (not all texts are self-critical – just as not all are naive), it is distinct and prevalent enough to serve as a characteristic marker for the period and its philosophical self-definition. Such a procedure includes a wariness of homogenising Romanticism, and insisting that its differentiations contain the strength of its movement. While this project does not want to proclaim sufficient distance to make a statement like McGann's, this need not be the result of a lack of *critical* engagement with Romanticism's self-representations.

Another major school of thought that has shaped Romantic Studies over recent decades, and is relevant in this context, is associated with the work of deconstruction. The regular invocation of philosophy on the one hand, and the contingency of interpretation on the other, may have created the impression that this book also is a 'deconstructive study'. It is not. While I pay attention to language and writing, I do not conceptualise, interpret, or write, in terms of differ*a*nce, logocentrism, or *arche*-writing. Some readers may nevertheless feel that my interpretations follow what is often described as a 'deconstructive move'; that is, they tease out contradictions through very close readings, and reveal a counter-logic in certain texts. They also pay special attention to language and the philosophical assumptions that are in place when we, and others, use it. However, to scrutinise inherent contradictions in texts, ponder the philosophical implications of a particular trope, or attend to the wider linguistic assumptions of a poetic work, are not specifically 'deconstructive' moves. These analytical interests and techniques are as familiar to Plato as they are to Coleridge (or at least the 'Plato' and 'Coleridge' that we believe ourselves to be familiar with). Many of Romanticism's most important authors continuously think and write about these aspects of linguistics and thought. This is not to say, as has been argued by some, that some Romantics produce deconstruction *avant la lettre*. In fact, often the contradictions Romanticism uncovers escape the temptation of mythologising concepts such as 'textuality' or 'poetology', which deconstructive readings so regularly employ. This study resists the claim that a method that pays philological and philosophical attention to the conceptual assumptions a text exhibits is something that a very particular school of contemporary continental thought teaches us.[17] Rather, such methods have a venerable historical trajectory, which also leads through Romanticism.

The sophistication and quality of much Romantic thought leads me to suggest that it should play a more active role in consciously shaping our method of reading it. This suggestion refers to the textual and philosophical (rather than the historical) dimensions of our sources. The period's *way* of reading itself, its linguistic analysis and philology, can provide many insights that are instructive for us as contemporary critics. And I hope that the readings in this volume illustrate these dimensions. My stress on the tensions, contradictions, and broken origins of thought and language, then, is not a continuation of a deconstructive tradition. Rather, it is an attempt to use certain aspects of Romanticism's own criticism as adequate critical tools in relation to itself. As a side effect, it also shows occasionally where deconstruction might suffer crucial limitations.

A good practical illustration of this book's relation to deconstruction is to single out the figure of Paul de Man. He is closely associated with that school of thought as well as with a philological approach to the Romantic Period. His immensely instructive and influential work, and especially his methodology of rhetorical readings, underpins many of the hermeneutic decisions of this volume. However, while the book endorses many of de Man's suggestions, it is not de Manian in slavishly following his methodology. Even more importantly, it does not believe that his most important critical contributions are detached from the Romanticism that feeds them. Ultimately, the volume steers away from de Man when he provides an account of some of his own central linguistic assumptions. According to de Man, these assumptions, or a very similar set, allow and enable the production of texts and readings we have come to associate with him. Crucially, he also claims that they are in place for Romantic writing (including Walter Benjamin). The final chapter discusses this argument, and how it is mounted, at length. The reader will have to decide whether it succeeds, but its main thrust is relevant here. According to my reading, de Man is helpful where he is consciously Romantic, and positions himself as such in a typically sophisticated manner. He is unhelpful where he denies and ignores the sources that allow him to produce such an analysis. Those are the moments when he replaces his sources with a fervent antagonism that results in readings which lack the care and quality that generally distinguish them. It is not entirely coincidental that the detailed analysis of this differentiation in de Man's work occurs by relating it to Benjamin's oeuvre. While de Man attempts to purge Benjamin of the theological aspects of his Romanticism it becomes clear how much de Man's subtlety elsewhere depends on precisely those dimensions. Because both de Man and Benjamin are highly important in my own account, and their work stands in a fertile relation to one another, some readers might assume that I use them interchangeably. However, as this general sketch indicates, and as the final chapter shows in detail, their differences turn out to be far more important for my analysis than their similarities. Benjamin is able to incorporate fragmentariness as a condition of philosophy that is productive, despite the impossibility of its redemption. This compares favourably with de Man, whose reading of fragmentariness leads him to present a disenchanted, but ultimately restricted, secularism of forced coherence.

This book is about different gaps, losses, and breaks. Over the last few pages I have tried to sketch how it also forms part of a general framework of scholarship. A number of projects attempt to work towards a fresh understanding of how such fissuring dynamics can be fruitful in describing and defining categories like 'Enlightenment' or 'Romanticism'. *Fracture and Fragmentation* forms part of a heterogeneous group of scholarly attempts to reawaken interest in returning, once again, to the question what Romanticism might be. It wants to do so without falling into the stifling opposition between formalism and historicism. However, such a generalised commitment about avoiding (already mythologised) ideologies has itself already become a cliché. Therefore I want to provide a slightly more accurate map of this project, including its attempt to show the relevance of what Andrew Benjamin calls a 'reworking of key elements' or the 'truth of Romanticism'.[18] Apart from the figures already mentioned, other scholars of Romanticism such as John Barrell, James Chandler, Frances Ferguson, Ian Balfour, Marc Redfield, William Keach, and Leon Chai, to name but a few, have recently provided us with very insightful, astute, and coherent, readings of historical material as well as with shrewd assessments of their own positions towards it.

Evidently, all of these scholars pursue very different goals. Barrell remains one of the single most important authors on Romanticism. His recent work is as acute as ever on the interplay between historical source and contemporary description. In *The Spirit of Despotism* (2006), Barrell focuses on instances as 'complex manifolds of events, discourses, and narratives, which allow us to see historical change in all its messy and material confusion; as knots which as we disentangle them are discovered to be made up of threads leading backwards and forwards in time'.[19] Invoking Lessing, he focuses on the respective '"central point" of a process of change, one which contains within itself the traces of what led up to it and intimations of what will follow'.[20] Many of the fractures and breaks described here are similar to such 'central points', albeit resisting their potentially teleological aspects. Alongside Barrell's earlier work, Chandler's magisterial study *England in 1819* (1998) allowed a large number of projects to redefine themselves as historically minded while maintaining an interest in the formal and philosophically charged aspects of particular literary works.[21] His work permeates the thinking of all the other critics I have mentioned. Chandler's claim 'that we most invoke the terms of a historicism that is emergent within Romanticism when we make the historicist critique' is particularly relevant here.[22] Its self-critical aspect stands in a productive relationship with Ferguson's precise and eloquent interventions on Romanticism. She reminds us that 'the special pressure that romanticism brings to bear on memory is the pressure of an expanded moral obligation, an obligation to reexamine one's own past actions to see if their value has been altered by subsequent events'.[23] It is evident that both discussions are as much an attempt to define Romanticism as they are a comment on the critical history of such a project. Balfour's *The Rhetoric of Romantic Prophecy* (2002) remains one of the most intelligent and original recent interventions in Romantic Studies.[24] He successfully takes up Hamilton's invitation to provide deeper ways in which to think about how ideas in and of European Romanticism can help (rather than hinder) a historically accurate textual interpretation that is sensitive to the particularities of its own national tradition. In his comparative work, Marc Redfield combines rhetorical reading of the de Manian kind with a highly developed sense of the historical specificity of the texts he analyses. His seminal discussion of ideology and aesthetics prefaces a work that is aware how often 'many stories of Romanticism move uneasily between historical and formal concerns, seeking to explain the history of their own representational possibility'.[25] In his subtle *Arbitrary Power* (2004), Keach sees his project as directly complementary to Chandler's, wanting to 'extend unfinished work on Romantic theories of linguistic agency, practice, and institution and to show how deeply implicated they are in defining social changes and conflicts'.[26] His study does indeed concentrate on language and its theorisation, but never loses the sense of how its dialectical relation with a historical setting provides a scene of production that is still dominant today. Albeit in a different context, Leon Chai's *Romantic Theory* (2006) alerts us to Romanticism's contemporaneousness in similarly effective ways. Although he is receptive to the difficulties of certain idealistic impulses in Romantic thought, Chai suggestively states that 'if Romantic theory lay at the source of our present impasse, it might also point to a way out of it'.[27]

My descriptions of these projects must remain highly simplistic here, given the depth and strength of each of the studies. However, even in such general terms some important markers of their critical impetus emerge. They all make a theoretical and historical investigation of their own assumptions an integral part of their hermeneutic approach. This strengthens their own position against a certain form of naivety, and guards against some forms of ideological blindness. Furthermore, all these projects have loose commitments to larger critical frameworks, which compete with one another, or to which they stand in direct opposition. That does not mean, however, that they cannot be instructive. Often, it is precisely the *type* of conflict they engender with one another that is important. Thus it is the method and structure of their arguments, their methodology and praxis, that make these studies so important here. The innovations they offer through their original readings of literature are not only tied to a specific authorship. Their additional impact lies in the way they perform, structure, and conceptualise these readings. On the one hand, these books aim to construct or refine the literary and historical period of Romanticism. On the other hand, they continuously insist that part of this construction must be to attend to the ways in which the philosophical overlaps with the historical, both in the period and today.

All these studies attempt to navigate the scholarly impasses that are created by some traditional scholarship in the area of Romantic Studies. The present volume wants to build on their work, and champion fragmentation as a particularly successful notion and tool for doing so. As I have already indicated, questions of the fragment, or fragmentation, are of particular importance during, and for, the Romantic period. The sustained interest in this topic remains closely linked to the writings of Jena Romanticism as well as the commentary it engenders (from the Romantics themselves, through Benjamin's first book, his *Dissertation*, up to contemporary philosophy). It would be foolish and unnecessary to claim that the projects of the *Athenaeum* or Novalis's *Pollen* are not important for considering how central questions are circumscribed here. However, as I have already indicated, and notwithstanding this general intellectual debt, there are many relevant differences to the precise formulation of my argument. A slightly more technical delineation considering the prolific nature of 'the fragment' as a term in Romantic scholarship will clarify this point. *Fracture and Fragmentation* stands in relation to, but also differs from, a number of works that discuss the fragment as a distinctive Romantic genre. Here I am thinking most prominently of studies by Marjorie Levinson, Thomas McFarland, Sophie Thomas, Anne Janowitz, and Elizabeth Harries in the field of English studies, but also of theoretical discussions by Jean-Luc Nancy, Philippe Lacoue-Labarthe, and Maurice Blanchot that focus mostly on German or French sources. While all of these accounts have influenced my readings, there is a crucial distinction between these engagements with the fragment and my approach.

For all their differences, these critical discussions centre on the fragment as a (mostly literary or philosophical) *genre*. In fact, the two most acclaimed monographs exploring this dimension in the study of British Romanticism starkly enact a critical dichotomy regarding the question of genre. On the one hand stands Thomas McFarland's psychoanalytically and phenomeno-logically inflected *Romanticism and the Forms of Ruin* (1981), which reads the fragment as typical of the Romantic Period because it best articulates that 'Incompleteness, fragmentation, and ruin – the diasparactive triad – are at the very center of life.'[28] McFarland's account takes an eclectic range of European theorisations of the fragment as a basis for an engagement with Wordsworth and Coleridge. While presenting an impressive number of sources on the fragment, McFarland comes close to homogenising them, so as to fit his specific narrative about the interdependence of Wordsworth and Coleridge. McFarland claims that his study's 'most paradoxical ambition is to seem the first instance of a "genre", that Friedrich Schlegel described as not yet existing, one that is "fragmentary both in form and content, simultaneously completely subjective and individual and com-pletely objective"'.[29]

At the other end of the critical spectrum stands Levinson's early work *The Romantic Fragment Poem* (1986), which argues in opposition that 'we should no longer elucidate English practice by German aesthetics'.[30] She complains that 'the fragment poem [...] has escaped demystification' and instead attempts to place her readings of Coleridge, Byron, and other Romantic poets in relation to their relevant contemporary British influences (such as the Ossian fragments).[31] A number of accounts can be situated in between these two poles. Janowitz combines a focus on the fragment as genre with the theme of the ruin-poem. Her analysis of the relation between the collapse of architectural and linguistic forms anticipates certain aspects of Harries's account of the 'deliberate' formalisation of the category of 'the unfinished' in the eighteenth century. Most recently, Sophie Thomas has stressed the status of certain literary fragments in relation to the link between antiquarianism and ruin.[32]

The common assumption of these different accounts of English Romanticism is that (in Elizabeth Cook's words) the fragment is 'a recog-nised [or recognisable] genre'.[33] Lacoue-Labarthe's and Nancy's interest in the form of the fragment shares this approach. Their widely cited study, *The Literary Absolute* (1978), focuses on the fragment as theorised in the *Athenaeum*.[34] Early Jena Romanticism also stands at the centre of Maurice Blanchot's complex engagement with the form of the fragment in Friedrich Schlegel's work, most famously articulated in *The Infinite Conversation* (1969) and *Writing of the Disaster* (1980).[35] The later work in particular has been the focus of wide critical attention and, in turn, has provoked commentary by both Nancy and Lacoue-Labarthe, who set it back into relation to Romanticism.[36] A detailed discussion and identification of the numerous shades of these and other rich and influential accounts is yet to be written.

The crucial point of departure and difference of the present study is that it sidesteps any identification of the fragment as a *genre*. By contrast, my readings emphasise fragmentation and fracture as processes or principles (be they rhetorical or conceptual). In other words, this book wants to shift the focus from the question of 'the fragment' as genre to 'fracture' or 'fragmentation' as notions that create a new explanatory or exploratory grid through which to understand broader categories such as Romanticism. Thus I mobilise fragmentation as a notion whose multifacetedness and intricacy enable conceptual and textual analysis of texts not normally thought of in relation to brokenness. The catalyst of my argument is conceptual rather than generic.

Fragmentation encourages us to look for details, and to perceive the importance of minuteness anew. It requires of us a certain attentiveness that reminds us how each fracture, textual or phenomenological, demands scrutiny in its relation to a larger structure. The relation between the two might uncover the impossibility of the broken piece to be reabsorbed into an original totality. Nevertheless, the initial fantasy of plenitude, of wholeness, can turn out to be enabling and creative. Its failed representation through language, however, always reminds us of the ultimate impossibility of fulfilling this desire. As I have indicated, the chapters of this book often revolve around such fantasies of wholeness that turn out to be broken in their origin or hide a fracture at their centre. The kaleidoscopic structure of the volume reflects this insight, openly hiding Romanticism as its own broken origin. The details that form the patterns in the kaleidoscope are observations on how a particular Romantic aesthetic comes into being by its own negation.

What are at stake, then, are the different forms an opening of Dickinson's 'Gap' can take. These might range from a small detail to larger assumptions about how textual constructs operate. One of the aims of this book is to present material that has not previously been thought of or discussed in relation to the fragmentary. This explains, amongst other things, the omission of the 'obvious choice', Samuel Taylor Coleridge. The readings also attempt to show how different forms of fragmentation play themselves out in the detail of the text. Thus, one of the goals is to illustrate the multilayered aspect of fragmentation. The interpretations are not the result of a rigid theoretical framework which fits literary texts to an argument. In using fragmentation as a critical category, the analysis often proceeds from the microlevel to more general arguments and conclusions.

The overall structure of the book falls roughly into two parts. The first three chapters provide a theoretical frame, discussing accounts of language and aesthetics that shape the second half of the eighteenth century. Here I deal with concerns that emphasise the broader outlines of Romanticism; for example, how questions of language-theory (the origin and fall of language) or categories of aesthetics (the sublime) are generated and find their way into both poetry and theoretical writing. The second part comprises four chapters. It concentrates on how some of these theoretical issues can be identified in writings by William Wordsworth, John Keats, Thomas De Quincey, and Paul de Man. Specifically, I have chosen to locate how rhetorical strategies such as the use of parenthesis or citation are connected to autobiographical and critical writing, how epistolary writing is linked to the creation of a poetic corpus, and what part fracture and fragmentation play in contemporary constructions of Romanticism. It should be clear, however, that this general division merely provides a rough frame of reference for the structure of the book, rather than suggesting the wholesale separation of theoretical framework from specific readings.

The first chapter discusses how the notion of fragmentation plays itself out in the literature of the eighteenth century when understood through the image of the Tower of Babel – a powerful signifier for the fundamental fragmentation of language. Following Walter Benjamin, I understand Babel as symbol of a fundamental rift within the 'history' of language that dooms subsequent linguistic expression to fragmentariness. Close readings show how the language of Wordsworth's poetry and prose makes this concern explicit. His attempt to negotiate the fundamental fracture between the human and the natural in poems such as *The Ruined Cottage* (1798) mirrors the break between the human and a language of plenitude. This is a condition that pervades all of Wordsworth's writing and constitutes its central predicament. A discussion of his *Essays upon Epitaphs* (1810–12) shows how this problematic invades both the argument and the language of Wordsworth's theoretical writings.

In the second chapter, the insights gained in relation to Wordsworth's writing are set in the wider context of the pan-European late eighteenth-century preoccupation with theories of the origin of language (as shown in many texts, including those of Johann Gottfried Herder and Hugh Blair). A rhetorical analysis of works by figures such as Georg Hamann, Lord Kames, James Beattie, and James Harris illustrates that their arguments point towards the impossibility of overcoming a rift within language at its origin. This fundamental break is associated with the figure of anthropomorphism, normally taken to be limited to its rhetorical function. By examining its wider meaning and implications, both as a literary as well as a philosophical and theological term, I show how anthropomorphism becomes a concentrated figure for an inescapable rupture within language, which is of such concern to a number of Romantic poets and theorists.

The next chapter takes reports on the 1755 Lisbon earthquake as its starting point in order to make explicit the deep-seated link between conceptions of fragmentation and the category of the sublime. Here, fragmentation is conceived as both external and internal fracture (the external, actual fragmentation of the city, and the consequent collapse of imagination). A discussion of the eye-witness accounts of the earthquake via Edmund Burke's *A Philosophical Enquiry into the Origin of our Ideas of the Sublime and Beautiful* (1757) shows the relevance of the notion of fragmentation to this pivotal work of British aesthetics. By reading Immanuel Kant's account of the dynamic sublime as developed in the *Critique of Judgement* (1790, rev. 1793 and 1799) in relation to his wider corpus, especially his writings on the Lisbon disaster, I show that fragmentation lies at the heart of this supposedly rationalising account of an important category of the aesthetic. The wider claim is that fragmentation is located at the centre of a rationalising process that leads from the moment of the sublime to its representation, and, also, at the centre of a narrative of secularisation which takes the 'scientific' response to the Lisbon earthquake as a marker in European Enlightenment.

The fourth chapter links the general problem of the hermeneutical gap between experience and narration to the notion of fracture in autobiographical writing. It does so via the grammatical and rhetorical figure of parenthesis. A reading of crucial moments and episodes in *The Prelude* (1850) establishes the connection between parenthesis and fracture. I identify parenthesis as the rhetorical and conceptual sign of Wordsworth's difficulties when negotiating the breaks of a supposedly organic narrative of 'growth'. The analysis shows that some of the most important moments of *The Prelude* – moments identified by Wordsworth himself as sources of the creative process – are parenthetical in nature. Fracture, paradoxically, becomes the structuring principle of autobiographical coherence in *The Prelude* as well as the figure that shapes some of its culminating episodes.

The chapter on John Keats's letters is closely related to the idea of fragmentary self-construction. It considers how the letter's dialogic form negotiates the problem of the gap between writer and reader. Simultaneously, the letter maintains its position within a larger system of epistolary writing which can be theorised through the framework of gift-theory, following the rhetoric of economics in the letters. The classification of the letters becomes one of the main ordering principles for an understanding of the literary entity 'Keats'. Here, the notion of the archive is of crucial importance. Fragmentary by definition (no archive is ever complete), it stands in a productive relationship with documents that provide literature and its critics with the possibility of constructing literary bodies such as Keats's. In this case, his fragmented letters form the basis for the literary corpus of Keats.

The sixth chapter investigates the status of citation, understood as a fragmenting moment, as it informs the project of Thomas De Quincey's critical writings on Wordsworth. The fracturing power of citation works in two ways: it fragments the text that contains it, and the text the citation is taken from. De Quincey's writing, in the way it cites Wordsworth, puts fragmentation at the centre of his project. My reading here is linked to a philosophical understanding of citation theorised in the writings of Walter Benjamin. Citation is identified as a crucial mechanism in the archivisation and construction of categories such as Romanticism, of which Wordsworth becomes the representative poet. De Quincey's strategy of citation archives the fracturing and double-sided force of this citational dynamic as an aspect of the category of Romanticism itself. Together with Benjamin (the bracketing figure of the book) this archiving moment exemplifies how the topics, areas, and texts that are discussed here relate to general questions about Romanticism, as well as to more local, literary-critical concerns.

The final chapter turns to the importance of linguistic fracture in the recent constructions of Romanticism offered by Paul de Man. Especially in his later work, a curious tension between systematicity and the insistence on fracture determines de Man's theoretical position. The fracture between language and subject becomes one of the most important conditions of his thinking. However, locating fracture at the heart of a systematic account results in difficulties for de Man. A close analysis of his lecture on Walter Benjamin reveals a reluctance to acknowledge the destabilising consequences of putting a disruptive figure, such as fracture, at the centre of linguistics.

This has significant consequences for conceptualising the category of Romanticism through language, as de Man attempts to do in *The Rhetoric of Romanticism* (1984). A reading of the preface to this work illustrates the way that, via the Romantic legacy of de Man and Benjamin, fracture finds its way into a contemporary account of Romanticism. The book closes with an explanation of why the assumed weakness of such an account might be better understood as a part of its methodological strength.

CHAPTER I

A brotherhood is broken: Babel and the fragmentation of language

NATURE'S MOURNING AND WORDSWORTH'S
THE RUINED COTTAGE

And the Lord said, Behold, the people *is* one, and they have all one language; and this [the building of the Tower of Babel] they begin to do: and now nothing will be restrained from them, which they have imagined to do. Go to, let us go down and there confound their language, that they may not understand one another's speech. So the LORD scattered them abroad from thence upon the face of all the earth: and they left off to build the city. Therefore is the name of it called Babel; because the LORD did there confound the language of all the earth: and from thence did the LORD scatter them abroad upon the face of all the earth. (Gen. 11.6–9)[1]

The story of the Tower of Babel is one of the most poignant and powerful images for the fragmentation of language. It is a condensed trope of an ideal Language of plenitude and understanding being broken, scattering with its fragmentation peoples, their communication with each other, and their position as subjects in the natural world. This first chapter will use the image of Babel to explore several different dimensions of linguistic fracture and scattering, and think about how they are negotiated in the poetry of William Wordsworth. It proposes to understand Babel as a trope or conceptual springboard that goes further than the first narratorial layer of the biblical story. This approach also makes it possible to explore an important link between Wordsworth's poetry and Walter Benjamin's early writings on language. The analysis follows a curious double move in Wordsworth's *The Ruined Cottage* (1798) that is mirrored in a powerful way in Benjamin's quasi-theological essay 'On Language as Such and on the Language of Man' (1916). To follow such mirroring is not to argue for an 'application' of one text to the other but rather to observe that the interaction between these two works can illuminate certain dimensions of Romantic writing and thinking. Wordsworth and Benjamin, in their very different ways, share a deep conviction that language stands at the very beginning of an understanding of the world and its representation. While it is important to keep in mind their differences, it is fruitful to examine some conceptual and poetical crossing-points in their writings, especially considering the importance of these two authors for the links between linguistic theory and Romanticism. It can help us to reread the Wordsworthian text, and allows us to see how powerfully Benjamin continues to think in a particular Romantic tradition.[2] Their different ways of negotiating how poetic language exhibits a linguistic predicament, namely its fragmentariness, which defines how the human subject situates itself in the world, offer new insights into Wordsworth's poetical practice as well as shed light on Benjamin's analytical claims. One text here can help illuminate the other without having to neglect their respective historical, conceptual, and formal specificities, or wilfully harmonising their relation.

Benjamin himself mentions the story of the Tower of Babel in 'On Language as Such', arguing for its dimensions beside the purely exegetical or revelatory:

If in what follows the nature of language is considered on the basis of the first chapter of Genesis, the purpose [*Zweck*] of this is neither to pursue biblical interpretation nor, here, to ground thinking on the Bible as objectively revealed truth; rather, what shall be discovered arises from the biblical text itself in regard to the nature of language.[3]

We can see how understanding Babel as an image of and for linguistic fragmentation serves as an enabling fiction for thinking about the consequences of this shattering and how its different dimensions play themselves out in a variety of texts.

The most immediate way of understanding the myth of Babel is as a prime image for the fragmentation of what one might call an *Ursprache* (an Ur-language). This Language is – if it can be at all thought of as a system of signification – a mode of communication in which there is no possible misunderstanding, where there is a perfect match between signifier and signified. The idea of this pre-Babelian or Adamic Language (despite their different locations in Genesis, these two are often equated) in its various forms has been a constant concern in the history of western linguistics.[4] Often the shortcomings or failings of natural languages, our linguistic predicament or condition, implicitly contrast with an idea of an original Language of plenitude as the ultimate source of poetical language. For the Benjamin of 'The Task of the Translator' (1923), this 'pure Language' is the ideal but irrecoverable realm that serves as the intentional object of natural languages, thereby making translation between them possible.[5] By figuring its original loss as a mythical linguistic fall, Benjamin in 'On Language as

Such' follows a tradition of literary-philosophical forms that during the Enlightenment and Romanticism actively attempt to satisfy a yearning for this pre-Babelian *Ursprache*. These include, to name but a few, poetic practice, linguistic theory, biblical hermeneutics, and philosophical thought. Inversely, the Tower of Babel becomes the ultimate image of the poetic condition, fragmentation of the *Ursprache* standing at the beginning of all linguistic or poetic formulation. As part of this wider framework, Benjamin's statements on language and Wordsworth's poetical practice offer important instances for understanding why the specific notion of fragmentation is especially powerful in relation to Romantic writing. While the fragmentary condition of language is ultimately irrevocable, this need not be as negative as it first seems. We will see how a certain Romanticism successfully defines itself through that fragmentation, understanding it as a productive and self-cognitive category. This also explains my reading of Benjamin here, which to some might seem rather melancholic. It concentrates on his discussion of linguistic limitations rather than focussing on the seemingly more optimistic gestures towards a redemptive theory of language. As I insisted in the introduction, such an acknowledgement of limitations, including the impossibility of attaining redemption, does not necessarily result in a defeatist version of melancholia or compensatory idealism.

The juncture that I want to emphasise in Wordsworth and Benjamin lies in the relation between nature and the linguistic subject – categories of paramount importance to Romanticism. I will begin by following a double movement that parallels and mirrors Benjamin's text with, and in, Wordsworth's *The Ruined Cottage*. This double movement centres on the negotiation of the relation between nature and language. At a crucial moment, Benjamin's essay mysteriously states:

It is a metaphysical truth that all nature would begin to lament if language was conferred on it. (Though 'to confer language' is more than 'to make her able to speak'.) This proposition has a double meaning. First it means: nature would lament about language itself. Speechlessness: that is nature's great grief (and it is for the sake of her redemption that life and language of *Man* – not solely, as one often suspects, the language of the poet – are in nature). Secondly, the proposition states: she would lament. Lament, however, is the most undifferentiated, impotent expression of language, it almost only contains the sensuous breath; and wherever there is only a rustling of plants, a lament always resonates within it. Because she is mute, nature mourns.[6]

Nature suffers and mourns because of its own muteness. And, Benjamin adds, one of the objectives of human language, as a language that can also be *within nature*, is to redeem nature from this condition. Secondly, Benjamin remarks that nature would *mourn*. The 'impotent expression' [*ohnmächtige Ausdruck*] only contains the breath of presence belonging to any utterance; it is, however, far from being differentiated, articulate, or eloquent. Through his example Benjamin openly invokes general parallels with Romantic poetry. As Geoffrey Hartman succinctly remarks, the trope of 'woods and waters mourning in the poet's mode' has long surpassed the status of the traditional and can already be described as a 'cliché'.[7]

Benjamin's twofold explanation for why nature would lament if endowed with language is paralleled at a crucial moment in Wordsworth's *The Ruined Cottage*. The beginning of the old pedlar's story about Margaret, her abandonment, and her eventual death serves as an epigrammatic moment for his speech as well as the poem as a whole. The narrator recounts the old man's speech about how when mourning and 'lamenting the departed', '[T]he poets' call nature to their help 'in their elegies and songs'.[8] This calling takes the form of an invocation, assimilating nature to the traditional *topoi* of the muse: not only Wordsworth and the narrator of *The Ruined Cottage*, but also the narrator within it (the old man telling his story to the narrator) are firmly located within Romantic ideas of nature. The poets,

> in their elegies and songs
> Lamenting the departed call the groves,
> They call upon the hills and streams to mourn,
> And senseless rocks, nor idly; for they speak
> In these their invocations with a voice
> Obedient to the strong creative power
> Of human passion. (*RC*, 73–9)

Nature in all its entirety is said to mourn with the poet: wood (grove), earth (hills), water (streams), and stone (rocks) are all the objects of the poet's call. It is remarkable how the text reinforces an unease about the inanimate, since we think of rocks as 'senseless' in two ways. On the one hand, they illustrate that some constituents of nature (especially inorganic ones) are fundamentally lacking in complexity of feeling: they do not have senses. Secondly, and as a result, they cannot express these feelings; they are senseless: they cannot use their senses, cannot see, touch, feel, or speak. It is not clear at all, then, how they could possibly mourn, and, furthermore, why the poet would 'call' these 'senseless' stones to mourn in the first place. This apparent difficulty is immediately resolved. We read that, contrary to our common assumption, the invocation, the 'call' of the poet, is not idle. In effect, 'they [the groves, hills, and streams] speak / In these their invocations', echoing the poets' calls. It is crucial that this plural ('they') can refer not only to the poets but also to the different parts of nature. Nature, previously thought to be 'senseless', speaks in its multitude 'with a voice'. This 'voice' will be mourning, but is also 'Obedient to the strong creative power / Of human passion'. It thus follows the poet's 'call'; it obeys him. It is in this way that human language, the poet's language, as a language *within* nature, redeems nature from its senseless condition. Nature suddenly obeys a 'strong creative power' and, as a result, speaks a language filled with lamentation. A few lines later this grief encompasses the human figure too. We read that the old man stood beside 'yon spring' (*RC*, 82) and 'eyed its waters till we seemed to feel / One sadness, they and I' (*RC*, 83–4). Nature here mourns, but in an inarticulate way. Crying does not allow for eloquent speech or differentiated expression: the second moment of Benjamin's thought finds its parallel here.

This, however, is not where the analysis ends; Benjamin expands or rather rethinks his argument:

But the reversal of this proposition leads even deeper into the essence [*Wesen*] of nature: the sadness of nature makes her become silent. All mourning contains the deepest tendency to speechlessness; and that is infinitely more than the inability or reluctance to communicate. That which mourns thus feels known through and through by the unknowable.[9]

A variant reading in MS. B of *The Ruined Cottage* provides the possibility of expanding the comparison drawn so far. Here the poem takes back some of the assuredness it exhibited in regard to a speaking nature: the old man stands next to the spring and exclaims that 'The waters of that spring if they could feel / [M]ight mourn' (*RC*, MS. B, 135–6; my emphasis). In the same way that 'the poets' have disappeared in this draft, the assuredness that nature can respond has gone too: 'They [the waters] are not as they were' (*RC*, MS. B, 136). Instead of mourning in the same manner, the waters of the spring are not the same as the waters of the old man's tears. We find in this an echo of the previous reading. There the old man 'eyed its [the spring's] waters' (*RC*, 83); however, even at its most extreme they only '*seemed* to feel / One sadness, they and I' (*RC*, 83–4; my emphasis). As much as the 'I' attempts to merge with the waters through an alteration in its 'eye', the two stay distinct. The tears remain salty, the river sweet.

In both versions of the poem, the reason for this separation is the same: 'a ['the', MS. B] bond / Of brotherhood is broken' (*RC*, 85). The brotherhood between nature and man has been fractured. This break goes further than William Ulmer's suggestion that Wordsworth's pantheistic vision 'was always less confident and complete than critics often contend'.[10] In fact, here nature and human do not even speak a uniting language anymore, and it is impossible for them to mourn in the same manner. Note that just as the reversal of Benjamin's sentence allows him to read his statement more profoundly, this does not contradict the reading above, but rather turns it around. In all mourning there is a drive towards silence, and nature exhibits this drive; this is the deeper meaning of Benjamin's initial statement. Importantly, the broken brotherhood between nature and the human subject results not only in nature's mourning, but also in its subsequent muteness. It is important to contextualise this fracture of the brotherhood between nature and man. Through a further reading of Benjamin, Wordsworth, and sources surrounding them, I will place this moment of rupture in relation to the Babelian myth.[11]

If the 'bond' was originally intact, it seems reasonable to suggest that man and nature once communicated without the insurmountable barrier of nature's silence. As *The Ruined Cottage* puts it: 'They [the waters] are not as they were' [*RC*, MS. B, 136]. There were times '[W]hen every day the touch of human hand / Disturbed their stillness, and they ministered / To human comfort' (*RC*, 86–8). The human hand was once able to disturb the stillness, the muteness, of the waters. 'Disturbed' here is not necessarily negative. It means that communication could take place between the waters and the human in the past. The 'stillness' is complementary, if read as a muteness which could be 'disturbed' or interrupted by human action, and answer intelligibly in return. The lines suggest that the bond of brotherhood is a reformulation or a rethinking of the past in which such communication was possible. In one case it is a dash, in the other a colon that separates the break of the 'brotherhood' and the remembrance of a previous state. The waters 'ministered' to human comfort, but not only by providing essential water. They also ministered in the sense of 'communicating' (*OED*); they 'communicate' human comfort, speak to the human. Now, however, 'A spider's web' hangs over the well 'And on the wet and slimy foot-stone lay / The useless fragment of a wooden bowl' (*RC*, 89–91). Communion is prevented. This is the lasting legacy of the pride of Babel's inhabitants who wanted to 'make themselves a name'. They make an affirmation that is inherently self-contradictory because the people of Babel (which literally means 'confusion') build the tower so as to make themselves a name – the only thing that linguistically unites them as a group.[12] The bowl is thus not only a symbol of the former inhabitants of the cottage and their brother-hood with the waters. It also represents the vessel of the pre-Babelian language that is fragmented.[13] The bowl, a human product, lies next to the well with which it is impossible to communicate anymore. It does not serve as a closed vessel in order to 'minister'; its fragmentation prevents the successful carrying of water or signification. The biblical associations are unmistakable.

The most direct reference is to Ecclesiastes, a part of the Old Testament that is deeply concerned with fragmentation. One of its central passages reads: 'Or ever the silver cord be loosed, or the golden bowl be broken, or the pitcher be broken at the fountain, or the wheel broken at the cistern. [...] and the spirit shall return unto God who gave it. Vanity of vanities, saith the preacher; all *is* vanity' (Eccles. 12.6–8).[14] There are further links between these passages from the Bible and *The Ruined Cottage* under the sign of Babel. Ecclesiastes reminds us that 'That which hath been is named already' (6.10) and that the memory of the dead is 'forgotten' (9.5). In fact, 'Also their love, and their hatred, and their envy, is now perished; neither have they any more a portion for ever in any *thing* that is done under the sun' (9.6). The old man, whose direct speech will take up most of the poem, begins thus:

> we die, my Friend,
> Nor we alone, but that which each man loved
> And prized in his peculiar nook of earth
> Dies with him or is changed, and very soon
> Even of the good is no memorial left.   (*RC*, 68–72)

The fragments of earth, the 'nooks', special to 'each man', and the memories that he connects with them, will vanish with his death. But worse, 'very soon / Even of the good is no memorial left'. This is the moment where the poets have to bond with nature to preserve the memory of the deceased in 'elegies and songs'. The proximity of these passages reinforces the presence of the biblical text in Wordsworth's poem. The biblical myth of Babel – in which vanity and pride result in the fragmentation of a God-given language – is an implicit condition for the poem.

To pause, reiterate, and look forward: communication between man and nature has become impossible; the confusion of tongues is also a sign for the break between the natural world and man. In human terms, Babel results in confused babble and noise; for nature, the linguistic fall results in silence. Babel not only thematises the incapacity of human subjects to communicate with each other. It also becomes a sign for the divide between the human subject and the natural world. Following Benjamin, if an understanding of the language of nature were possible, it would only occur through instances of mourning. This mourning is a result of the silence brought by the Babelian confusion. The second part of this chapter will show how we can identify certain strategies in *The Ruined Cottage*, as well as Wordsworth's wider oeuvre, that are designed to overcome a comparable impasse of non-communication and muteness. *The Ruined Cottage* does not start with the assumption that nature is silent or mourning. In fact, at the beginning it is negative on the first point and neutral on the second. The narrator describes the old man in the following manner:

> He was a chosen son:
> To him was given an ear which deeply felt
> The voice of Nature in the obscure wind,
> The sounding mountain and the running stream.
>
> (*RC*, MS. B, 76–8)

Given the biblical overtones, this is a bold description – and not only for referring to the old man as a 'son'. He is a 'chosen' son of God, a special human being; although not a Christ-like figure, he has a divine gift. Intriguingly, this gift is a special sense: an 'ear' is 'given' to the man that 'deeply' feels the 'voice of Nature'. The 'chosen son' can decipher with a God-given gift the hieroglyphic nature around him. Even if the wind is 'obscure', he can 'feel' the 'voice of Nature' in it. We remember that, according to Benjamin, 'to confer language' is far more than 'making speak'. This chosen son can decipher the obscure noises of the winds as language, just as he can understand 'The sounding mountain and the running stream'. Nature not only speaks to him through sounds but also connects them to a 'running stream'. The text closely links this sense-ability of the old man, his special 'ear', to another power:

> To every natural form, rock, fruit and flower,
> Even the loose stones that cover the highway,
> He gave a moral life; he saw them feel
> Or linked them to some feeling. (*RC*, MS. B, 80–3)

The old man sees nature feel, his ear feels deeply; he thereby deciphers nature's language or links it to 'some feeling'. The last qualification is, as we have seen, vital in the remainder of the poem. It is this link that will be broken.

This affective power, however, is not the end of the old man's sense-abilities. His command over nature's mysterious cyphers includes the use of other sensory organs too:

> he had an eye which evermore
> Looked deep into the shades of difference
> As they lie hid in all exterior forms,

> Which from a stone, a tree, a withered leaf,
> To the broad ocean and the azure heavens
> Spangled with kindred multitudes of stars,
> Could find no surface where its power might sleep,
> Which spake perpetual logic to his soul,
> And by an unrelenting agency
> Did bind his feelings even as in a chain.   (*RC*, MS. B, 94–103)

Any reading of this sentence will confront the partial unintelligibility of its mixed metaphors. But this should not impede attempting to understand its sources. It is clear enough that the old man's eye has special powers, putting it in a realm similar to the divine gift of his hearing. The eye, like the ear, can decipher nature's language, and 'look deep into the shades of difference'. It can therefore distinguish between the different constituent systems within language and can read the 'shades', the representations within 'difference'. These shades 'lie hid in all exterior forms'; that is to say that they are somehow behind (lie hidden in) natural phenomena. The exterior forms are described as 'a stone, a tree, a withered leaf', representing nature through single and particular examples. The 'shades of difference' reside in a reading of nature's microcosmic instances (a stone, a tree, or a dying leaf). However, they also encompass the most sublime aspects of nature, 'the broad ocean and the azure heavens / Spangled with kindred multitudes of stars'. The old man, then, has the ability to read and see into the mysteries of the entire natural world. He can read the 'exterior forms', and, thus, all natural phenomena. But his special senses provide him with an even deeper reading. The 'chosen son' can look into the 'shades of difference', the structure, which lies beneath the surface. The old man understands nature's language and what lies behind it: he knows its grammar. The structure of the language read by the old man seems to be located in a transcendental source. A cosmic order reigns behind the 'exterior forms' and is understood as akin to language – language in a deeper and wider sense than usual, but language nevertheless. We can understand this structure to correspond to a perfect Language without confusion and scattering. It is in this sense that we can call it pre-Babelian. The old man, at first, seems to have access to this structure. There is little doubt that he is a positive and powerful figure throughout the poem. His senses, allowing him to read the language of nature, are fulfilling and enabling: 'Though poor in outward shew' (as a result of passing his life in a 'poor occupation'), the old man is 'most rich' (*RC*, MS. B, 86, 68). His wealth lies in the gift his creator has given him and, as a result, 'He had a world about him – 'twas his own' (*RC*, MS. B, 87). And, being the sole inhabitant of this world (because nobody apart from God can read it in an adequate way), he is the owner of the entire cosmos, down to the stones that cover the highway, just as much as the oceans and the heavens with their stars. The ability to *read* and understand the language of nature through special sense-awareness is the method by which this understanding can be achieved. The poem insists that the special eye is 'Flashing poetic fire' (*RC*, MS. B, 71), thus suggesting that the power of deciphering has itself a poetical quality to it.

However, the reading of this passage is not as straightforward as this first glance might indicate. After referring to the 'multitudes of stars', the sentence becomes very hard to follow.[15] Until then it is elaborate and intricate, but not convoluted. Suddenly, it is not clear grammatically what certain parts of the sentence refer to. Presumably it is the eye which finds 'no surface where its power might sleep'. But the narrator has already lost the initial localised metaphor which dealt with 'a stone, a tree, a withered leaf'. It is as if, after expanding over the regions of sublimity, the sentence loses its hold and collapses. Consequently, the suggestion of order ('perpetual logic') becomes double-edged. Naturally, this is not the only grammatically ambiguous sentence in *The Ruined Cottage*. Through its specific context in the poem, however, its 'confusion' points, maybe inadvertently, towards a structural aspect which is easily overlooked. During these lines, the sentence loses its hold and the referent becomes unclear. This grammatical collapse occurs at a moment when the potential insight into a much larger structure is advertised. The narrator wants to advocate the old man's ability to look into the mysteries of natural phenomena and read them fully. During the description of this procedure, the narrator's own language suddenly collapses. He is not able to structure the description adequately (not in poetic, but in purely grammatical terms). In view of his gifts, the old man is able to express the ability to read nature. The poetic persona, however, who relates this ability, does not perform his task successfully. Consequently, the unstable status of the narrator as an intermediary immediately suggests itself.

The insistence on narratorial unreliability at this particular moment in the poem is important, if only because most of *The Ruined Cottage* is related by the old man himself (or at least is quoted in direct speech). Thus the convoluted sentence is trying to describe something that is impossible to describe. The alleged reading of nature in the terms that the narrator ascribes to the old man is not (and cannot be) successful. After the narrator finishes describing the old man's sense-abilities, the latter actively denies the powers that have been ascribed to him by the narrator. As we have already seen above, he responds negatively to his ability to decipher nature. In fact, it is he who announces that 'the bond / Of brotherhood is broken'. The status of this claim is problematic, but no more so than the report the narrator gives us. This report, the reader understands, is at least partly a projection. It is an ideal that the narrator himself cannot achieve, not even when describing it. The reason for this failure is voiced by the object of his ideal projection, the old man himself: nature cannot be read as successfully as we wish or imagine, even when there is a significant effort to connect with it (think of the old man crying next to the well). This relates both to the content of the old man's speech and to its position in the poem. Not only is *The Ruined Cottage* itself fragmented into large quotations and narratives but the misreading of the old man's qualities also leaves its trace, both in minute terms (the convoluted sentence) and in a larger contradiction (the old man ruling out the narrator's report by definition). In short, the narrator misreads the nature of the chosen son. It is no surprise, then, that this error should precipitate a moment of structural disintegration.[16] This interpretation of the passage leaves us with a question about what *kind* of misreading the narrator enacts. In the wider context of the present concern, the idealistic terms of the misreading are of importance. The ability that the old man is supposed to have is presented as a gift to be valued above any material wealth. It characterises itself by a total understanding of nature and the ordering principles behind it. In terms of language and its origin, this kind of understanding and vocabulary refer to the realm of the prelapsarian.

Babel is a rupture in the 'history' of language, the symbol for the fragmentation of an *Ursprache* accessible for all peoples. One way to understand this rupture is to comprehend it as an event which conditions all subsequent poetry. This totalising claim is not to be understood as covering the entirety of the subjects available to poetry. It does stress, however, that poems like *The Ruined Cottage* point towards the condition of rupture as an underlying prefix rather than towards a 'basis for community in the errant instabilities of mortal experience'.[17] The awareness of this prefix is discovered through the language of the poem itself, which exhibits the very limitations it is aware of. The remainder of this chapter will explore some forms that the desire takes to overcome this necessary fragmentation (what was termed 'yearning' at the start). This yearning is a desire for a Language as a perfect medium of communication without the dangers of confusion and scattering.

One attempt to overcome our linguistic condition has already been located in Wordsworth's *The Ruined Cottage*. Although finally the yearning is not fulfilled (after all, 'the bond / Of brotherhood is broken'), the suggestion remains that an answer might lie in the complexity and depth of the natural world. It might be the function of poetry to mediate a solution that lies all around us. Remember that it is the 'poetic fire' which allegedly makes the old man's eye so special. This is not to be confused with the idea that the language of nature is inherently perfect. As we have seen in Wordsworth's poetry, nature's utterances are often mournful. Invoking Benjamin again, I want to explore how elsewhere in Wordsworth an expression of this mourning is related to speechlessness, and how, thereby, the yearning for a Language of plenitude is connected with silence.

THE PENTECOSTAL FANTASY AND SILENCE

The motive for the mourning of nature is the fundamental rift between her and the human subject. The ensuing silence causes melancholy and its expression in mourning. It is the lack of communication that is at the heart of nature's lamentation. And even within recognition and aesthetic description of this melancholy by the human subject, it is not possible to bridge the gap. Not even the old man of *The Ruined Cottage* can merge with the stream; they continue to talk in different languages. However, it is nature itself that also points towards a possible solution. This occurs in a variety of ways. First, I will concentrate on how the 'Arab Dream' of Book 5 of *The Prelude* (1805) explores the desire to overcome the poem's linguistic condition. This attempt is tied to another biblical image of communication, namely Pentecost. Secondly, I will show how Wordsworth's *Essays upon Epitaphs* (1810–12) and two of his poems thematise a merging with nature as an attempt to surpass linguistic confusion in a meaningful silence.

The initial anxiety about the perishable nature of human achievements expressed in Book 5 of *The Prelude* gives way to the famous dream about the figure of the Arab. The narrator's friend, having read *Don Quixote*, falls asleep next to the sea and passes 'into a dream' in which he sees 'before him an Arabian Waste / A Desart'.[18] The lines move straight to the joyful encounter with the Arab; the dreamer is happy to have 'a Guide / To lead him through the Desart' (*1805*, 5. 81–2). He follows the Bedouin, who carries a mysterious stone and a shell. The explanation of the significance these objects hold is one of *The Prelude*'s best-known passages:

> the Arab told him that the Stone,
> To give it in the language of the Dream,
> Was Euclid's Elements; 'And this,' said he,

> 'This other,' pointing to the Shell, 'this book
> Is something of more worth.' And, at the word,
> The Stranger, said my Friend continuing,
> Stretch'd forth the Shell towards me, with command
> That I should hold it to my ear: I did so;
> And heard that instant in an unknown Tongue,
> Which yet I understood, articulate sounds,
> A loud prophetic blast of harmony,
> An Ode, in passion utter'd, which foretold
> Destruction to the Children of the Earth,
> By deluge now at hand.   (*1805*, 5. 86–99)

Before discussing the nature of the shell in detail, we should direct our attention towards a line at the beginning of the passage. The sentence about 'the Arab' who 'told him that the stone [...] / Was Euclid's Elements' is interrupted and broken by a strange qualification: 'To give it in the language of the Dream'. All that follows as reported speech from the Arab is a translation (this is the implication of 'to give' here). This qualification reinforces the point, not only that there are different kinds of languages (the language of the dream as opposed to the language of nature, of men, or a pre-Babelian Language), but also that the difference really is one in kind rather than simply of degree.[19]

Even within the language of the dream, the differences between spheres are remarkably unstable and contradictory. The senseless stone will be the book of 'Euclid's Elements', the work describing nature geometrically and rationally. There is, however, something above the book and stone that represents coherent systematicity – 'something of more worth': the shell of poetry that the Arab carries. The Arab commands, like a biblical figure, that 'I should hold it to my ear'. The dreamer follows the command ('I did so'), and this triggers what I want to call the text's Pentecostal fantasy. Without being able to resist, once the shell is held to his ear, the dreamer hears 'A loud prophetic blast of harmony, / An Ode, in passion utter'd'. It is important precisely how this ode foretells destruction. The instant the dreamer holds it to his ear, he hears the prophetic blast 'in an unknown Tongue, / Which yet I understood, articulate sounds'. The abundance of biblical imagery in these lines is remarkable. What started off with an ambiguous 'command' turns into 'prophetic blasts'. The proceedings are just like those described in Acts 2: the tongues of fire appear to the Apostles, rest on them, and they then are all filled with the Holy Spirit. As a consequence they start speaking in tongues but are understood by everyone. Although in *The Prelude* it is an 'unknown tongue' that the dreamer understands (whereas the Apostles suddenly speak in tongues previously unknown to them), the result is similar: the Babelian confusion of language is resolved. Despite their uniting qualities, both prophesies speak of destruction: *The Prelude*'s 'Destruction to the Children of the Earth' echoes the biblical vision that 'it shall come to pass in the last days, saith God, I will pour out of my Spirit upon all flesh […] And I will shew wonders in the heaven above, and signs in the earth beneath; blood, and fire, and vapour of smoke' (Acts, 2.17–19). Yet again, however, the Wordsworthian text varies the biblical imagery when its prophetic vision tells of a universal 'deluge'. This is the drowning which in Genesis immediately precedes the story of Babel and links these two myths intimately.[20]

Wordsworth's text overlaps the biblical text with his own. The 'prophetic blast' is an instance where linguistic confusion is overcome; not only can the language of a dream be understood, but also, within it, an unknown tongue speaks in articulate sounds. The location of this vision within the dream indicates a condition of its possibility. It is only within a dream that the speaker overcomes his Babelian predicament. And, most importantly, it is through nature that he does so. The *shell* speaks in a multitude of tongues, an apocalyptic vision in which it foretells destruction 'by deluge now at hand'. Although it is the figure of the Arab who declares 'That all was true' (*1805*, 5. 101), the shell's voice, the 'prophetic blast', is primary. It is through nature, even if through nature in a dream, that the Babelian condition is overcome.[21] The image of the shell (poetry) as the apostolic speaker offers a strong, very insistent image of a pre-Babelian restoration. It is further reinforced a few lines later when the 'book' (the shell) is described as:

> a God, yea many Gods,
> Had voices more than all the winds and was
> A joy, a consolation and a hope.   (*1805*, 5. 107–9)

These multilingual and divine winds are akin to the 'strong driving wind' coming from the sky and filling 'the whole house where they [the Apostles] were sitting. And there appeared to them tongues like flames of fire, dispersed among them and resting on each one' (Acts, 2.2). In the Pentecostal fantasy, the barriers between language and nature are resolved in the prophetic blast of the shell's ode.

However, all this occurs in the 'language of the dream', along with any Pentecostal attempt to resolve the contradictions governing poetic language. That the stone and shell are suddenly books and 'I wondered not' (*1805*, 5. 111) – that they simultaneously remain both stone and shell – makes

the reader wonder in turn. The ontology of the Arab is equally problematic
to grasp. He simultaneously is Don Quixote and the Arab, but, at the same
time, neither of these two:

> I fancied that he was the very Knight
> Whose tale Cervantes tells, yet not the Knight,
> But, was an Arab of the Desart, too;
> Of these was neither, and was both at once.   (*1805*, 5. 123–6)

The language of the dream and the Pentecostal experience make it possible
for the shell or the Arab to 'escape' the law of the excluded middle – they
can be x and not-x at the same time. Only in a divine sphere that belongs
to the 'Gods' can such a state be achieved. Unless language enters the
sphere of the dream or the divine it stays bound to the conceptual and
linguistic necessities that describe the predicament of a fallen language.
It is at the most basic level, through its own means, that *The Prelude*
reminds us that the Pentecostal moment cannot occur within the realms
of a human language. The shell is already twice removed. First by the
'language of the dream', and, secondly, by the post-Babelian terms that
describe it in a poetic text. The predicament of post-Babelian language
includes a need for the language of difference: to describe existence any
violation of the law of the excluded middle results in impossibility. The
language of *The Prelude* cannot itself be Pentecostal. Within its sphere,
nature and poetry can be portrayed as the most likely candidates for the
achievement of linguistic harmony. But in the end it must capitulate
before the shortcomings of its own medium, while retaining the fantasy
of poetry as apostolic.[22] Once again, Wordsworth's text mournfully
reminds us that the Babelian condition draws a distinction of kind and
not of degree.

The second essay of *Essays upon Epitaphs* inadvertently reveals how poetry
is affected to the core by the condition of linguistic fragmentation.
Wordsworth illustrates his argument for the stylistic importance of the
epitaphic with a number of examples. Notoriously, these include a
German inscription taken from Coleridge. It is, writes Wordsworth:

thus literally translated. "Ah! They have laid in the Grave a brave Man – he was to
me more than many!"

> Ach! sie haben
> Einen Braven
> Mann begraben –
> Mir war er mehr als viele.[23]

The commentary in W. J. B. Owen's standard edition of the *Prose* points out that 'Wordsworth's version of the German is nearer to Coleridge's translation than to his version of the German' (*Prose*, 2. 107). This may be so, but the notes fail to mention a strange and (in this context) telling circumstance. The translation Wordsworth gives, and announces as literal, falls prey to his difficulty with the German language. Wordsworth's translation is rather misleading. 'Brav' generally means 'well-behaved' or 'worthy' (there is an etymological link to 'brave', but it is rather weak). 'Brave' translates as 'mutig' – the meaning of the epitaph is quite different from what Wordsworth takes it to be. I draw attention to this point not to criticise Wordsworth's language skills – that would be foolish – but rather to suggest that this unnoticed slippage attains a special significance in the context in which it occurs. The Babelian confusion, which all poetry must labour under, is exhibited over the course of an argument that approximates epitaphic expression and poetical expression per se. That this slippage takes place in the *Essays upon Epitaphs* foregrounds it all the more. The close connection of Wordsworth's poetry to the genre and theme of the epitaph is well known. Its significance ranges from identifying all of Wordsworth's poetry as essentially epitaphic to more moderate claims that, through the alteration of traditional epitaphic form, Wordsworth creates the form of his own, and Romanticism's, lyric.[24] Geoffrey Hartman long ago claimed that 'what Wordsworth did is clear: he transformed the inscription into an independent nature poem, and in so doing created a principal form of the Romantic and modern lyric'.[25] Thus, Wordsworth's small mistranslation concentrates two lines of the present concerns. Babel haunts not only the epitaph Wordsworth cites, but also, by extension, the argument he makes about poetry, style, and nature. It serves as a powerful reminder of the poetics within which Wordsworth operates. However, the epitaph is also located closest (in both thematic and physical terms) to a realm in which linguistic confusion can supposedly be overcome: the grave, which marks both death and the subsequent merging of the human with the natural.

At the beginning of the *Essays*, Wordsworth reminds us that the epitaph presupposes a monument. The grave is a place where nature and the human merge, a nexus where mourning, monument, and nature overlap. In the grave, subject and nature become 'one'; their differences collapse, and the corpse, through death and decay, becomes a participant in nature's mourning. When the human becomes one with inanimate nature, both start speaking the same language, thereby transforming the remains into part of nature's language. As *The Ruined Cottage* vividly reminds us about

Margaret, 'The worm [is] on her cheek' (*RC*, 158); the body of the human merges with its natural surroundings. We might recall how many of Wordsworth's poetic landscapes contain burial grounds or graveyards. 'We Are Seven' and the 'Matthew' poems are two familiar examples. In relation to the theme of the fragmentary and the epitaphic, the reader is strongly reminded of 'Michael' and the 'straggling Heap of unhewn stones' (line 17) to which (similar to the 'fragment of a wooden bowl') the poem's narrative and its central motif belong ('And to that place [the heap] a Story appertains' [line 18]). This gravestone becomes the origin of the poem but remains a memorial for fragmentariness, being left 'unfinished when he [Michael] died' (line 481).[26] In all of these contexts, the dead alter the language of nature that constitutes the context of the living by becoming one with, and therefore part of, the landscape. A contemplation of these natural surroundings in turn affects how we envisage our own limitations. Wordsworth remarks that 'when death is in our thoughts, nothing can make amends for the want of the soothing influences of nature, and for the absence of those types of renovation and decay, which fields and woods offer the notice of the serious and contemplative mind' (*Prose*, 2. 54). The agglomeration of negatives here clearly illustrates Wordsworth's vision of the diminishing effect of urban life (or, rather, Wordsworth's version of it) on the mind. However, the sentence also suggests, more positively, that as long as the reader has not fallen into such urban alienation, it may indeed be possible for him to develop a satisfactory awareness of the languages of both nature and man. Crucially, Wordsworth locates the grave as a site for the possible merging of these languages through death. He concludes his *Essays* with a suggestive self-citation from *The Excursion* (1814):

> And yon tall Pine-tree, whose composing sound
> Was wasted on the good Man's living ear,
> Hath now its own peculiar sanctity;
> And at the touch of every wandering breeze
> Murmurs not idly o'er his peaceful grave.   (*Prose*, 2. 96)[27]

Having become one with nature, being buried in the 'peaceful grave', the deaf dalesman now is part of the 'composing sounds' not accessible to him before. But, as we know, the language of this 'murmuring' is not straightforward. Merging with nature is not a simple transference from human to natural language.

Wordsworth's writing reminds us throughout of the extreme difficulties of dealing with the limitations of human language (not only vis-à-vis nature but also in relation to communication between humans). The boy of

Winander, in his attempted dialogue with the owls, is probably the best-known example of an effort to bridge the communication between the natural and the human. The silence of the grave in the 'Matthew' poems and the 'dolorous groan' (line 134) of the water in 'Hart-leap Well' are two other familiar instances. The poem I want to concentrate on, however, is 'The Solitary Reaper' (1805).[28] While wandering through the wild Scottish landscape, the poetic persona encounters the figure of a young woman singing a passionate and mournful song:

> Behold her, single in the field,
> Yon solitary Highland Lass!
> Reaping and singing by herself;
> Stop here! Or gently pass!
> Alone she cuts, and binds the grain,
> And sings a melancholy strain.   (lines 1–6)

This solitary singer, though not quite a deathly reaper, becomes an epitaphic figure ('Behold her'; 'Stop here'). Her song overflows the valley with sounds of lamentation sweeter than a 'nightingale' (line 9). It captivates the narrator and he becomes an attentive listener. But the narrator faces a fundamental problem: however distinct the reaper's human song might be from the nightingale's, he still has no access to its meaning. Because he does not understand her Gaelic, he has to ask:

> Will no one tell me what she sings? –
> Perhaps the plaintive numbers flow
> For old, unhappy, far-off things,
> And battles long ago:
> Or is it some more humble lay,
> Familiar matter of today?
> Some natural sorrow, loss or pain,
> That has been, and may be again!   (lines 17–24)

These lines thematise the topic of linguistic confusion as well as the link between mourning, nature, and survival. The poet insists that he does not know what the girl is singing about; he can only identify the 'flow' of the melancholy metre ('plaintive numbers'). Not grasping the words implies a deep uncertainty about the understanding of lyrical expression in language per se. It is not only that the poet is uncertain about the subject of her complaint (whether it concerns present or past, and whether it will occur again). More importantly, poetical language in the wider sense is at issue when the narrator can only take away the memory of the song's music, without its linguistic content:

> The music in my heart I bore,
> Long after it was heard no more.   (lines 31–2)

The lament can only be internalised in a non-linguistic and silent form. The shortcomings of language for the poetical are emphasised through silence. What is recorded and will survive 'in [his] heart / Long after it was heard no more' is the memory of the music rather than the words. The epitaphic lyric collapses its linguistic nature into a silent musical memory. For the poet, this can be no solution; after all, his is a linguistic medium. Thus, the anxiety about how his own song (like the reaper's) will be silent 'Long after it [is] heard no more' deeply informs the mournful subject of Wordsworth's poem.

Silence emerges as a major dimension to, and concern within, Wordsworth's poetry. The sources that inform his contemporary context share this preoccupation. Within the wide variety of eighteenth-century linguistic theory, silence and muteness stand in a vital relation to language and style. In his *Elements of Criticism* (1762), for instance, Lord Kames constructs an entire system of 'natural languages' and rhetorical analysis that includes silence. Despite characterising human beings as essentially communicative, he considers silence to be the strongest and most extreme form of reaction to communication (this last point is important: silence itself forms part of the 'language' of signification). Thus, Kames argues, 'a man immoderately grieved, seeks to afflict himself, rejecting all consolation: immoderate grief accordingly is mute: complaining is struggling for consolation [...] When grief subsides, it then and no sooner finds a tongue: we complain, because complaining is an effort to disburden the mind of its distress.'[29] Immoderate and inconsolable grief is mute; it seems unsurprising that nature has become silent, since it is immoderately and constantly mourning. Whenever it *does* speak, which is only when 'grief subsides', it mourns.

In a similar argument to Kames's, James Beattie includes what will become one of the prime topoi in Romantic poetry. In his 'Illustrations on Sublimity' (1783) he argues: 'It may seem strange, and yet it is true, that the sublime is sometimes attained by a total want of expression: and this may happen when by silence, or by hiding the face, we are made to understand that there is in the mind something too great for utterance.'[30] In reaction to natural powers, these theorists argue, silence is the appropriate response, since expression is overwhelmed and made redundant. Simultaneously, albeit inversely, part of nature's sublimity is the silence it exhibits; its feeling of sadness is too overpowering to be able even to mourn.

The reason for this mourning is the speechlessness and muteness of nature. Peter Larkin's worried conjecture in relation to *The Ruined Cottage*, namely, that there 'may be no way of translating nature's ambivalent response to suffering into meaningful grief', is more than fulfilled.[31] Nature's response turns out to be to her own condition alone, and to perpetuate its intensely mournful form. To invoke Benjamin: 'the sadness of nature makes her become silent' because 'All mourning contains the deepest tendency to speechlessness.'

As we know, the grave in Wordsworth is identified closely with images and invocations of silence. The narrator in *The Prelude* stands in front of the burial ground of the boy of Winander and remembers: 'I believe that oftentimes / A full half-hour together I have stood / Mute – looking at the Grave in which he lies' (*1805*, 5. 420–2). At this point, the narrator is so overcome with grief that he cannot utter a word. It is not possible to put his mourning into language. There is nothing more mute and silent than death. Not only is the grave quiet in itself, but it also results in silence. We find this imagery throughout the Wordsworthian corpus. Margaret in *The Pedlar* (1804) is 'Forgotten in the quiet of the grave' (line 441). There is no sound because no memory triggers mourning. Margaret has been forgotten, and even the grave containing her body has been obliterated from memory. This lack can have several causes and may take a variety of forms. In *The Ruined Cottage* it is described at the beginning of the old man's speech. He explains that 'very soon / Even of the good is no memorial left' (*RC*, 71–2). The loss of memory, the circumstance that Margaret's body has been 'forgotten', is directly linked to the lack of memorial. No epitaph records her and reminds the surroundings that there is a body for which it speaks. Similarly, the 'silent trees' in 'Nutting' stand as markers of the relationship between the human and the natural, broken by the boy's 'merciless ravage' (line 43) that brought the hazel crashing down. The 'Thoughts that do often lie too deep for tears' (line 206) are part of the oblique and overwhelmed response presented in Wordsworth's great 'Ode' ('There was a time').[32] Despite the evident memorial and epitaphic functions that poetry assumes (and many of Wordsworth's poems are actively interested to prevent lack of memory, functioning as epitaphs both for language and for the poet), silence plays an important part in Wordsworth's poetics. The tension between the appropriateness or necessity of silence and its counterpart, both human and natural, is constantly being negotiated in Wordsworth's texts.

Wordsworth's self-citation from *The Excursion* in the *Essays* illustrates this dynamic well. The quotation is from Book 7 of the poem, which is entitled 'The Churchyard among the Mountains, Continued'. In the churchyard lies the 'monumental Stone' which was placed there after the death of the sixty-five-year-old dalesman 'From whom, in early childhood, was withdrawn / The precious gift of hearing' (*Prose*, 2. 94).[33] The monument takes the place of a memorial for a human who, in contrast with the old man of *The Ruined Cottage*, is denied the divine gift of a special sense-ability: he is deaf.[34] The monument is a reminder that the dalesman was born 'To the profounder stillness of the grave' (*RC*, 2. 95). The silence here performs two functions. First, it is renewing; Wordsworth himself implies through the choice of the verb 'born' that there is an understanding by which the moment of death (or the burial) is also the beginning of a new life. Secondly, the stillness of the grave is *profounder*. The comparative only makes sense in relation to a clarification that the dalesman is deaf. The stillness, the silence, of the grave is more profound because it is deeper, and is more meaningful. It can only be so within a system of signification. This system of signification is the silent language of nature. The stillness is more profound because it is part of a more radical silence which expresses nature's character, rather than being an unnatural impediment. Once more, the most profound form of mourning is silence.

However, the negotiation of this silence is no easy task. In Wordsworth's ''Tis said that some have died for love', a man is about to commit suicide because 'He loved – The pretty Barbara died' (line 9). He 'makes his' mournful and eloquent 'moan' (line 10) which constitutes most of the poem. His plea for silence invokes nature *not* to mourn with him:

> Oh! What a weight is in these shades! Ye leaves,
> When will that dying murmur be suppress'd?
> Your sound my heart of peace bereaves,
> It robs my heart of rest.   (lines 21–4)

This is not solely a desire for immediate death, as the following lines suggest:

> Roll back, sweet rill! back to thy mountain bounds,
> And there for ever be thy waters chain'd!
> For thou dost haunt the air with sounds
> That cannot be sustain'd;
> If still beneath that pine-tree's ragged bough
> Headlong yon waterfall must come,
> Oh let it then be dumb! –   (lines 29–35)

The mourner is far from being soothed by the surrounding nature, as Wordsworth had suggested in the *Essays*. However, this is not due to nature's failure to provide a 'contemplative field to the pensive mind'.

Rather, it is the kind of soothing that nature supplies here which becomes a problem. The lover cannot bear the speaking of nature which 'robs [his] heart of rest'. His mourning reaches such an extreme that the only thing he can bear is silence. Although still addressed in a friendly or pastoral mode ('sweet rill'), nature is asked to stop fulfilling its 'normal' function. The rill is supposed to 'Roll back', reversing its natural flow. The speaker wants the waters to be 'chained' – something that is only possible through icy silence. The river haunts 'the air with sounds' producing effects 'That cannot be sustain'd' and which prove unbearable. Its waters should be 'dumb', corresponding to the speaker's desire for muteness. Ultimately, he will not be able to bear the sounds and will take his own life – silencing himself. By committing suicide he himself becomes dumb, only to merge with nature. It seems that silence is understood both as the most powerful emotional reaction and also as the ultimate *result* of nature's mourning.

The double-sidedness of the poem's ending, however, becomes apparent when we consider that the silence is only achieved by self-destruction. The speaker is enacting a reversal when he becomes part of nature's mourning because nature here is not mute. The eloquent subject can only silence a supposedly inarticulate nature by becoming part of her lament and by becoming silent himself. His mute grave will form part of nature's 'murmuring' in turn. The tropologies of speechlessness and lament become indistinguishable in the epitaphic poem that nature presents after merging with the human. Neither human language nor the rustling of plants finds an expression that can escape their respective limitations. Arno Borst's statement is incisive when he writes that 'in the end, language could be the inner word and that deep silence which marry mystically in the origin'.[35] In Wordsworth, this is both the language of the human and the language of nature around him, which constantly reciprocate their juxtaposed forms of mourning. Reading the early Benjamin and Wordsworth side by side allows us to reflect on the wider insights of this dual movement. The double-edged concern with how the subject negotiates its relation to both the linguistic and the natural world is figured under the fragmented sign of Babel.

CHAPTER 2

Figuring it out: the origin of language and anthropomorphism

FIGURATIVE LANGUAGE AND ANTHROPOMORPHISM

Jean-Jacques Rousseau begins the second chapter of his *Essai sur l'origine des langues* (1753) with a meditation on the invention of speech. He maintains that we often misconstrue the fundamental character of the origin of language by mistaking the primacy of passionate poetry for a more rational geometry: 'The language of the first men is put before us as though it were the languages of Geometers, while we see that they were the languages of Poets. This must have been so. We did not begin by reasoning but by feeling.'[1] This assertion about the pre-eminence of the poetic is part of a longer story about the broken origins of language and Romanticism. This chapter is, in part, about that story. It shifts our attention from linguistic-architectonic fragmentation (the Babelian tower) to a tropological linguistic fracture, namely anthropomorphism. This provides us with a different case study of how fracture is a particularly powerful notion through which to grasp Romanticism. Within the context of this larger framework, the chapter begins by asking how and why the origin of language and poetry are so often identified with one another. The figural and conceptual strategies employed by Romantic poets, rhetoricians, and philosophers who advocate this conjunction reveal that the fracturing trope of anthropomorphism occupies a special place in the field of linguistic theory and historiography. Anthropomorphism emerges not 'just' as a rhetorical figure, but as a linguistic move with deep philosophical implications. This move is present in a number of theoretical texts of the period, from Hume, via Kant and Hamann, to Herder and Wordsworth. The analysis of the figure, and its subsequent location at the origin of language, explains why fracture emerges as a powerful category with which to describe its peculiarly Romantic condition and ramifications. Framed by the link between the question of origin and the question of anthropomorphism (both as a trope and as a philosophico-theological problem), the discussion will formulate some of the central preoccupations resulting from this connection, and illustrate how British theorists of language, such as Thomas Blackwell, James Harris, or Hugh Blair, attempt to solve them through various conjectural histories of linguistic progress.

Anthropomorphism poses some of the oldest and most fundamental philosophical and theological questions dealing with the relation and status of the human subject vis-à-vis the physical world as well as the metaphysical realm. Importantly, anthropomorphism encompasses two distinct but connected spheres: first, the projection of human qualities onto nature, and, secondly, the projection of human qualities onto the divine. The trope describing these relations concentrates linguistically a central problem of philosophy and theology that finds one of its most pressing expressions in the late eighteenth century. The collapse of the rhetorical figure and the philosophical difficulty is significant here. The figure is deeply wedded to the philosophical problem through its conceptual connotations and implications. Furthermore, this crossing moment is located within and around discussions about the origin of language. The nature of this origin (and its particular relation to figurative language) plays a major role in its analysis. The readings will make clear the extent to which the conceptual implications of the figure, and its inevitable use, are important in describing the origin and nature of both language and poetry.

As is widely known, questions surrounding the origin of language are a major concern of the European intellectual community during the Enlightenment and Romanticism. It is, in fact, the obsession of a generation. Much of this territory is well documented and has received extensive commentary.[2] Given the concerns of this chapter, my own contextualisation concentrates mainly on the writers in whose works anthropomorphism represents a major concern. A focus on the philosophical and rhetorical dimensions of their language distinguishes my approach from more historically minded studies in this field such as Hans Aarsleff's, Robert Norton's, James Stam's, or Sabine Hausdörfer's.

Throughout the *Essai* quoted at the beginning of the chapter, Rousseau presents a theory that collapses the origin of language and the origin of poetry. This is a standard move in language theory of the period. It functions as a common denominator and link between an otherwise heterogeneous group of linguistic histories and theories. For all of these accounts, as Hamann puts it in *Aesthetica in Nuce*, 'Poetry is the mother tongue of the human race' or the 'Ur- and mother-Art' (A. W. Schlegel).[3] Early British examples of this collapse between poetic and linguistic origin include the writings of Thomas Blackwell, William Warburton, and James Burnet (better known as Lord Monboddo). All these thinkers identify the origin of language as coinciding with the beginnings of poetry. This is in accordance with several other figures in the pan-European debate about linguistics, whose participants are very much aware of each other's contributions. In his *Du contrat social* (1762) Rousseau refers to Warburton's standard work on the history of language entitled *Divine Legation of Moses* (1738). Herder writes a laudatory preface to Monboddo's *Of the Origin and Progress of Language* (1773–92) after completing his own essay on linguistic origins. Famously, in the prize-winning *Abhandlung über den Ursprung der Sprache* (*Essay on the Origin of Language*) of 1772, Herder also refers to John Brown, another British leading theorist of language, who in his work *The History of the Rise and Progress of Poetry, through it's* [*sic*] *several Species* (1764) defends the common origin of language and poetry. Hugh Blair, in the enormously influential *Lectures on Rhetoric and Belles Lettres*, argues much the same.[4] All of these works identify linguistic with poetic origin and, in turn, define poetical language as passionate speech characterised by a high degree of figuration. Importantly, these signposts, common throughout the eighteenth century, also become part of a much larger historical narrative by which these accounts begin to overlay poetics and history.

In his *Lectures* Blair maintains that in its earliest stages language is hyperbolical and metaphorical. He admits that 'there seems to be no small reason for referring the first origin of all language to divine teaching or inspiration'.[5] However, he reconsiders his position, and qualifies that God instructed the first people in 'only such language as suited their present occasions'.[6] By enlarging its vocabulary, the human race begins to communicate with each other through cries and other utterances that are of a 'strong and passionate manner'.[7] At its very beginning, language is metaphorical, strong, and passionate. Additionally, these figural and passionate aspects are inextricably tied to each other. In effect, language is metaphorical because it is passionate; the passionate cry leads to a figural expression. Blair writes:

As the manner in which men first uttered their words, and maintained conversation, was strong and expressive, enforcing their imperfectly expressed ideas by cries and gestures; so the Language which they used, could be no other than full of figures and metaphors, not correct indeed, but forcible and picturesque.[8]

He insists that there '*could* be no other' language at the beginning than one 'full of figures and metaphors' (my emphasis). There is a necessary connection between the linguistic origin and the figurative. And, according to Blair, this necessary connection arises through its 'manner', which is 'strong and expressive'. Tellingly, Blair insists that this language, because of its figurative qualities, was 'not correct indeed'. Despite this qualification, his account places the figurative and tropological at the very heart of the origin of language. Through linking poetry and language in one and the same origin, this origin itself becomes at once tropological and a figure for 'origin'.

However, Blair assures his reader that when 'Language, in its progress, began to grow more copious, it gradually lost that figurative style, which was its early character'.[9] This enlightening process allows a replacement of hyperbolic language with a more rational discourse: 'The ancient metaphorical and poetical dress of language was now laid aside from the intercourse of men and reserved for those occasions only, on which ornament was professedly studied.'[10] Blair, along with a number of other linguists believes that language was 'metaphorical' as long as it was poetry or passionate speech. The tropological and the poetical are inextricably bound up with each other. In itself, this is not a very contentious claim. The reason given, however, is noteworthy: poetry and trope are connected to each other because poetical language is passionate. Through an account of poetry as passionate speech, and passionate speech as inherently tropological, these three aspects are tied together. That, however, makes language tropological within and at its origin. To avoid a potential misunderstanding: this is not about tripping up eighteenth-century linguistic theory; rather, it is to take seriously that, as contemporary critics, we can learn a great deal from how and why the conflicting ideas that are being articulated within these projects find their ways into the rhetoric of their arguments.[11] It is difficult to imagine how, if language is figurative at its very heart, it would fundamentally change. Considering that the figurative is identified with both the origin and the nature of language, it remains unexplained how this nature could be reversed. That Blair later wants to call language's figural quality an 'early character' is indicative of the problem. His vocabulary betrays the impasse: the shape of the sign might change over time, but that does not alter the argument that the sign itself is still a figure, a character with figurative qualities which has to remain so by definition.

Thomas Blackwell prefigures Blair's argument by describing the '*Original*' of language as 'expressive commonly of the *highest Passions*'.[12] And, like Blair after him, he makes a necessary connection with the figurative nature that this origin carries within itself (language being expressive of the highest passions). In fact, he argues that 'From this Deduction, it is plain that any Language, formed as above described, must be full of Metaphor; and that Metaphor of the boldest, daring, and most natural kind […]'.[13] The boldness of metaphor is natural to language since it lies at its

The figure of anthropomorphism holds a prominent position in the literature of the Augustan period, but even more so in Romanticism. Considering the importance of the categories of 'nature' and 'the natural' for Romanticism, it is inevitable that a trope endowing nature with human attributes acquires special significance. It is not surprising that it also exhibits one of Romanticism's deepest conundrums and imports the problem into the conceptual framework with which we construct this historical or literary category. Through the figure of anthropomorphism, the speaker endows nature with human attributes, often even going so far as to personify 'her'. In other words, the speaker projects human qualities onto animate and inanimate objects around him. This move is, supposedly, part of a project of merging with nature. However, the problematic circularity of description and meaning is evident. Nature is conceived of and proposed as the ultimate possibility and means to overcome human limitations. But, at the same time, this proposal describes nature as having human attributes. Any additional stress on the importance of the unity with nature only intensifies the problem. This is not to suggest that rhetoricians or poets make a 'mistake' when they employ the figure of anthropomorphism. Rather, through exhibiting this circularity, anthropomorphism calls attention to itself as a significant marker that allows for a reconsideration of the category 'nature' or, indeed, 'Romanticism'.

The problem of anthropomorphism, as a puzzle of likeness, is one of the most ancient ones in philosophy. A continuous concern exists about the status (visual, linguistic) of the relationship between gods and humans in the world. With Xenophanes, anthropomorphism finds one of its earliest and harshest critics. His conjecture that, were animals to conceive of gods, these would be depicted in the form of animals has become a commonplace. However, anthropomorphism also finds champions such as Ovid and his celebration of the human as built in the image of the gods. The advent of monotheistic Christianity both restricts and intensifies the importance of anthropomorphism understood as a western philosophical or theological problem. This includes anthropomorphism in both directions: humans giving god(s) human qualities and humans giving nature and inanimate objects human qualities. A brief discussion of a few major eighteenth-century landmarks in this long and complicated history will help to explain the relevance of this issue here.

One of the most influential critiques of anthropomorphism and its philosophical significance is David Hume's posthumous *Dialogues concerning Natural Religion* (1779). Hume presents the problem of anthropomorphism from within natural theology. In Part 8, Philo, one of the interlocutors, counters various different versions of the argument from design. Significantly, one of the most important and philosophically acute passages of Philo's conclusion concerns the problem of anthropomorphism as a necessary part and consequence of any argument from design. Philo, summarising the common weaknesses of his adversary's deductions, states:

You have run into *anthropomorphism* […] In all instances which we have ever seen, ideas are copied from real objects, and are ectypal, not archetypal, to express myself in learned language: You reverse this order, and give thought the precedence. In all instances which we have ever seen, thought has no influence upon matter, except where that matter is so conjoined with it, as to have an equal reciprocal influence on it.[20]

The problem for Philo is clear: the origin of any coherent conceptual understanding of the world implies that there *cannot but be* an anthropomorphic conception of God. He considers this a severe limitation of the tools that philosophy uses to inquire about the nature of the divine. The radicalism of Philo's argument lies in denying that the main problem is an ignorant anthropomorphism of the object of knowledge. Instead, he stresses that the anthropomorphic *origin* of all means that are necessary for epistemological inquiry makes it impossible to construct, create, or discover a non-anthropomorphic conception of God or the world around us. The problem of anthropomorphism becomes a fundamental epistemological stumbling block of, and in, philosophy. This radically sceptical position, although it is countered later in the dialogue, comes to be the central point of reference not only for Kant, who wants to repudiate it, but also for Hamann, who defends Philo's position against an overrationalised solution. Both, however, recognise that the central problem of anthropomorphism poses itself most poignantly in terms of language. The rhetorical figure of anthropomorphism becomes a concentrated signifier for the philosophical dilemma.[21]

In the *Critique of Pure Reason* (1781, rev. 1787), for whose inception Hume is so important, Kant draws an important distinction between a natural and a transcendental theology. Crudely put, the first employs the idea of 'highest intelligence'. This conception, which leads to the idea of God as the ultimate cause of the world, is evidently borrowed from man himself. It leads to the animated God of theism. The second establishes the idea of God through pure concepts as the necessary cause of the world. This leads to abstract deism. Correspondingly, this division results in two kinds of anthropomorphism. On the one hand, there is a dogmatic, and, on the other hand, a symbolic, anthropomorphism. The first remains in the realm of the 'world', attached to the objects and concepts surrounding us. This is the anthropomorphism many of us are familiar with. Symbolic anthropomorphism departs from a framework of abstract deism and relies on identifying a correspondence of two seemingly different concepts, such as the world and God. Kant attempts to solve the problem posed by Philo via the second route. For Kant it is the understanding of a relational correspondence between (a set of) different and dissimilar objects rather than a correspondence between similar objects that characterises what he calls 'the symbolic'. As Hans Graubner puts it: 'Thus, it is not God's nature that resembles man; rather, His [God's] relation to the world resembles man's relation to his [man's] artificial products.'[22] It is this 'symbolic' relationship which, according to Kant, answers the most pressing questions connected to the problem of anthropomorphism as posed by Philo.

Hamann, in turn, objects strongly to Kant's elaborate construct on the grounds that it misunderstands the fundamental impossibility of adequately describing the relation between God and man in linguistic terms. Kant's distinction overlooks or underestimates the fundamental importance that inevitably results from any human projection. Kant has certainly removed the problem of anthropomorphism from the sphere of crude misunderstandings about the 'human' nature of God. However, Hamann maintains that this is only a gain in degree and not in kind. What Kant has done is to turn the screw one more time – but it cannot possibly alter the problem that his conceptual tools and organising principles, in his case language, are of anthropomorphic origin. As Philo insists, the very means of gaining knowledge spring from the anthropomorphic. They must remain, 'symbolic' or not, human projections because, for Hamann, they are given in anthropomorphic language. Hamann, via Philo, simply refuses to accept the adequacy (or independence) of the Kantian terms. He argues, just as Philo does in the *Dialogues* (which Hamann eventually translates), that for all of Kant's sophistication, the means of his conceptual inquiry – language and thought – necessarily remain anthropomorphic. In other words, Hamann accuses Kant of anthropomorphising reason itself in his account, thereby undercutting reason's paradigmatically 'enlightened' and independent nature.[23]

The significance of all these arguments for my particular analysis emerges through the pivotal role all three authors assign to language. Hamann is strongest in insisting on the inherent link between the problem of anthropomorphism and the linguistic. For him, Kant's rationalistic concept of God is empty because it catapults the deity out of language itself. Kant's attempt to rationalise anthropomorphism disregards that language must be anthropomorphic; otherwise it would lose God out of itself and thereby fail even more in its descriptive power for the world and its creator. The occasion of Haman's writings links this problem to the earlier concerns of this chapter. Hamann presents some of his views on anthropomorphism in the wider context of defending a divine origin of language. He insists that as the origin of the tools of any inquiry about the world is anthropomorphic (and because these tools are constituted by language), anthropomorphism lies within the origin of language itself. Thus the problem of anthropomorphism and its conceptual implications are directly related to the central questions around the origin of language and poetry.

The famous dispute between Hamann and Herder on the origin of language elegantly focuses this concern. Herder, Hamann's pupil, colleague, and friend, in his celebrated *Abhandlung über den Ursprung der Sprache*, not only proposed that poetry and language shared their origin, but furthermore advanced his central thesis of a 'human' origin of language. In a striking moment, Herder argues that the assumption of a divine origin of language, rather than stressing God's importance, inversely, 'diminish[es] God with the smallest, most imperfect anthropomorphisms'.[24] The argument is ingenious, to say the least: to assume a divine origin of language is being ungodly, and, what is more, it is to deny the true nature of the divine. It would be preposterous to assume a divine origin of language, as this implies that God Himself will reach down like a human and hand us the ability to speak. For Herder this argument diminishes God, precisely through an anthropomorphic move. By implication, such a view is caught up in misconceptions, both of God and of the nature of the rational human agent. The latter's definition as a being with an appropriate sense of the divine leads Herder to conclude that language, if it is correctly understood, must be of human origin. More so, it actually is part of a definition of the human. The origin lies within the nature of both language and man. To misunderstand language as something given by the divine is to misapprehend God as an entity with human attributes. Herder argues that it is through understanding the creative power of the human soul in the development and 'invention' of language that the fundamental character of this rational creature is expressed. As such it can serve as an adequate reminder of God, who has made man in his own image. Language lies within us and only when we realise it as such can we grasp its true character. Language and poetry are thus human in their origin too. Because Herder's wider argument maintains the importance of figurativeness within the origin of language, anthropomorphism must lie very much at the heart of language. However, the figure points, as we have seen, towards a fundamental rift between man

and the divine. This rift becomes visible at the very point where Herder is
defending the piety of his argument. Anthropomorphism is both: it is
within the very origin of language and, at the same time, woefully inadequate in its description of God.

Herder, unwillingly, has to place anthropomorphism at the very centre of
language and, simultaneously, insist on the inadequacy of this figure. This
leaves only the conclusion that language always is, and must be, witness to
the torn and broken relations between the human and the divine. Not only
that, however. It transpires that the figure of anthropomorphism itself
exemplifies this fracture. In order for it to fulfil its rhetorical role adequately,
it needs to assume the deep and fundamental rift between the natural and
the human, akin to the 'broken brotherhood' that Wordsworth laments in
The Ruined Cottage. Thus language reflects as itself (within its origin and
whole structure) the fundamental break which exists between human and
deity, and between human and nature. Language also reflects this fracture
microcosmically, within itself, in its grounding rhetorical tropes: anthropomorphism, as a figure, is only possible through the assumption that there is
an insurmountable gap between the spheres it pretends to connect. As Paul
de Man puts it when examining the conceptual presuppositions of the
figure:

'Anthropomorphism' is not just a trope but an identification on the level of
substance. It takes one entity for another and thus implies the constitution of
specific entities prior to their confusion, the *taking* of something for something else
that can then be assumed to be *given*. (*RR*, 242)[25]

The 'confusion' here is equivalent to the fracture between nature and man.
What Herder's argument suggests, however, is that considering language
there is no state that could possibly be 'prior to confusion'. Language, in its
coming into being, is, and must be, anthropomorphic. It thereby exemplifies the deep and irreversible fracture between the subject and nature.
Language carries this fracture within itself, at its very heart. The conclusion
must be that language is, in its origin, fractured. It comes into being as
already carrying within itself the rift between language and nature.

Herder's account understands anthropomorphism to be at both centre
and origin of language. It insists that the rhetorical figure is inadequate for a
fitting description or characterisation of the deity. As he argues:

The higher origin is, as pious as it might seem, quite ungodly: with each step it
reduces God through the lowest and imperfect anthropomorphisms. The human
origin shows God in the greatest light: His work, a human soul, which, through
itself, creates and continues to create a language because it [the soul] is His work, a

human soul. The origin of language thus only becomes godly in a dignified way insofar as it is human.[26]

Hamann, Herder's most prolific critic and reader, launches his attack precisely against this conceptual double bind. In his review of Herder's essay, Hamann's first focus is the question of the anthropomorphic origin of language and its relation to the divine. Immediately after quoting the passage above, Hamann exclaims in typically opaque and ironic fashion:

Here! Here! (by the life of Pharaonis!) here is *God's finger*! This apotheosis Αποκολοκυντωσις or also apophtheirosis tastes more like galimatias than the lowest and undignified but nevertheless privileged anthropomorphism.[27]

Hamann, albeit in a playful mode, mounts a sustained critique of Herder's presuppositions. He argues that Herder has only been begging the initial question: his explanatory framework can only be successful after an apotheosis of the human, which in effect does not have explanatory power. While pretending to argue for a truly 'human' origin of language, Herder has simply elevated man to the position that God traditionally occupies in the creation of language. But he has not changed the structure of the argument. Stam discusses this aspect of Herder's reception in his own *Inquiries into the Origin of Language* (1976): 'If all phenomena are explained in strictly immanent terms, Hamann contends, it is necessary to introduce more ad hoc miracles than if one simply accepted the divine creation of a reasonable natural order: It is a solution worse than Deism.'[28] In fact, I believe that, for Hamann, it is not a solution at all. For him, Herder misunderstands the nature of both the divine *and* the human. There cannot be an apotheosis of the human, and certainly not a linguistic one, which would reach God successfully. One of the most powerful reminders of this human limitation is precisely the linguistic fragmentation of the Babelian tower. Man should not and cannot climb to his deity, reach up, and elevate himself to it. If he does, the result is a Babelian 'galimatias', a 'meaningless talk' in a 'confused language' (*OED*). Hamann argues that the reverse of Herder's argument holds true. It is exactly the other way around. God always reaches down – we never meet him half-way up.

Hamann suggests that his differences with Herder regarding anthropomorphism are the most compelling illustrations of this crucial point. There is, we can see, a deep awareness of the role of anthropomorphism as a figure with major conceptual implications. It becomes both image and problem, located in the origin of language, working its fracturing power into the linguistic. More than a master-trope, it becomes a shorthand for the necessarily fractured nature of human language and the doomed attempts to overcome this condition. That is also why, for Hamann, Herder's solution of the problem of anthropomorphism is fundamentally misguided. In trying to escape the practice of anthropomorphising God, Herder deifies man instead. This not only is an essentially mistaken approach to the problem of the origin of language, but also deeply misunderstands God's relation to man. It is connected with Hamann's earlier insistence that anthropomorphism lies at the very heart of language. Hamann argues that we cannot conceive of the formation of our analytical tools and terms of inquiry independently of this figure.[29] Language must, *in its origin*, be anthropomorphic if it wants to be intelligible and recognisable as language to the human. In other words, any human language will have anthropomorphism at its heart, hence will be fractured and will exhibit its brokenness from the very moment it comes into being. This sounds very similar to the conclusion we reached with Herder's argument. In effect, a reading of Hamann offers, albeit by a very different route, a parallel moment to Herder's thesis. Anthropomorphism, with all its conceptual implications, remains the sign at the origin of language that language is necessarily fractured. The rhetorical figure itself exemplifies a fundamental rift in all language, from the very moment it comes into being.

To recapitulate: after formulating the problem of anthropomorphism in a general way, and particularly in relation to Romanticism, it becomes clear that its significance goes far beyond that of a 'mere' rhetorical figure. In fact, the theologico-philosophical problems arising in connection with it are absolutely fundamental, not only concerning wider philosophical issues, but specifically in relation to the origin of language and poetry. The conceptual implications of anthropomorphism can be located not only *within* the origin of this language but also as offering the inescapable conclusion that this origin is in itself already fractured. The fundamental break between the divine and the human, as well as between the human and the natural, lies within all language itself, because it lies in that language's origin. The debate between Herder and Hamann, largely centring on the problem of anthropomorphism, illustrates two very different approaches to this question. Both positions, however, ultimately result in concluding that anthropomorphism (and the philosophical implications it stands for) is located at the very origin of human language. It therefore permeates the linguistic with the implicit fracture, making this master-trope a powerful signifier and constant reminder of such a break. The rest of this chapter discusses how a number of British linguistic theorists negotiate the figure of anthropomorphism and some of the attendant complications of its meaning I have just presented.

THE GREAT NATURAL DISTINCTION

A number of theories of rhetoric and language attempt to counter the anxieties connected with linguistic fracture. One strategy they employ is to seek refuge in a fictional genealogy designed to obliterate the unsettling within the figural. Some of the most important examples of these histories focus on anthropomorphic elements within linguistics and how they act as reminders of the inherent brokenness of language. These accounts form part of the much larger framework sketched out above, namely a narrative that recounts language's history as a development from passionate poetry to rational philosophy. The most extreme instance of this argument in the British tradition attempts to relegate the smallest trace of anthropomorphism to history. It presents the gendered article, the most basic instance of anthropomorphic language, as figural and distorting, and, consequently, as an element to be banished from the English language. This is not as obscure an argument as it may sound. Gendered articles are a constant concern within many British and European theories of language, and a reminder of just how fundamental the question of anthropomorphic language can be. As Lord Kames argues in *Elements of Criticism*, the 'chastity of the English language, which in common usage distinguishes by genders no words but what signify beings male and female', both allows for a more philosophical discourse and also leaves open a 'fine opportunity for the prosopopoeia [*sic*]'.[30]

James Harris, in his enormously influential *Hermes: or, a Philosophical Inquiry concerning Language and Universal Grammar* (1751), provides an early instance of this type of argument. First, he makes the very basic observation that

Besides *Number*, another characteristic, visible in Substances, is that of Sex. Every Substance is either *Male* or *Female*; or *both Male and Female*; or *neither one nor the other*. So that with respect to *Sexes* and their *Negation, all Substances conceiveable* [*sic*] are comprehended under this *fourfold* consideration. [...] Language [...] considers *Words denoting Substances* to be either MASCULINE, FEMININE or NEUTER.[31]

As a general description or even as criterion for classification, this seems very straightforward. Harris, however, elaborates further that 'In the *English* Tongue it seems a general rule (except only when infringed by a figure of Speech) that no Substantive is *Masculine*, but what denotes a *Male animal Substance*; none *Feminine*, but what denotes a *Female animal Substance*; and that where the Substance *has no Sex*, the Substantive is always *Neuter*.'[32]

If this statement is to be rescued from the simply obvious, Harris must be taken as saying that what is special about the English tongue is that, *because of its neuter articles*, it only genders words that really denote sexed 'animal Substances'. The ambiguity of the term 'animal Substance' already indicates the problems that Harris faces. If he is correct in his banishment of anthropomorphism, then he must assume that there cannot be a sexed and animated substance that is not human. However, he must realise the complications of this view and also that it is, as an observation, plainly inaccurate: we divide the entirety of the animal world into gendered categories. Harris makes another concession, which in this context is even more important. The parenthetical qualification of '(except only when infringed by a figure of Speech)' will prove to be a paradigmatic example for attempting to explain the continuing presence of anthropomorphisms in language as a purely rhetorical and controllable device. Harris's use of parenthesis shows that he assumes this statement to be obvious (every anthropomorphism is a 'figure of Speech'). It also suggests that the 'infringement' on the English tongue is discernible as unnatural and it can be removed, if so desired. Harris is anxious to assure the reader that the power of figurative speech in undermining the accounts of 'neutral' discourse can be controlled. Whenever the English language is discussed in detail, it is praised for its philosophical neutrality, exemplified through the ungendered article. However, whenever the ungendered article is mentioned, the possibility of figuration undermining it always looms in the background. Horne Tooke's *Diversions of Purley* (1786–1805) puts it succinctly: 'Figure apart, in our Language, the names of things without sex are also without gender.'[33]

In his *Lectures*, Blair reiterates that it is peculiar to the English tongue that it has no gendered articles and that it avoids putting 'all […] names of inanimate objects […] upon the same footing with living creatures'.[34] Blair links this directly to the superior status of English as a philosophical language in comparison to other tongues. This is a fairly predictable conclusion which follows from identifying anthropomorphic language, including gendered articles, as passionate and poetical (and thus clouding objective judgement and its neutral expression). What Harris implied is here expressed with the utmost bluntness: 'The English is, perhaps, the only Language in the known world […] where the distinction of gender is properly and philosophically applied in the use of words.'[35]

A number of linguistic theorists, especially during this period, state with conspicuous repetition that only intentional manipulation of language makes rhetorical infringement through passionate figures possible.

According to this narrative, we have entered the age where our rational and linguistic abilities allow us to distinguish between, and manipulate, different kinds of language. For Blair, the sharp division between the passionately poetical and the neutrally philosophical is immediately understood and controlled. The clear divide even enhances the heightening effect of an unusual poetical style. Immediately after insisting on the superiority of English due to its neutral gendering, Blair writes: 'Yet the genius of Language permits us, whenever it will add beauty to our discourse, to make the names of inanimate objects masculine or feminine in a metaphorical sense.'[36] It is the 'genius of language', language itself, which permits us to manipulate it for aesthetic reasons.

Anthropomorphism, being at the very heart of figural language, is thus banished from 'rational' discourse. The listener or reader is, according to Blair, absolutely aware of this distinction. When we use anthropomorphism 'we are understood to quit the literal style, and to use one of the figures for discourse'.[37] Through figural language or poetry, our language adopts 'a higher tone', and 'By this means, we have it in our power to vary our style at pleasure. By making a very slight alteration, we can personify any object that we chuse to introduce with dignity; and by this change of manner, we give warning, that we are passing from the strict and logical, to the ornamented and rhetorical style.'[38] The link between anthropomorphism and the language of the passions becomes evident again. The 'higher tone' as part of the 'ornamented and rhetorical style' is the controlled difference between philosophy and poetry. In a 1763 review of the fragmentary *Ossian* poems, Blair insists that apostrophe and personification, and hence anthropomorphism, 'as in all ages' are part of 'the languages of passion'.[39] Beattie had already argued in his *Dissertations* that 'It may now be remarked in general, that the sublime is often heightened, when, by means of figurative language, the qualities of a superior nature are judiciously applied to what is inferiour. Hence we see in poetry, and in more familiar language, the passions and feelings of rationality ascribed to that which is without reason, and without life, or even to abstract ideas.'[40] Lord Kames discusses anthropomorphism in a similar vein: 'The converting things inanimate into sensible beings is so bold a figure, as to require, one should imagine, very peculiar circumstances for operating the delusion. And yet, in the language of poetry, we find variety of expressions, which, though commonly reduced to this figure, are used without ceremony, or any sort of preparation; as, for example, the following expressions, *thirsty* ground, *hungry* churchyard [...].'[41] In all of these accounts, poetry and anthropomorphism represent the areas of controllable figuration.

This continuous insistence on intentional control over the figurative language may make the reader suspicious. Beattie, in a slippage of vocabulary, equates poetry and unceremonious language. The passionate and figural language of anthropomorphism slyly finds its way back into what Wordsworth will call the 'real language of men'. Similarly, in Kames's text the qualification explaining the common occurrence of anthropomorphisms within language ('and yet') is a hint as to why these accounts struggle to effect a neat division between philosophy and poetry, and have difficulties in construing a fantasy of a non-anthropomorphic language. Although there is still the delimitation of figural language to 'the language of poetry', anthropomorphism has the potential to invade all language. It is all the more significant, then, that Kames himself observes that the reason for these slippages is located in the passions, which rule part of the human character. According to him, 'the mind, prompted by passion, is prone to bestow sensibility upon things inanimate. This is an additional instance of the influence of passion upon our opinions and belief.'[42] Alternatively, anthropomorphism is part of the human imagination and still clearly distinct from objective reality: 'What then is the nature of this personification? [...] I discover that this species of personification must be referred to the imagination: the inanimate object is imagined to be a sensible being, but without any conviction, even for a moment, that it really is so.'[43] The conceptual circle highlighted at the beginning of this discussion keeps recurring. We use figurative language when under the influence of irrational passion. This language ascribes 'the passions and feelings of rationality [...] to that which is without reason'.[44] In other words, the capacity of the human for passion is central for endowing nature with exactly the quality that sets the human apart from nature in the first place, namely rationality. However, the division of the figural and the non-figural seems impossible because of the unintentional manipulation of language. The initial assurance that, because of man's rational nature, an intentional separation of the two spheres would be entirely under his control is destabilised.

The uncontrollable infringement on language represented by anthropomorphism haunts all the arguments so far discussed. This often occurs at moments when these accounts attempt to formulate criteria for the employment of rhetorical figures. Speaking of adequate and appropriate uses of anthropomorphism, Harris makes this noteworthy comment:

In some Words these distinctions [gendered nouns] seem owing to nothing else, than to the meer [*sic*] casual structure of the Word itself: [...] In others we may imagine a more subtle kind of reasoning, a reasoning which discerns, even *in things without Sex*, a distant analogy to that great NATURAL DISTINCTION, *which* (according to *Milton*) *animates the World*.[45]

The distribution of gender within a language is supposed to be entirely arbitrary.[46] This seems unsurprising considering that gendered language allegedly makes anthropomorphic distinctions where 'Sex never had existence'.[47] Anthropomorphism is used either as a controlled trope, or in an arbitrary way, when it is known not to have any 'real' relation to the inanimate world. However, Harris's second claim thoroughly contravenes this strategy. Within his qualification he involves several aspects that directly counter his initial argument. Through the 'more subtle', and therefore presumably more desirable, reasoning one 'may imagine' a scenario which is totally distinct from the assumption of the arbitrary assignation of gendered articles. For all the qualifications that Harris inserts, it is clear that this is a not just a fanciful, but rather a deep and meaningful, alternative to the initial account. He suggests that there exists a fundamental and underlying distinction which can be captured successfully via gendered language. This anthropomorphic language 'discerns' and differentiates within the world of unsexed objects and entities an 'analogy', a figural resemblance, to male and female. Somehow, there is 'even *in things without Sex*' a 'NATURAL' differentiation that corresponds to the human sexes. According to this argument, anthropomorphism is neither misguided nor arbitrary. Rather, it serves as a helping device in achieving a correct correspondence between the world and its linguistic representation through figurative language. Harris's suggestion that the tension between these two accounts is resolved because there are two different kinds of words (some which are 'naturally' suited to anthropomorphism and others in whose case arbitrary distinctions suffice) only intensifies it.

More interesting than the tension in Harris's argument in itself is his stress on the 'more subtle' reasoning that leads to anthropomorphising inanimate objects *correctly*. The implication is that anthropomorphism, perhaps through its location within the origin of language, can reveal an insight about the nature of the world and language within it. Harris's example of Milton and 'the great NATURAL DISTINCTION' is telling.[48] What is remarkable here is that the distinction is characterised both as 'natural' and as responsible for all life. The projection of this 'natural' distinction is the most basic instance of anthropomorphism. And even if Harris admits that in some cases it is 'correct' to anthropomorphise (because, after all, there is 'an analogy'), it comes as an even bigger surprise that one can or should do so 'naturally'. This must be possible through discovering the 'great analogy', for which Harris gives instructing examples. According to him, terms and concepts are anthropomorphised adequately according to their 'nature'. It is not altogether surprising that nouns which are 'conspicuous for the Attributes of imparting or communicating; or which were by nature active, strong, and efficacious, and that indiscriminately whether to good or to bad' are to be masculine.[49] In contrast, nouns are anthropomorphised into the feminine if they are 'conspicuous for the Attributes either of receiving, of containing, or of producing and bringing forth; or which had more of the passive in their nature, than of the active'.[50] The 'nature' or 'character' of the object will determine which sex its linguistic characters have.[51] Harris uses biblical themes and imagery to explain that the earth's 'natural' character is always feminine, as she is the 'receiver' or 'container'. Further examples illustrate how inanimate objects can and should be anthropomorphised according to their 'natural' character:

Among *artificial* Substances the SHIP (Ναῦς, Navis) is *feminine*, as being so eminently a *Receiver* and *Container* of various things, of Men, Arms, Provisions, Goods, *&c.* Hence Sailors, speaking of their Vessel, say always 'SHE *rides at anchor,*' 'SHE *is under sail.*' A CITY […] and a COUNTRY […] are *feminine* also, by being (like the Ship) *Containers* and *Receivers*, and farther by being as it were the *Mothers* and *Nurses* of their respective inhabitants.[52]

The structural problem of this argument is evident. Harris insists that 'substances' are anthropomorphised according to their 'nature'. Their 'nature' or character, however, is only intelligible when already anthropomorphised. This goes beyond Harris's earlier 'substances'. For him, time is 'justly' considered masculine, as is death: 'Even the Vulgar with us are so accustomed to this notion, that a FEMALE DEATH they would treat as ridiculous.'[53]

With an anthropomorphic somersault, Harris finally reaches the conclusion that 'the supreme Being […] is in all languages *Masculine*, in as much as the masculine Sex is the superior and more excellent; and as He is the Creator of all, the Father of Gods and Men'.[54] Virtue, on the other hand, is feminine, and so are fancies, caprices, and fortune. Harris's 'more subtle kind of reasoning' discovers whichever 'analogy' it put into the objects to begin with. The (de facto judgemental) prefiguration of certain qualities in terms of gender shows most starkly how some of these conjectural histories are both complicit with, and resistant to, ideological forces. Language here forms part of and continues a long history of delimiting gender and its roles along specifically motivated lines. Rather than concentrating on the issues of sexual politics that these texts perpetuate, however, this reading will veer in a slightly different direction. I want to conclude the chapter by reconsidering the professed conjunction between language and the logical origin of history.

It is doubly telling that Harris insists on a link between anthropomorphism and 'nature'. The 'nature' of the nature surrounding him corresponds to the human 'character', and is captured via the characters of the trope. We are a long way away from the controlled figuration of language that can be clearly demarcated as passionate poetry. Rather, the fracturing figure of anthropomorphism seems not only to invade language, but also to do so because this is language's *nature.* Language, with anthropomorphism at its origin, irrevocably fractures and breaks the human's relationship to the natural world. Harris's ambivalent reasoning finds its epitome in an instructive example:

As to the OCEAN, tho' from its being the *Receiver* of all Rivers, as well as the *Container* and *Productress* of so many Vegetables and Animals, it might justly have been made (like the Earth) *Feminine*; yet its *deep Voice* and *boisterous Nature* have, in spite of these reasons, prevailed to make it *Male.*[55]

The 'natural distinction' that allegedly enabled man correctly to anthropomorphise objects and nouns finally collapses. The ocean, because of its 'nature', could easily have been female. However, according to its nature, it is designated male. This strange instance is the extreme upshot of an argument that wants to proceed in two directions simultaneously.

Harris is by no means alone in his way of reasoning on this point. Kames's *Elements of Criticism* argues in much the same way: 'The winds in their impetuous course have so much the appearance of fury, that it is easy to figure them wreaking their resentment against their enemies, by destroying houses, ships, & c.; but to figure them love-sick, has no resemblance to them in any circumstance.'[56] The double sense of 'figuring' points towards the connection between the creation and the understanding of a concept, including its 'original' anthropomorphic figuration. Blair's *Lectures* also follow Harris's account in their description and assessment of this issue. He states that: 'This assignation of sex to inanimate objects, this distinction of them into masculine and feminine, appears often to be entirely capricious; derived from no other principle than the casual structure of the Language, which refers to a certain gender, words of a certain termination.'[57] Blair admits that he is deeply influenced by Harris here, and openly refers to this debt in the *Lectures*:

When we employ that liberty which our Language allows, of ascribing sex to an inanimate object, we have not, however, the liberty of making it of what gender we please, masculine or feminine; but are, in general, subjected to some rule of gender which the currency of language has fixed to that object. The foundation of that rule is imagined, by Mr. Harris, in his 'Philosophical Enquiry into the Principles of Grammar,' to be laid in a certain resemblance, or analogy, to the natural distinction of the two sexes.[58]

Blair adopts Harris's model of the taxonomy of 'proper' anthropomorphising based on a 'certain resemblance or analogy'. Of prosopopoeia he writes that 'it is a figure, the use of which is very extensive, and its foundation laid deep in human nature'.[59] If used in the correct way, without 'ridiculous effect', the figure is 'found to be natural and agreeable; nor is any uncommon degree of passion required, in order to make us relish it. All poetry, even in its most gentle and humble forms, abounds with it.'[60] Significantly, it is because anthropomorphism itself is 'natural' that it agrees with us. Evidently, this problematic argument relates back to the circularity that haunts the trope of anthropomorphism. By extension, it also explains why it enforces the general argument of this chapter. The 'natural' 'resemblances' or 'analogies' stand in the same circular relation to anthropomorphism as anthropomorphism relates to a Romantic longing of merging with an anthropomorphised nature.

   All the accounts discussed so far involve strategies of negotiating the anthropomorphic origin of language, and continuously rephrase its fracturing 'nature'. These writers repeat the trope's divisive power down to their argumentative movements and terms. Entirely conscious and controlled manipulation is impossible, not least because the breaking force is located at the very origin of language, which is prior to linguistic control. With this in mind, I want to reverse de Man's observation that 'Anthropomorphism seems to be the *illusionary* resuscitation of the *natural* breath of language, frozen into stone by the semantic powers of the trope' (*RR*, 247; my emphases). If, as the readings above suggest, anthropomorphism is understood as a 'natural' trope, its signification and implications are also 'natural' consequences. But these implications mainly concern the fracturing power of anthropomorphism that forever marks the rift between man and nature. The ultimate conclusion must be that this fundamental break, the fragmenting quality of the origin, is also a 'natural' one. This gives new impetus to the assertion that the division between nature and the trope (a trope that simultaneously sets us apart from it and wants to unite us with it) is located at the origin of language. Accordingly, language already contains this fundamental break within itself. The fracturing anthropomorphism is a 'natural' one in the sense that it pertains to the character and nature of language. By the same token, one can describe the divide that resides within the coming into being of language as 'natural' or adequate to it. And what would be better to represent this dynamic than the rhetorical figure that always captures this fracture – anthropomorphism. The trope of anthropomorphism concentrates the essential difference located at the linguistic origin.

Blair insists that anthropomorphism is not only 'natural' in relation to the description of certain specific objects (owing to their supposedly inherent qualities). He goes further, arguing that its use is natural to man:

Indeed, it is very remarkable, that there is a wonderful proneness in human nature to animate all objects. Whether this arises from a sort of assimilating principle, from a propension to spread a resemblance of ourselves over all other things, or from whatever other cause it arises, so it is, that almost every emotion, which in the least agitates the mind, bestows upon its object a momentary idea of life.[61]

In other words, it is part of our nature to endow our surroundings with human qualities, to anthropomorphise. Blair explains that prosopopoeia (including his own, presumably) 'is a figure, the use of which is very extensive, and its foundation laid deep in human nature', making it 'natural and agreeable' to man.[62] This is the extraordinary reverse side of the controlled figuration with which we started. Anthropomorphism, with all its power to divide, is the 'natural' mirror and explanation of the relation between the human and the natural. That it is through one of the master-tropes of poetry that this divide can allegedly be bridged only reinforces the tensions in Blair's account:

One of the greatest pleasures we receive from poetry, is, to find ourselves always in the midst of our fellows; and to see every thing thinking, feeling, and acting, as we ourselves do. This is, perhaps, the principal charm of this sort of figured style, that it introduces us into society with all nature, and interests us, even in inanimate objects, by forming a connexion between them and us, through that sensibility which it ascribes to them.[63]

This is a wonderfully adequate description of the psychological propensity to anthropomorphise. However, it is, also, an admission of how far this rhetorical move exhibits the impossibility of fulfilling its ultimate fantasy. The assimilation of nature ('thinking, feeling, and acting, as we ourselves do') forms a 'connexion' between nature and us. However, that assimilation is, as Blair's syntax already suggests, made by language itself. It is the 'figured style' that forms the 'connexion' and 'it' also ascribes human qualities to nature. Language itself keeps up the divide, however pleasurable it might be to think of an unfractured relationship between the natural and the human. In reaction, the subject defines itself through its natural propensity to anthropomorphise. This is a definition *against* what the trope promises to unite the subject with (i.e. nature – which is also what makes the figure supposedly pleasurable). Man 'naturally' anthropomorphises because he wants to merge with nature (and this is what the trope promises to do); anthropomorphism is the constitutive figure for human nature. However, as the figure also reminds him, man is *by nature* fundamentally divided from nature. Anthropomorphism performs the double function of pretending to overcome this division and, at the same time, insisting that it is impossible to do so. The longing rhetorics of anthropomorphism constantly remind us that both language and subject are fractured in their origin.

CHAPTER 3

Forces trembling underneath: the Lisbon earthquake and the sublime

'Have you heard of the earthquake in Lisbon?'[1]

THE PROGRESSIVIST NARRATIVE

In the opening book of his autobiography, *Dichtung und Wahrheit* (1811–32), Goethe records one of his most important childhood experiences by taking a distancing look at himself in the third person:

[T]he boy's tranquillity of mind was deeply shaken for the first time by an extraordinary event. On the first of November, 1755, occurred the great earthquake of Lisbon, spreading enormous terror over a world grown accustomed to peace and quiet.[2]

Just as this date shakes and severs Goethe's biography, the tremendous impact of the earthquake of Lisbon is a defining moment for the entire century. In what follows, I want to take seriously Goethe's image of the disruptive power of this well-known disaster.[3] The argument of this third chapter presents the Lisbon earthquake as an event whose metaphorical force provides a conceptual springboard for a reading of some central texts on the sublime. Although my point of departure is the material circumstance of 1755, its role in these readings is primarily that of conceptual and rhetorical catalyst.

The earthquake of Lisbon has captured the imagination of people throughout the centuries in many ways.[4] In recent times we have become familiar with the journalistic strategy of linking disastrous events such as 9/11 or the Asian tsunami in 2004 with the eighteenth-century disaster. Most extended commentary generally understands the earthquake, at least in some aspect, as an event which marks a crucial and initiating moment in a history linking modernity and increasing secularisation, in both the sciences and the humanities (as far as these divisions apply here).[5] Correspondingly, the *meaning* of the event was, and indeed is, most often theorised in relation to the multidisciplinary complex of issues surrounding the ancient discussion of theodicy. Crudely put, there are two main ways in which Lisbon is presented as a marker of modern European history. First, as swinging general trust from a best of all possible Leibnizian worlds to a less optimistic view of a life defined by inexplicable suffering. Or, secondly, as an incentive to show that we should abandon the idea of a wrathful deity that makes the earth tremble in order to adopt a more convincing account that is based on the analysis of natural causes.

In either case, the link between the Lisbon earthquake and the development of our contemporary literary or scientific outlook has proved to be hermeneutically powerful and lasting.[6] It has had a constant presence in scholarly literature in a variety of fields. A recent example is Susan Neiman's widely discussed study *Evil in Modern Thought* (2002), in which she locates 'the modern as beginning at Lisbon' and calls the earthquake the 'birthplace of modernity'.[7] A number of important thinkers and authors are often enlisted as the most distinguished and illustrious proponents of conceptualising Lisbon in these terms. Goethe, William Blake, and Mary Wollstonecraft write about the earthquake; Heinrich von Kleist and Thomas Mann use it in their masterpieces; Theodor W. Adorno, Walter Benjamin, and Bertrand Russell continue the attempts to understand the catastrophe philosophically.[8] Most of these accounts see the importance of the rupturing moment which the earthquake comes to represent as an exemplary position within a narrative that describes the eighteenth and nineteenth centuries as developing a more secular outlook, particularly in response to natural phenomena. I will refer to this view as the 'progressivist narrative'. Even the many theologically inflected responses to the calamity, which directly link the disaster to a divine act or word, retrospectively also form part of the framework for this story. Whether as independent contributions or as part of the discussions on theodicy, they are dismantled and superseded by more enlightened arguments (or so the story goes).

The specific literary context of the catastrophe is constructed, at least in part, as a chapter of this progressivist story. Alexander Pope's *An Essay on Man* (1733–34) and its mocking reception by Lessing and Mendelssohn prepare the literary field before the catastrophe hits European intellectual life. In assessing the immediate aftermath, Voltaire's reaction generally serves as the paradigmatic example. His influential *Poéme sur le désastre de Lisbonne* (1756) – a classic case of an argument-poem defending a particular position in the debate on the problem of evil – becomes the point of reference for Rousseau's reply on the subject as well as innumerable other voices.[9] The earthquake retains its power throughout the period as a general foil for imagery, such as in Kleist's *Erdbeben in Chili* (1807). Despite their differences, the representative nature of these 'enlightened' texts is firmly established in and through secondary sources.[10]

The argument of this chapter is situated against this general background. It will focus on the role played by the aesthetic, specifically the Romantic sublime, in the outlined field of responses. The chapter will fall into three parts, moving from the particular to the general. In the first section, I will look at reports from the immediate scene of the disaster. The second and third steps link these readings to a much larger complex of aesthetics, via the category of the sublime. By looking closely at texts by Burke and Kant, I will attempt to unravel the double nature of the sublime as a taming and domesticating force that ultimately relies on the destructive power of fragmentation. Lisbon and its shattering power haunt the secular and 'progressivist' character of Burke's and Kant's arguments that has often been taken for granted in secondary literature. Fragmentation frames and captures precisely the theoretical as well as the more immediately empirical aspects of this dynamic. Thus introducing the notion of fragmentation is a specification and precision of David Simpson's general remark that 'if the earthquake [of Lisbon] can be said to have exposed the dubious status of the doctrines of rational self-sufficiency which the public voice of Enlightenment thought put forward, then it could also be said that it re-emphasised the priority of the gaps upon which that voice was founded'.[11] The chapter will show via the notion of fragmentation that the reaction to the Lisbon earthquake allows new insights into the structural position of the Romantic sublime, especially within a larger Kantian framework. The fragmentation of ideas, to return to Goethe's remark, can be read as the necessary condition for the subsequently rationalising categories of the sublime, one of the most central categories of Romanticism. Correspondingly, the common critical narrative allows for its reversal: the 'progressive' power of Lisbon relies on something altogether negating and exceeding rationality or secular description. The earthquake's ripples remain more destructive than has been assumed.

CLASSIFICATION AND EXCESS

Eye-witness accounts of the Lisbon earthquake rank among the most impressive documents of the eighteenth century. Letters written by inhabitants, travelling merchants, and other survivors of the catastrophe, struggle for words to represent the absolute terror and destruction of the disaster. While the event exceeds classification, the reports attempt to find a language in which to present the destruction that surrounds them. The lack of available vocabulary transpires in a variety of failed attempts to classify the event geographically, historically, and psychologically. An example from each of these areas follows.

The difficulty contemporary observers have in attempting to categorise the disaster is striking. It should really have been different. At least England's distant observers seem superficially prepared. In 1750 a mild trembling of the earth in London leads to a publication of an extensive special appendix to the papers of the Royal Philosophical Society dedicated to reports about the event.[12] Hence it is not surprising that the Society is open to papers about the new scene and that earthquakes become a dominant subject of the proceedings for over a year.[13] However, the natural catastrophe in Portugal proves to be of such proportions that its trembling cannot be fixed in an appendix. The Lisbon earthquake, rather than being limited in its location and consequences to one place, immediately becomes a European catastrophe felt throughout the western world. The Society stresses that reports about the trembling of the earth arrive from places as diverse as Madrid, Cadiz, Tetuan, and other locations on the Iberian peninsula. There are letters from Tangier, Arzila, Salle, Fez, Mequinez, Morocco, Sarjon Hills, Madeira, and Tasso – the impact of the earthquake is truly intercontinental. And the disaster is not only exoticised: Lisbon is also felt in Derbyshire and Scotland. Once the earth moves from Africa to northern Europe, its aftershock cannot be contained in a single volume. The following years see a continuing interest in geological catastrophes. Reports on movements of the earth reach the Royal Society from Neuchâtel, Geneva, New York, Boston, Pennsylvania, Glasgow, Dumbarton, Leiden, Brussels, Dover, Brigue, and Maastricht. It is evident that Lisbon is not simply a localised catastrophe. The event has its epicentre in a particular place – its impact, however, is far wider. A geographical localisation of the event becomes impossible, its power is beyond containment. Lisbon cannot be confined to one geographical space; suddenly it is all over Europe.

The difficulty in fixing Lisbon within conventional parameters becomes even clearer when reports attempt to articulate its exceptional status by means of temporal images. The catastrophe is catapulted out of normal history. A letter from an English merchant resident in Lisbon writing back home makes clear that the event does not belong to the generally accepted narrative within which we live:

[The earthquake] reduced the whole Metropolis to Ashes; rendering it such a Spectacle of Terror and Amazement, as well as the Desolation to Beholders, as perhaps has not been equalled from the Foundation of the World.[14]

The singularly disastrous character of the catastrophe cannot be 'equalled' by anything in the annals of the world. It cannot be domesticated within a common taxonomy of known, memorisable, historical events. It becomes an event of biblical proportions, a 'disaster' in the most radical sense of the Old Testament. As the eye-witness insists:

I have past through the Ruins of the principal Parts of the City, and they are dreadful indeed to behold. I believe so compleat a Destruction has hardly befallen any Place on Earth, since the Overthrow of *Sodom* and *Gomorrah*.[15]

Normal classification will not do here. Although the beholder does not turn into a pillar of salt, the dimensions of the destruction are suggestive enough. The event is of proportions that go beyond modern records. Through the mythical allusion it escapes the status of a historically locatable event. The reference to Sodom and Gomorrah suggests how far the 'compleat Destruction' breaks the usual frame of history. John Biddulph's *Poem on the Earthquake at Lisbon* (1755) puts it in a similar way when describing the miseries of the Portuguese King:

> Lo! The good King from out the ruin'd Heaps,
> By Providence Divine, Like *Lot* escapes;
> But *Lot's* Command, while yet the City burn'd,
> The weeping King had disobeyed and turn'd:
> There in Salt Tears congeal'd, he fix'd had staid,
> And, like the Woman, a new Pillar made:
> Forbid his dear *Eurydice* to view,
> Like *Orpheus* he had look'd and perish'd too.[16]

The wild and jumbled mixture of biblical and Classical imagery unwittingly reflects the chaos represented in the scene. In the remainder of the poem the King is confusedly likened to Moses on Ararat, Job, and Aeneas beholding 'his burning Troy'. Not only are these disordered comparisons but they also defy coherent classification of collapse and destruction under traditionally historical rubrics. People involved in the earthquake, such as the actual King, are taken out of history and transformed into mythical figures. Note that these are examples that fall outside discourses with open theologico-didactic goals (where one might expect, and indeed finds, an abundance of biblical vocabulary, most notably in the innumerable sermons that use Lisbon as 'proof' for the wickedness of its Roman Catholic inhabitants).

Thus, I want to suggest, the earthquake pervades and exceeds the language of its textual reception, catapulting the event out of time and place. Geological science is not immune from this move either. In a letter passed on to the Royal Society, a 'Mr Perry' confirms that 'The earthquake at Lisbon, which you gave me an account of, was certainly the most awful tremendous calamity, that has ever happened in the world. Its effects are extremely wonderful and amazing; and it seems, as you observe, to have been felt in all parts of the globe.'[17]

More localised reports from the scenes of Lisbon's destruction illustrate the extent to which fragmentation ends in ruin and formless graves. The merchant's report already quoted attempts to capture the process of devastation from the midst of its chaos:

Not long after my Arrival at the Place I have mentioned, a general Pannic [*sic*] was raised from a Crowd of People's running from the Waterside, all crying out the Sea was pouring in and would certainly overwhelm the City. [V]ast Numbers of them [the inhabitants] ran screaming into the ruinated City again, where, a fresh Shock of the Earthquake immediately following, many of them were buried in the Ruins of falling Houses.[18]

The already 'ruinated City' becomes, through a second quake, just as deadly as the nearby sea, locking the inhabitants of Lisbon into a prison of shock, horror, and death. The material fragmentation of the city is repeated twice over. 'Ruinated' already, it buries 'many' of the 'vast Numbers' under its fragments ('the Ruins of falling Houses'). These letters insist on the earthquake's power to form a deadly tomb under which the inhabitants are 'buried'[19] or by which they are 'dashed to pieces'.[20] In the same vein, another eye-witness, Anthony Pereira, reports that 'the houses, the streets and alleys were strewed with dead bodies: some had their brains dashed out with the falling of the arches, other were crushed by the tumbling of the walls, most of them were overpowered and suffocated with the weight of the rubbish, in such a heap of rafters and stones'.[21] In its collapse, Lisbon becomes a mass grave – in fact, a 'third part of its inhabitants was buried in the ruins'.[22]

Neither mind nor body can cope with these dimensions. In the most extreme instance, the city's total destruction and collapse is mirrored in the bodily annihilation of its inhabitants, as this anonymous letter gruesomely describes:

Mr. Vincent […] never left the house he slept in, being suddenly crushed to death before he was dressed, and buried in ruins, which is the only tomb he is ever like to meet with; for his friends, after many fruitless searches, having discovered as they supposed the remains of his body, they found them so putrified, broken and scattered that 'twas impossible to remove them.[23]

The human form is reduced to shapelessness, its body mutilated beyond representation. The very shape of the human subject is 'broken and scattered' beyond recognition. 'Mr Vincent', just like Lisbon, 'is no more'. His corpse has been so crushed that it becomes futile to attempt its 'reconstruction'. The only thing left to contemplate and behold are the ruins that function as his memorial. Importantly, the reports correspondingly insist how this material collapse goes hand in hand with a mental breakdown. The reports from Lisbon repeatedly make the 'Horrors in the agitated Minds of the Populace' responsible for their running into 'ruinated' graves.[24] The mental collapse lies at the epicentre of the disaster:

It would be a vain Attempt to endeavour describing the numberless Miseries, and terrible Distresses of all kinds, occasioned by this dreadful Calamity, as well as the shocking Effects that it had on the Minds of all people.[25]

The subject's mind is taken over in the apocalyptic scene, sometimes dangerously close to melodrama. A total breakdown of coherence makes orderly writing impossible. The descriptions emphasise the correlation between mental and material fragmentation throughout. The material collapse of the city's buildings, churches, and symbols is paralleled by a collapse of inner structures. While the capital is 'scattered' its inhabitants suffer from mental breakdowns and 'various Distempers'.[26] Mirroring the ruined buildings, people are said to be 'sinking under the Anguish of Despair'.[27] Descriptions like these – and there are many more – insist that there is a close and complex relationship between the victims' actions, their faces, shouts, general confusion, and the already encountered 'Horrors in the[ir] agitated Minds'.[28] The reason why the mental aspect of these jumbled descriptions is particularly important is that it provides the first, most obvious, but (as we shall see) problematic link to the aesthetic category of the sublime. The insistence on the mental quality of the experience immediately tempts us to figure the catastrophe and its representations in terms of the sublime, thereby following a number of authors who use earthquakes as an illustration of the sublime.

The rhetoric of the eye-witness reports from Lisbon suggests that it is impossible to find a vocabulary for such an event: geographical, temporal, and mental classifications no longer hold. This excess also becomes a self-conscious subject in the record itself. We already know that it is a 'vain Attempt to endeavour describing the numberless Miseries, and terrible Distresses of all kinds, occasioned by this dreadful Calamity'.[29] Another witness argues similarly that 'It would be impossible to pretend justly to describe the universal horror and distress which every where took place.'[30] There is no space here that could be reserved for controlled representation. An anonymous letter confirms that the earthquake 'has made such a scene of desolation and misery, as words cannot describe', and yet another source succinctly states that "Tis not to be expressed' what degree the suffering takes.[31] The Nuncio in Lisbon assures that 'our Grief and Consternation are unutterable', just as another anonymous victim reports that, when arriving at the sight of a ruined house, 'The new scenes of terror I met with here, exceed all description.'[32] Unsurprisingly, the confusion and breakdown are reflected in the texts themselves. The total breakdown of the city is said to make the activity of structured recording impossible. Mind and body no longer provide a stable background for the writing of letters: 'the scene of misery and destruction is so horrible, that one's blood grows cold at giving you a description of it'.[33] Writers often 'must humbly beg your pardon, Sir, for the disorder of this letter, surrounded as I am by the many in distress, who, from one instant to another, are applying to me either for advice or shelter'.[34] Their writing must be 'imperfect' because they are in 'Hurry and Confusion' while mirroring the fragmentation of the city in their writing.[35]

Nevertheless, we might say, these records exist; while they insist on the difficulty of their production, they are still there. And that is partly because, during and before their writing, a certain distance from the event itself is generated. Only distance allows for the development of a vocabulary that might adequately describe the dimensions of the catastrophe. This distancing may be temporal, spatial, or mental. In the realm of aesthetics the sublime is the category that theorises the creation of this type of distance, and develops a terminology of representation. The two most important accounts of the sublime in the period, Burke's *A Philosophical Enquiry into the Origin of our Ideas of the Sublime and Beautiful* (1757) and Kant's *Critique of Judgement* (1790; rev. 1793 and 1799), both insist on this move as vital. In what follows, I want to show how the creation of distance leaves behind the insistence on excess and breakdown in the eye-witness accounts from the scene. Simultaneously, however, it also transpires that the initial importance of ineffability becomes a difficulty which haunts these more theoretical accounts. The emphasis of my analysis will be on the aesthetic-philosophic dimensions of these two canonical texts. This focus permits me to acknowledge, but ultimately sidestep, approaches that also thematise the interaction of psychic and material events in the realm of language.[36]

BEHOLDING THE RUINS

Burke's *Enquiry* offers an instructive and condensed example of how the mental experience of terror is connected to pleasure, and what makes the strange and disturbing delight we take in scenes of horror (a central part of the sublime) possible. In a well-known passage he conjectures that

This noble capital, the pride of England and Europe, I believe no man is so strangely wicked as to desire to see destroyed by a conflagration or an earthquake, though he should be removed himself to the greatest distance from the danger. But suppose such a fatal accident to have happened, what numbers from all parts would croud to behold the ruins?[37]

Burke chooses London as the imagined setting of his thought-experiment. However, it is very likely that the inspiration behind it is the very real Lisbon earthquake, which, having occurred only a year before this passage was written, was still fresh in Europe's mind.[38] The imagined transposition of Lisbon into London is, in fact, a common rhetorical strategy at the time. For example, James Hallifax in a 1756 sermon reminds his congregation of the almighty powers of the Lord who has stricken Roman Catholic Lisbon: 'Let us look back with Horror upon our Lives and Actions, and see whether, if *London* and *Lisbon* had fallen in the same Instant, we should have been duly prepared for such a sudden Destruction? How few are there of us that must not shudder at the Thought!'[39] And the anonymous *Address to the Inhabitants of Great Britain; occasioned by the late Earthquake at Lisbon* (1755) insists that 'Awful as it [the earthquake] is, *we* might have felt it, and LONDON instead of LISBON might have been a *Heap of Ruins*.'[40] Thus, on first inspection, the reports on Lisbon's 'Spectacle of Terror' seem indeed a straightforward (if anachronistic) illustration of the stereotypical Burkean sublime.[41]

However, things are not that simple. What is most striking about the context of Burke's passage is how far the catastrophe forms part of a larger taxonomy of the aesthetic and how it presents an imaginary London earthquake (which reminds the reader of the real one in Lisbon) as part of the construction of an aesthetic category such as the sublime.[42] Burke's argument that we take pleasure in scenes of destruction relies implicitly on the moment of fragmentation exceeding all description. Thus the representation of the consequences, even when sufficient distance is gained, depends on a moment which denies the possibility of representation. An articulation of the ruins through the sublime domesticates the imagined catastrophe into a framework of manageable concepts. These form, or are part of, a larger taxonomy of philosophy in general and of aesthetics in particular.

It is a given in secondary literature that nearly all theorisations of the sublime insist on distance as necessary to allow for the development of a vocabulary that adequately describes the aesthetic experience. Whether this distancing may be temporal, spatial, or mental, we have to be in a position to 'behold' the sublime, or rather its aftermath – the ruins it leaves behind. In the realm of aesthetics, the sublime is the category that theorises the creation of this type of distance and develops a vocabulary of representation around it. Once Lisbon is categorised as 'the sublime' (or rather, its representation), it is conceptualised, rationalised, and framed in a systematic account. (An extreme example of how this systematisation takes place is precisely the terminology of 'beholding the ruins', which reoccurs with such frequency in the eighteenth century that it becomes a standard phrase in aesthetic discourse.) Both Burke and Kant stress the importance of distance in their respective texts. It is instructive to see how in the creation of this distance they leave behind the insistence on excess and breakdown we encountered in the eye-witness accounts from the actual scene. They replace the breakdown with a ruin. Crucially, the ruin is already viewed from the distance; we 'behold' it – it is *already* aesthetic. Hence, the subsequent classification of the event as sublime domesticates it, while enabling an orderly and framing discussion of it in aesthetic terms. The ruins become foundational, and serve as a stabilising grounding in creating a discourse *on* the sublime. The sublime, understood in this sense, is a taming category. A letter by a James O'Hara, a captain visiting Lisbon in 1755, written to his sister in the aftermath of the disaster, provides an example how the sublime can be understood as taming or 'domesticating':

P.s. Since writing the above, I have accompanied Admiral Broderick over most part of the ruins of this city, lately famous for its wealth and commerce. Never did any eye behold so awful, so tremendous a scene. The moon, which was then at the full, shining resplendently on the Tagus, gave us a night view of this wreck of nature.

The howling of the dogs, the stench of the dead bodies, together with the gloom which now and then diffused itself around, from the moon's being sometimes obscured, gave me some idea of that general crash, when sun and moon shall be no more; and filled my mind with meditations, that only such a scene could inspire.[43]

O'Hara's text is a postscript to the inexpressible. The transformation from indescribable scenes to panoramic view is remarkable. The scene on Lisbon's stage has changed utterly. Not that it is a purely pleasant one. In the nearly gothic description it is still 'awful' – but also 'tremendous'. The city that – like Burke's London – is famous for its splendour and richness has been shattered, and suddenly looks like a heap of ancient ruins, waiting for the visitor to enjoy the 'sublime' moonlit scene. Even natural might, which just a few days ago had struck so mercilessly, helps to elevate the aesthetic scene of ruin. The full moon shines, reflected in the river, lighting up a 'wreck' of nature and sometimes, 'being obscured', gives a perfect lighting to this premature illustration of Burkean sublimity.

For the writer, the scene engenders notions which link it to the most paradigmatic instance of the sublime, the apocalypse. Here chaos reaches such dimensions that fundamental distinctions break down. Even the very beginning of creation, light, whose representation Longinus had already held up as *the* paradigmatically sublime moment, and which creates the division into night and day (the most basic of all classifications), supposedly collapses. Only a scene as terrible, confused, and obscure as Lisbon can 'inspire' the imagination to such thoughts and feelings. But the path taken by these thoughts and feelings is familiar. In this report they are not jumbled, terrified, and confused at all. This is precisely because, as Burke will later insist, they are being formed in front of a 'scene', with sufficient distance to aestheticise the 'ruins'. James O'Hara is Burke's imaginary disaster-tourist *avant la lettre*. The vocabulary, imagery, and register make it plain that this is at once a controlled and controlling scene. The rationalisation of the shattering moment into the sublime (through the distance demanded by Burke's account) ensures the upholding of a psychology that works within the framework of its aesthetic categories. The letter on the sublime scenery of Lisbon again provides a good example. The observer is removed through controlled perspective; he uses what will become conventional topoi (the obscure moon over the ruins), and he even creates a formal distance by severing his description from the main body of the letter (a post scriptum). O'Hara's highly formalised response and its reliance on an ordering principle are epitomised by the coherent subject who controls and holds the experience together.[44] The standardisation of this response in literary works throughout the following century reinforces the suspicion that the ruins often are more foundational than is usually assumed.

Reading O'Hara's letter in conjunction with the earlier eye-witness reports and theorisations of the sublime, it becomes evident that there is a tension between the domesticating quality of representations of sublimity, and that such representations ultimately rely on a moment which escapes any categorisation at all. The simultaneity and interdependence here are significant. At one level, Lisbon escapes the modes and possibilities of classification per se, be they temporal, geographic, or aesthetic. At another, this stands in immediate tension with the subsequent mechanisms of control, such as packaging the ruins as a sublime scene. At the very core of the domesticating effect of the sublime that creates the 'scene' of Lisbon lies a shattering moment of fragmentation that exceeds all order and qualification. This interdependence, it seems, is sufficiently strong for the fragmentation to be considered structurally and logically necessary for the sublime. Not only does Lisbon find its way into the *Enquiry*, but Burke's text can be read as a rationalisation of the disaster within a psychology of the aesthetic. The moment of fragmentation becomes the *sine qua non* for the aesthetic pleasure achieved through the domesticating effect of the sublime. So, once the process of distancing rationalisation has begun, there still remains the force that generated the necessity for an ordering movement in the first place. This goes further than Burghard Schmidt, who in his study on post-modernity offers a related genealogy of the link between fragmentation and the sublime. He suggests that, at least until Arthur Schopenhauer, they are coextensive, and define themselves together in opposition to the beautiful.[45] However, Schmidt downplays their crucial differences by ignoring the excessive character of fragmentation, on the one hand, and the domesticating nature of the sublime, on the other. By contrast, I want to argue that the fragmenting moment exceeds the possible taxonomies of a discourse of aesthetics, including the sublime.

Two instances in Mary Wollstonecraft's imaginative writing vividly present how the ambivalent nature of this dynamic is negotiated when the earthquake is used as a literary trope. On the one hand, we read about the protagonist Mary in the novel *Mary: A Fiction* (1788), who flees England and chooses to go to 'Lisbon rather than France, on account of its being further removed from the only person she wished not to see'.[46] In this novel Lisbon is all sublime, recalling O'Hara's letter, which set the 'tremendous' scene in the moonlight: 'When the weather began to clear up, Mary sometimes rode out alone, purposely to view the ruins that still remained of the earthquake: or she would ride to the banks of the Tagus, to feast her eyes with the sight of that magnificent river'.[47] Here the disaster has become a 'feast' to be consumed after the parting of the clouds, and which can also be relied on to elevate one's thoughts. Without being overwhelmed, Mary rides (but only 'sometimes') to view the aestheticised remains ('ruins') in peace and quiet. The earth is certainly not shaking anymore; the viewing can be arranged and undergone 'purposely'. In Wollstonecraft's posthumous fragment *The Wrongs of Woman; or Maria* (1798) the main character, Maria, confined in a madhouse, discovers an utterly different type of ruin. 'Sometimes, from her window, she turned her eyes from the gloomy walls, in which she pined life away, on the poor wretches who strayed along the walks, and contemplated the most terrific of ruins – that of a human soul.'[48]

Maria can contemplate the mental equivalent of material destruction without moving from her prison. The next sentence makes a direct link that stresses the dissymmetry between the two: 'What is this view of the fallen column, the mouldering arch, of the most exquisite workmanship, when compared with this living memento of the fragility, the instability, of reason.'[49] However, further reflection on the part of the narrator reveals that the relation between material and mental is not quite so clear cut: 'It is not over decaying productions of the mind, embodied with the happiest art, we grieve most bitterly.'[50] Minds here *are* embodied. Wollstonecraft's narrator continues to describe the dialectic between the two:

The view of what has been done by man, produces a melancholy, yet aggrandizing, sense of what remains to be achieved by human intellect; but a mental convulsion, which, like the devastation of an earthquake, throws all the elements of thought and imagination into confusion, makes contemplation giddy, and we fearfully ask on what ground we stand.[51]

Here the earthquake provides a conceptual image for the total collapse of thought and imagination. The 'fearful' reaction hints at the link to the sublime before which '*all* the elements of thought and imagination' (my emphasis) are thrown into confusion. No conceptualisation or halt is possible. Only later can we 'ask on what ground we stand' – the devastating force of the earthquake is complete.

These two passages by Wollstonecraft uncover the multifaceted ways in which the image of the earthquake (and the earthquake *as* image) operates. They also provide a concrete illustration of how this paradigmatic example for the natural sublime is presented in non-theoretical writings. *Mary* offers an illustration of the fully domesticated Burkean scene that is ready for touristic inspection. On the other hand, *The Wrongs of Woman; or Maria* advances the earthquake as an image of mental fragmentation and breakdown that denies all rationalisation. We can see how fragmentation becomes a notion that escapes the realm of the aesthetic. It also comes to occupy an unexpectedly central position in Burke's account. His covert allusion to Lisbon becomes an anxious indicator for an important dimension underlying his theory: namely, that at the very core of the psychology of coherence (which makes an aesthetics of the sublime possible) lies a fragmenting force that exceeds its ordering categories. The Burkean sublime relies on this breaking force because it structurally and logically precedes the process of reconstruction within the framework of the aesthetic. Burkean distance ultimately relies on a shattering of relations.

The fundamental tension uncovered in the Burkean account of psychology intensifies when we transpose it to a more formal argument such as the Kantian one, which similarly sustains distance as a prerequisite for the representation of the sublime. In the remainder of this chapter, I shall attempt to unravel two aspects of Kant's account in the *Critique of Judgement* and show how productive it is to consider them in connection with the events in Lisbon. First, the analysis will focus on the formal dimension of fragmentation in relation to the dynamic sublime as posited in the third *Critique*. Secondly, the attention will turn to some of Kant's pre-critical writings and their reception which invite us to reconsider the central position of this aesthetic category.

In the section 'On the Dynamically Sublime in Nature' Kant emphasises that it is only in safety and with enough distance that we can begin to enjoy (and judge) a scene which otherwise would be simply terrifying. In a well-known passage Kant writes to this effect:

Just as we cannot pass judgment on the beautiful if we are seized by inclination and appetite, so we cannot pass judgment at all on the sublime nature if we are afraid. (*CJ*, §28)[52]

Speaking further about natural might, Kant elaborates:

Yet the sight of them [the natural phenomena inducing fright] becomes all the more attractive the more fearful it is, provided we are in a safe place. (*CJ*, §28)

As in Burke's case, however, once the process of rationalisation is begun, there still remains the force that generated the necessity for an ordering movement in the first place. This force, which denies all conceptualisation, forms the basis for distance. This makes the process of rationalisation especially significant. The reader will remember that Kant spends some time explaining how far it is ultimately necessary and responsible for the pleasure connected to the sublime. Throughout the 'Analytic of the Sublime' Kant argues that both the moment of being utterly overcome and the subsequent rationalisation of such a moment are constitutive of the human subject. They provide a valuable way of affirming the special status of the human subject within the wider context of the natural world. This affirmation consists of, and is performed by, the category of rational thought.[53] The sublime, then, is for Kant an instance through which we can define ourselves as rational beings, albeit relying on the 'supersensible substrate' that Kant speaks of in §26 and 'which underlies both nature and our ability to think'. The stakes are high. Kant's account gives the sublime an important place in a larger framework that explains the human ability to make judgements and thereby attempts to explain how we place ourselves as rational agents within the natural world.

Kant insists that the pleasure connected to the sublime is the result of feeling elevated in relation to the nature that would otherwise crush us. And, as he explains in §28, it is our power and ability to reason [*Vernunftvermögen*] *through which and which themselves* make us feel this pleasure:

For although we found our own limitation when we considered the immensity of nature and the inadequacy of our ability to adopt a standard proportionate to estimating aesthetically the magnitude of nature's *domain*, yet we also found, in our power of reason, a different and nonsensible standard that has this infinity itself under it as a unit; and since in contrast to this standard everything in nature is small, we found in our mind a superiority over nature itself in its immensity. (*CJ*, §28)

The power of reason, in a crucial way, sidesteps natural might. That natural power exceeds human strength is undeniable: 'physische Ohnmacht' (physical impotence) are the words Kant uses in the original. Simultaneously, however, this is the very point where elevation over nature is possible, because we have within us

an ability to judge ourselves independent of nature, [which] reveal[s] in us a superiority over nature that is the basis of a self-preservation quite different in kind from the one that can be assailed and endangered by nature outside us. This keeps the humanity in our person from being degraded, even though a human being would have to succumb to that dominance [of nature]. (*CJ*, §28)

Kant has already insisted on the human ability to assert itself against nature when he discusses safety as a necessary condition for the positive experience of the sublime. Speaking of terrifying natural objects, he writes:

And we like to call these objects sublime because they raise the soul's fortitude above its usual middle range and allow us to discover in ourselves an ability to resist which is of a quite different kind, and which gives us the courage [to believe] that we could be a match for nature's seeming omnipotence. (*CJ*, §28)

It is thus the division between external might and the internal ability or power of reason that serves as a larger philosophical frame. This is also why Kant keeps insisting that the sublime is a state of mind – an inner moment – although we keep on using the term (including him, he admits) for the outer circumstances causing the mental state.

Even such a brief overview makes it evident that for Kant the sublime is a central part of a large and complex philosophical map. The sublime, in fact, has a deep connection with the epistemological and ethical aspects of the critical framework in terms of which experience is possible in the first place.[54] Leaving aside the extent to which the third *Critique* 'crowns' the *Critique of Pure Reason* and the *Critique of Practical Reason* (1788), Kant himself insists on how the complex knot of nature and the subject ties them together. This is particularly visible in the roles rational thought and subject-formation play in Kant's understanding of the sublime. It is a moment where crucial aspects of Kant's thought stand in dialogue with each other.[55] Correspondingly, an unsettling fragmentation will reverberate within both subject-formation and the construction of epistemological principles. Just as the sublime begins to connect up with other branches of Kant's thought, the fragmenting quality that underlies the sublime also invades them.

A lot of this has been a cornerstone of discussion in aesthetic criticism since the publication of the *Critique of Judgement*. In what follows, I want to leave this general discussion behind in order to concentrate on a specific aspect that follows from Kant's more general idea about the source of the sublime and how it is constructed *in ourselves* so as to become a defining feature of the subject. Kant, we know, insists that sublimity is not to be found in objects but only in our mind:

Sublimity is contained not in any thing of nature, but only in our mind, insofar as we can become conscious of our superiority to nature within us, and thereby also to nature outside us (as far as it influences us). Whatever arouses this feeling in us, and this includes the *might* of nature that challenges our forces, is then (although improperly) called sublime. (*CJ*, §28)

The centrality of this specific claim within the larger framework of aesthetic criticism is widely acknowledged. And once we finish Kant's sentence (Werner Pluhar's translation unfortunately breaks it in two, while Paul Guyer's version retains the semicolon that Kant's original places between the quotations provided here), we see that its final motive lies deeply within the subject's self-construction:

And it is only by presupposing this idea within us, and by referring to it, that we can arrive at the idea of the sublimity of that being who arouses deep respect in us, not just by his might demonstrated in nature, but even more by the ability, with which we have been endowed, to judge nature without fear and to think of our vocation as being sublime above nature. (*CJ*, §28)

This rich passage reflects back on Kant's concern to locate the sublime in a space that understands empirically experienced natural might as explicable within the framework of natural causes. The latter is an unspoken concern of the *Critique*, which, despite the innumerable commentaries on the role of nature in the text, has found little detailed attention.[56] Shortly before, Kant creates the background for his argument by positioning the sublime vis-à-vis the subject's relation to nature and creator. Kant explains that some people mistakenly interpret the idea or manifestation of natural might as a direct and anthropomorphised expression of divine powers:

This [Kant's] analysis of the concept of the sublime, insofar as [sublimity is] attributed to might, may seem in conflict with the fact that in certain situations – in tempests, storms, earthquakes and so on – we usually present God as showing himself in his wrath but also in his sublimity, while yet it would be both foolish and sacrilegious to imagine that our mind is superior to the effects produced by such a might, and is superior, apparently even to its intentions. (*CJ*, §28)

In order to give the sublime the position that Kant wants it to play, catastrophes or other manifestations of natural might have to be understood as divorced from higher intervention. An earthquake, albeit frightful, is devastating and disastrous, but not an expression of God's anger; to interpret it as such is to misunderstand the workings both of nature and of the divine.

Kant's general argument about the interpretation of natural disasters is not a new one. He openly and repeatedly rejects vulgar anthropomorphic thinking throughout his works. Even his reference to the earthquake sounds familiar. Remarkably, Kant already elaborates on the mistaken ethics resulting from anthropomorphising the cause of such events in his pre-critical writings:

But one contravenes very much against it [our compassion for the victims] if one regards such fates [natural disasters] always as imposed divine judgements, which strike the devastated cities because of their misdeeds, and if we regard these lamentable people as the target of God's revenge over whom all His righteousness pours out its bowl of wrath. This kind of judgement is criminal pertness.[57]

This statement, so very similar to the passage from the *Critique*, is taken from the final pages of a relatively unknown pre-critical essay entitled *History and Natural Description of the Remarkable Occurrences of the Earthquake, which at the End of the 1755th Year shook a Large Part of the Earth* – Kant's treatise on the earthquake of Lisbon. He writes and publishes this essay, and its second part, a year after the disaster together with another general treatise on earthquakes.[58]

The objection against interpreting a natural catastrophe, like the Lisbon disaster, as an expression of divine punishment links the third *Critique* and Kant's geological treatise. In both cases he implies that an 'outraged' reaction to an earthquake neglects to see it as part of a complex picture of natural phenomena. The Lisbon earthquake on All Saints' Day is the paradigm case of a natural disaster that was widely understood in terms of divine punishment or, alternatively, as evidence against traditional theology. Kant's move encourages the reader to sidestep this discussion, as he follows neither Voltaire nor the majority of contemporary clerical responses. In fact, he goes a step further than either of the parties who defend the 'obvious' meaning of the event (divine punishment or the evident impossibility of a benevolent God) and gives his apparently neutral account of natural causes a qualitative spin after all. Kant, outrageously for both the clerics and Voltaire, argues, first, that the horrors in Lisbon could have been limited by careful anticipatory reasoning, and, secondly, that, when contextualised in an adequate way, Lisbon's disaster even has a *useful* side to it. One section of his treatise is explicitly entitled 'Of the usefulness of earthquakes'. Acknowledging that this position will be intuitively unacceptable to most readers, Kant begins: 'One will be shocked to see such a terrible punishing rod for humans being praised as having a useful side.'[59] He then explains step by step. First, Kant makes the preliminary point that the extent of the catastrophe is partly due to the way the city was built. In other words, the Portuguese lack of foresight in matters of urban planning partly invalidates their claim to pity. Kant's argument here is a variant of Rousseau's rejoinder to Voltaire's famous *Poème* on Lisbon, his *Lettre à Monsieur de Voltaire* (1756). For Rousseau, too, modern urban planning, as the direct result and marker of questionable civilisatory developments, is responsible for the extent of the catastrophe.[60] Kant points out that the Peruvians, doubtlessly less civilised in the Rousseauan sense, build their cities with low houses, thereby reducing the risk of casualties in the great earthquake in Lima. And in his 'Concluding Observation', Kant echoes Rousseau, again in moralistic terms: 'Man is not born to build eternal huts on this stage of vanity.'[61]

This is an exemplary instance of Kant's argument from complexity and recontextualisation. It situates the specific earthquake of Lisbon in a scheme of natural phenomena, which, in their totality, ensure the world's continuous fertile existence. A first, 'outraged' reaction to a disaster like Lisbon neglects to see it as part of a bigger picture within a complex world. Hence, 'However much damage the cause of the earthquakes has ever provoked for humans on the one hand, it [the cause] can easily repair them with gains on the other.'[62] It does not matter that the particular basis for this move seems unconvincing to the contemporary reader. (It consists of conjectures about the revitalising nature of particles in the air and the continuous warmth in the inner regions of the earth, which guarantee fertility of soils.) What is important is the *type* of argument Kant is eager to construct and defend. For all his championing of contextualisation, Kant clearly limits his explanatory framework to an analysis of natural causes and what they can yield for him. The event, its context, and our possible interpretation of it (as useful, for instance), are all to be understood in terms of natural causes. This move helps to blur an underlying problem which comes back to haunt both Kant's aesthetic and its critical reception, namely, the ambiguous position that the Kantian sublime occupies in relation to the progressivist narrative sketched in the first part of this chapter.

Walter Benjamin's mythologising of Kant's treatise on Lisbon illustrates how the connection between Kant's aesthetics and the progressivist narrative becomes significant. In his essay 'Earthquake of Lisbon' (1931), Benjamin reconfirms the exceptional nature of the 1755 disaster. Not only does he point out the special status of Lisbon as a then-flourishing town (echoing the eighteenth-century fantasy, he states that the destruction of Lisbon would correspond to the annihilation of London in his day), but he also classifies the earthquake as 'the most extensive one has ever heard of'.[63] Despite dating the event historically, its status is still not totally clear: 'However, the earthquake that destroyed Lisbon on the 1st of November 1755 was not just a calamity like a thousand others, but in a lot of ways unique and remarkable.'[64] Benjamin also insists that 'At that time, nobody concerned himself more with these remarkable events than the great German philosopher, Kant.'[65] The special status of the material event combines with the eminence of the philosopher. According to Benjamin, it is none other than Kant who, with his treatise on Lisbon, inaugurates modern geology as we understand it: 'And a short paper that he [Kant] composed about it was really the beginning of scientific geology in Germany.'[66] Kant becomes the founding father of the discipline that helps us categorise the events in Lisbon in such a way that we understand them 'correctly'. Benjamin posits Kant as the founding father of *scientific* geology, not only geology as such. The secular character of Kant's text, its insistence on explaining the event in terms of natural causes, creates in its wake a modern discipline as we understand it. Already at its origin this new area of inquiry offers a taxonomy with which it can classify its own founding moment. According to this logic, scientific geology is born through the Lisbon earthquake, but immediately and retrospectively makes it subject to its rules. In Benjamin's account, Lisbon provokes a Kantian reaction eventually ending in the secular and scientific 'disciplining' of the catastrophe. This will result in a rationalised and domesticated discourse that is intelligible to us. Benjamin's essay is, in other words, a typical instance of the 'progressivist' position.[67]

These secular steps of thought find a parallel in the realm of the aesthetic. The rationalisation of the sublime follows a similar movement, insofar as it conceptualises an unrepresentable instance into a category that we can intelligibly manipulate. For this context, it is insignificant that the final object of a 'scientific' inquiry will be, according to Kant, conceptual knowledge, whereas the sublime cannot be based on straightforwardly epistemological categories. The account above stresses the importance of the posited moment that logically precedes the sublime as one of total shattering. This is an analogue to saying that the catastrophe of extraordinary proportions is necessary for the birth of the discipline that it will be understood by. Kant's own vocabulary hints at the destabilising dimension that underlies the domesticating tendency of the sublime. In §27 of the *Critique of Judgement* he writes:

In presenting the sublime in nature the mind feels *agitated* [Guyer: *moved*], while in an aesthetic judgment about the beautiful in nature it is in *restful* [Guyer: *calm*] contemplation. This agitation (above all its inception) can be compared with a vibration. (*CJ*, §27)

The agitation of the mind can be likened to a vibration, or a trembling. Kant uses the word *Erschütterung* (trembling) to describe and suggest the comparison, a sense that is lost in both translations. This trembling breaks and shakes the innermost moment of the *Gemüt*.[68] It is a similar tremor to the one with which this chapter began. Goethe's fracturing moment uses the same vocabulary (the *Gemütsruhe* or 'peace of mind' of the little boy is *erschüttert*, 'deeply shaken'), thereby mirroring the movement of the earthquake. Kant's argument for the rationalising logic of the sublime has an underlying trembling. The rationalised sublime depends on a shattering that does not allow representation. The foundational ruins in turn must rest on an abyss that cannot possibly form part of any architectural stability. In the same way as at the heart of the 'scientific reception' lies the disruptive moment of a mythologised secularisation, the sublime relies on the moment of total breakdown – a breakdown that, as Kant's own vocabulary betrays, resembles an earthquake. Here some of Kant's pre-critical writings, and Benjamin's mythologising of them via Lisbon, join hands with the explications of the dynamic sublime that we have already encountered in the *Critique of Judgement*. Considering the foundational character of this work for our understanding of the sublime in Romanticism, it is important to see how it is underwritten by a darker dynamic. The secular sublime, together with its ruins, discloses a disruptive and breaking quality at its core.

CHAPTER 4

A blue chasm: Wordsworth's The Prelude *and the figure of parenthesis*

> These kirkmen have done Scotland harm – they have banished puns
> and laughing and kissing (except in cases where the very danger and
> crime must make it very fine and gustful). I shall make a full stop after
> kissing for after that there should be a better parent-thesis: and go on
> to remind you of the fate of Burns.[1]

In the first chapter of this book I tried to show how an image of fragmentation such as the 'fragment of a wooden bowl' in *The Ruined Cottage* can play
a metonymic role in signifying a larger concern with fragmentation in
Wordsworth's poetry. The present chapter wants to illustrate how fracture
weaves itself into Wordsworth's texts syntactically, namely, by way of a
rhetorical and grammatical figure. The analysis will concentrate on the
figure of parenthesis. To ensure a clear focus, I will limit the reading of
this figure – at once rhetorical and grammatical – to some specific moments
in *The Prelude*.

Parenthesis is both a punctuation mark and a rhetorical figure. The
syntactical break in a textual structure by means of a parenthetical sign is
fundamentally disruptive in its effects. Grammatical treatises of the eighteenth century, which often include a section or chapter on parenthesis,
are as insistent on this as today's reference works. Parenthesis, both as a
grammatical unit and as a rhetorical move, produces a hiatus and a fracture
in thought and language. In his *An Essay on Punctuation* (1785), Joseph
Robertson discusses the link between thought and language when he
complains that 'in general they [parentheses] have a disagreeable effect,
being a sort of wheels within wheels, sentences in the midst of sentences, a
perplexed method of disposing of some thought, which the writer has not
the art to introduce in its proper place'.[2] Many of the complaints about
parenthesis in the period occur along similar lines, although often it is the
frequency of parenthesis, rather than its nature per se, that is the object of
criticism. F. [Francis?] Francillon's *Essay on Punctuation* (1842) offers a
concise and representative summary for the adequate use of the figure: 'A

parenthesis is a note and ought only be inserted in a sentence, when from its brevity, it does not distract the mind of the reader too long from the main proposition.'[3] Contemporary definitions of the figure show a continuity with these discussions in their fundamental assumptions about how parenthesis reflects a link between language and thought (and a rupture in both). Heinrich Lausberg's standard *Handbuch der literarischen Rhetorik* (*Handbook of Literary Rhetoric*) (1960) offers a definition in terms marked by the very figure it defines: 'The *interposition* "parenthesis" is the insertion – foreign to the construction – of a clause (and thus of an idea) into a sentence.'[4] Similarly, the *Encyclopaedia of Rhetoric* (2001) insists that the 'linguistic continuum' into which the parenthesis falls is 'thus disrupted', and sometimes this 'disrupture is probably violent'. The *Encyclopaedia* openly insists on its debt to earlier grammatical theory when it states that this is a reformulation of Fontanier's 'traditional treatise *Les figures du discours* (1821–30)'. The latter defines parenthesis as 'une insertion d'un sens complet et isolé d'un milieu d'un autre dont il interrompt la suite, avec ou sans rapport au sujet'.[5]

The interrupting and breaking quality of the parenthesis is not often commented upon in detail, although it poses questions of contemporary theoretical concern in a concentrated way.[6] One of the most evident issues it thematises is supplementarity (what is essential to the sentence and what is not?). Another, which this chapter focuses on, is linguistic disruption, understood in relation to the notion of fracture. Given that the syntactical structure of the parenthesis nearly always produces the effect of brokenness, this emphasis is not in itself surprising. What we put between brackets, whether they be (round) lunulae, [square] crotchets, or {curly} braces, is normally a fragmented sentence.[7] The present argument in relation to Wordsworth is that parentheses break the thought and flow of his language in instructive ways. The analysis will be restricted to one particular case of parenthesis, namely the lunulae (the round bracket). It is the most common and exemplifies well the fracturing quality that allows for a new reading of *The Prelude* as a cornerstone of Romanticism.

My approach thus far already indicates why fracture, rather than another term, is a productive critical category in this context. The figure of parenthesis illustrates particularly well the connection between language, thought, and their material representation in writing. It also insists on the importance and inevitability of rupture in that relation. Better than other grammatical entities, or marks of punctuation, it illustrates fracture, both visually on the page, in its conceptual-linguistic form, and in the phenomenology of reading (we always feel a break when we read a parenthesis). One of my contentions is that this punctuation is of major importance to Wordsworth's autobiographical poetry. This leads me to suggest the notion of fracture as a particularly adequate model with which to read *The Prelude*. Naturally, this is not to argue that the parenthesis itself is 'Romantic'; however, my readings will show that the specific way that Wordsworth employs lunulae in his poetry does tell us something both about his authorship and, via his writing, about the category of British Romanticism. First, his use of the figure sheds light on a neglected aspect of his work. Generally, scholarship that takes a sustained interest in Wordsworth's punctuation concentrates on editorial matters. There has been a constant investment in the autobiographical aspects of *The Prelude* since its publication. Only a few of these latter readings discuss fracture or fragmentation. None of them, as far as I know, describes Wordsworth's employment of a figure of punctuation as a stylistic decision of a grammatical order. In contrast, I want to show that attending to Wordsworth's use of parenthesis, especially through the notion of fracture, reveals an important aspect of this poetic practice and enriches our understanding of Romanticism. The chapter will illustrate that his use of lunulae is linked to central moments of his autobiographical and Romantic self-construction. Most likely, this is unintentional;[8] however, that does not prevent us from identifying it as forming part of a larger arsenal of concepts, figures, and strategies that make Wordsworth a representative Romantic poet. If lunulae are indeed linked to crucial moments of Wordsworthian poetry, then, by default, fracture is a particularly adequate notion with which to analyse this aspect of his writing. Thus, the readings want to show how the break of language and thought, which the parenthesis condenses, finds its way into the centre of Wordsworth's main work.

In a related discussion, John Lennard comments on the the figure of the round bracket in Romanticism by relating it to Coleridge's 'Dejection: An Ode'.[9] Lennard's argument foregrounds the graphical and etymological qualities of the lunulae, and how they make their impact on the poem. For instance, Lennard relates the form and appearance of the lunulae to the 'self-bracketing moon which hangs over "Dejection"' and speculates whether it may have become 'not only a symbol of his [Coleridge's] own condition and the inspiration of his talent, but also a richly funny intellectual joke'.[10] In contrast, the readings here want to explore how the conceptual import of the figure of the lunulae plays itself out in a larger autobiographical context, such as *The Prelude*. I want to pay special attention to how some of these cases relate to broader concerns at the heart of the poem and its construction. The chapter falls into three main parts. First, the readings concentrate on how some instances of lunulae in *The Prelude* perform, play with, and enforce the disruptive connotations of the rhetorical figure. The second part widens the focus, arguing that the issues raised by parenthesis can be extended to a reading of *The Prelude* as a whole. It emerges that key structural moments in *The Prelude* can be understood as both parenthetical and fracturing. Finally, the conclusion will outline how *The Prelude* negotiates the position of these structural moments within an autobiographical narrative.

BREAKING BRACKETS

In Book 1 of *The Prelude* the poetic persona recalls his childhood days and how the severing power of the cold winter winds impressed him. The way he remembers this event offers a simple but effective example of how parentheses, and lunulae in particular, pervade the poem to create a multifaceted and destabilising effect:

> Well I call to mind,
> ('Twas at an early age, ere I had seen
> Nine summers) when upon the mountain slope
> The frost, and breath of frosty wind had snapp'd
> The last autumnal crocus [...].   (*1805*, I. 310–14)[11]

The narrative breaks with the introduction of the parenthesis; the voice interrupts itself, thereby creating a highly self-conscious moment in the flow of recollections. The status of memory is openly thematised as the issue of narrative reliability comes to the fore. The voice calls 'Well [...] to mind', recalls, thereby opening up the narrative problem of autobiography and showing us the impossibility of being the same person he recalls. The problem of personal identity is partly made apparent through the visual break that the lunulae represent on the page itself. The problem of reliability is anxiously counteracted with the fiction that these lunulae increase the facticity of the narrative. By specifying that the 'early age' can be narrowed down to the more exact 'ere I had seen / Nine summers', the narrator insists on his reliability as well as his power of recall, suggesting that the poem's general statements can also be trusted. It implies that the narrator himself was there; nobody else could have had that specific experience – this is the poet's authoritative memory. The initial difficulty, however, invades the parenthesis. The moment the narrator recalls lies 'ere' he *had* 'seen' nine summers, thereby making both the future and the past his vantage points. The first moment reveals that the supposedly factual relies on the same mechanisms of temporal division that construct the subject who is relating. It is from a period *before* the nine summers that he *will have seen*, a period from which the narrator now wants to draw more concrete proof for his *present* recalling. Bracketing allows this attempted simultaneity and splitting of the different temporal and narrational perspectives of the poem. By breaking the text in such a manner, it becomes possible to switch time frames and thereby re-present the intricate problem of the temporality of one's self-construction in a condensed form. Specific changes in tense between the inside and outside of the lunulae are poignant instances of this dynamic. It is telling that in Book 2, for instance, Wordsworth parenthetically projects himself backwards while describing a crucial scene of human development:

> Bless'd the infant Babe,
> (For with my best conjectures I would trace
> The progress of our being) blest be the Babe [...]. (*1805*, 2. 238–40)

The blessing of the 'infant Babe' has to be reassured anxiously from the perspective of the present. Retracing the 'progress of our being' ruptures the organic growth before the baby even 'gather[s] passion from his Mother's eye!' (*1805*, 2. 243). The alliteration, together with the punning invocation of the infinitive ('b'/'be'), shows both Wordsworth's anxiety to insist on the success of the process, and its necessary failing: 'b' is second in order, and an alliteration always plays off the previous word, reminding us that the first has already passed. In reciting these lines from memory we often omit the qualifying abstract fragment that the lunulae contain. However, it represents a vital part of the 'progress of our being', which turns out to be much more ruptured than a harmonising false memory might suggest. The temporal breaks that Wordsworth describes repeat themselves on the reader's side too; first, through the visual 'reading' of a bracketed sentence that on its own is incomplete; and, secondly, through following the self-conscious moment in the narrative with parallel reflections about the reader's position. The reader is led to question his own reliability as a subject who recalls the past, including what he has read about others.

Another significant level on which the brackets operate here is also linked to the more general aspect of the problematic nature of autobiography as a document narrating the 'growth of a poet's mind'. The caesura that accompanies the bracket prepares for this problem. We pause in the flow of the story and realise that the round bracket introduces a parallel narrative which breaks the temporal cohesion of the account. It insists on the multifaceted nature of the auto-construction. The break emphasises narratorial unreliability at the very moment that the narrative appears to invest into its coherence. As with any moment of high self-reflexivity within a linguistic construction, these lines insist on our position as readers both outside of, and constituted by, the text. In this instance, the lunulae play a central part in the representation of the issues at stake in any autobiographical narrative. Parentheses draw attention to themselves at moments where they sever syntax and grammar both formally and conceptually, whether as rhetorical figures or as grammatical items. Their inclusion in the autobiographical narrative as a formal device allows it to insist that any such story must be fractured linguistically.

These structural and narratorial considerations fully come to the fore in the famous 'Analogy Passage', initially situated directly after the climbing of Snowdon in *The Five-Book Prelude*. This is a highly significant moment of parenthetical textual disruption. While not forming part of the two most canonical versions of *The Prelude*, these lines have repeatedly been identified as central to Wordsworthian self-understanding, especially in terms of the figurative nature of representation. In a well-known and important commentary, Mary Jacobus relates the passage's concerns with brokenness to the genesis of the whole of *The Prelude* in terms that are immediately relevant here. She argues that the passage 'represents in its own way a fracture in the text of Book 13 – as Wordsworth puts it parenthetically [...]'.[12] Jacobus is referring to the famous part of the 'Analogy'-passage that thematises precisely its own multilayered status as 'passage', narratorial and otherwise:

> Even yet thou wilt vouchsafe an ear, oh friend,
> [...]
> While with a winding but no devious song
> Through [ ] processes I make my way
> By links of tender thought. My present aim
> Is to contemplate for a needful while
> (Passage which will conduct in season due
> Back to the tale which we have left behind)
> The diverse manner in which Nature works
> Oftimes upon the outward face of things [...].[13]

Time and its breaks are thematised here. The passage starts with the imagined simultaneity of song and its hearing. This is a convention – we know full well that the scenario is fictional; there is never a 'friend' present while the lines are composed. The entire 'song' is 'winding' like a meandering river; it knows that it cannot be a straightforward narrative. This figure of the Heraclitean river into which no one can step twice is one of the oldest images for change and flux, already pointing at poetry's fluid relation to time. The 'windings' and 'processes' that are a part of the auto-construction of a changing subject openly find their way into the representation of this poetic persona. Neither the river nor the poet ever stays the same, however much they repeat their actions. The parenthesis reveals the fragility of the 'links of tender thought' that hold the poet's 'song' together. Although the thoughts are 'tender', and therefore invoke organic growth, they are still only as young and vulnerable as the fragile subject linking them. The narrator's 'present aim', his immediate goal, and also the intended receiver of the gift, is his own thought. The contemplation is 'needful' of this gift of a 'while'. Whereas the first 'while' indicates simultaneity ('While with a winding [...] song [...] I make my way'), the second is *a* specific while – and a needful while at that. The poet is trying to fix the flux of a process into the more contained mode of a noun that delimits the boundaries of contemplation ('My present aim / Is to contemplate for a needful while'). Meanwhile, the template, nature herself and her diverse workings, is broken up. The parenthesis severs both the contemplation *and*, more radically, the object of that contemplation, namely, nature and the analogy it provides to the mind of man.

The lunulae encapsulate an anxiety about potential disruptions to time in the poem, both structurally and philosophically. The '(Passage which will conduct in season due / Back to the tale which we have left behind)' does not supposedly break the 'tale'. But the poet appears to feel so anxious that this *might* be the case that he ends up digressing. In order to give the impression of unity, the parenthesis explains how in the future the narrator will come back to his main account. It thus concentrates the issues of temporality and narration, making visible the hermeneutic problem of narrative self-construction or writing itself. The parenthetical moment is marked by a difference from the main body of the text. It undermines the use of organic 'links of tender thought' to construct the passage's coherence. Rather, it does the opposite, severing an already complicated train of thought. Supposedly, the 'Passage' will be 'needful' and will wind recursively back to the main narrative ('in season due / Back to the tale which we have left behind'). The self-conscious 'you' with which 'the friend' is addressed at the beginning has changed into a 'we'. The highly wrought and fragile character of the fictional route to (and around) personal identity is openly acknowledged.

The problem of hermeneutic auto-construction is ostensibly resolved through an organic image. The lines suggest that when time has come ('in season due') the digression ('Passage') will flow back into the 'tale'. In other words, the 'Passage' will resolve itself naturally into the flow. But the isolation of the parenthesis itself undermines the organic nature of this succession. The temporal vocabulary of the 'Passage' first suggests a natural time frame with its 'seasons'. However, we have seen how the language of the text uncovers the constructed character of these changing 'seasons' and their development. Correspondingly, the spatial connotations of the narrative journey are also broken. The parenthetical 'Passage' is part of the traditional imagery of paths and roads marking the subject's life. Here it becomes a marker of fracture and disorder, much like a detour in the narrative of *The Prelude*. The 'Passage' turns out to be a moment of transition from one age to the next, at the same time as it encapsulates that process. Its digression, however, fractures the perspective of, and on, the poetic persona in too many ways for it to remain stable or link 'tender thoughts' in a 'tale'. Nevertheless, the act of recollection must be one of retrospectively building on such passages, however unstable. Later on, in Book 3 of *The Prelude*, Wordsworth looks back and surveys the contents of his memory: 'At this day / I smile in many a mountain solitude / At passages and fragments that remain' (*1805*, 3. 579–81). The 'passages' that are like 'fragments' of time and narrative act as 'tender links' that invite a knowing smile.

Through a parenthesis in the narrative, the present comes to precede the past. The multiplicity of perspectives reflects the complex temporal framework of Wordsworth's autobiography. Parentheses here provide microcosmic examples of how a rhetorical figure can point towards the complexities and brittleness of the construction of the present through the past, a construction necessarily fragmented in its representation. Where does that leave the meaning of these parentheses? We can read them as powerful examples of fracture in an autobiographical narrative that struggles to present an impossibly unbroken story of growth, tending (for all its breaks) towards the *telos* of 'a poet's mind'. The parenthesis instantiates the conceptual and rhetorical difficulties that accompany the representation of such a narrative of growth and representation. To the extent that these passages thematise time, the parenthesis illustrates how temporality is inevitably broken up in, and through, this autobiographical narrative.[14]

BRACKETING THE AESTHETIC

If we look at *The Prelude* structurally, it becomes apparent that language and arrangement of the poem insist that moments of brokenness and rupture are necessary in the construction of an autobiographical narrative. Moreover, it transpires that these breaks form important structural elements within the poem's production. This is to say, they are not just inevitable by-products, but rather moments of creative importance in relation to the narrative's inception. The 'spots of time' provide the most famous example for this dynamic. Their 'renovating' virtue is, albeit accessible throughout the poet's lifetime, the result of a fracturing event within his biography. Themselves 'scattered', they are inner events that reveal how 'the mind / Is lord and master, and that outward sense / Is but the obedient servant of her will' (*1805*, II. 271–3). There are two aspects of this rich passage that I want to highlight here. First, these experiences mark breaks within a biography, functioning as transformational moments that define the poet's subsequent life. Secondly, it is remarkable how much importance the poet gives to his *return* to these moments for the construction of his autobiography (not least because the moments 'interrupt' the reading process). There is a tension here between the demand for narrative coherence and the fracturing character of these structurally significant moments in an autobiographical poem. The conclusion of this chapter will elaborate further on this double movement.

Wordsworth's earlier 1799 *Prelude* already foreshadows these concerns. Here we read that 'All these [experiences in nature] and more with rival claims demand / Grateful acknowledgement.'[15] As these lines elaborate, Wordsworth constantly feels the pressure of choosing what to represent. If 'It were a song / Venial, and such as if I rightly judge / I might protract unblamed' (*1799*, I. 248–50), he might only have to speak about his immediate perception of the natural world. However, such an approach would simplify matters to a degree that cannot do justice to the project of *The Prelude*. As we know, Wordsworth amplifies the scope of his narrative far beyond the merely empirical. However, he articulates this vision via a plethora of reservations:

> but I perceive
> That much is overlooked, and we should ill
> Attain our object if from delicate fears
> Of breaking in upon the unity
> Of this my argument I should omit
> To speak of such effects as cannot here
> Be regularly classed, yet tend no less
> To the same point, the growth of mental power
> And love of Nature's works.   (*1799*, I. 250–8)

The shift from 'I perceive' to a pluralised 'we should ill / attain' and back to a singular 'I should omit' is indicative of the uncomfortable changes Wordsworth has to negotiate here. It illustrates how this shift is also a 'breaking' of the subject. The poetic persona here splits into two 'persons' in the same way that the autobiographical structure requires a fracturing of the subject. The ego as the 'rendezvous' of persons here reaches the level of grammatical confusion.[16] The necessary cut between 'I' and 'we' also fragments the sentence: the author must be neither and be both at once. The line 'Of this my argument' is a performative equivalent, which 'does' exactly what the author is pondering about. By reminding us of the fragility of any textual construction, such a moment of self-reference 'break[s] in upon the unity' of a narrative flow. The performative suggestion that the poem *must* be broken is also instructive. The 'object' of the autobiographical poem would be ill-attained if, out of 'delicate' and fragile fear 'of breaking' the coherence of the narrative, the oblique and fractured moments of the poet's life should be omitted. However, the 'effects as cannot here / Be regularly classed' are also moments of fracture that defy classification. No classification, no taxonomy, is possible for these points in a biography. They escape the framework of any (auto)biographical reconstruction which claims to be based on unity. Thus the passage also becomes a pointer to the 'nature' of such oblique moments of breakage while insisting on their importance.

Wordsworth's text creates an instructive background against which to understand some ways in which we have come to see a biographical puncture as central to the way we construct our roles as subjects. To think about how 'effects as cannot here / Be regularly classed' form part of a contemporary construction of subjectivity allows us to understand our own reading of Wordsworth's text better. Judith Butler's recent argument concerning how the understanding of another subject, conceptually and ethically, is connected to a familiarity with one's own obliqueness is a case in point. She shows how often the pragmatics and the organisational necessities of our circumstances lead us to assume that our lives follow coherent narratives. However, ultimately, connection, responsibility, and understanding are provided by an introspective admission that we know our own lives to be ultimately punctured by moments of interruption and parenthesis:

Indeed, if we require that someone be able to tell in story form the reasons why his or her life has taken the path it has, that is, to be a coherent autobiographer, it may be that we prefer the seamlessness of the story to something we might tentatively call the truth of the person, a truth which, to a certain degree, [...] is indicated more radically as an interruption. It may be that stories have to be interrupted, and that for interruption to take place, a story has to be underway.[17]

These interruptions and oblique moments, on which we ultimately rely, are helpful in relation to the events that have 'effects as cannot here / Be regularly classed' (*1799*, 1. 255–6). It is precisely the moments that 'tend' to that same goal which Wordsworth declares as the ultimate theme and productive principle of his poem. Their relevance for 'The growth of mental power / And love of Nature's works', that is for *The Prelude* and its author, is a way of describing a moment akin to 'the spots of time'. Several striking passages of the poem narrate such unrepresentable moments as paradoxical examples that escape a taxonomy.

The episode of the drowned man of Esthwaite is an instance of such a parenthetical moment of rupture. Several commentators have pointed out that this passage in Book 5 of *The Prelude* describes a moment that eludes categorisation. Nevertheless, as a spot of time, it also becomes a productive source for future poetry. While tracing Wordsworth's revisions of the episode, Susan Wolfson comments that his 'most powerful imaginative efforts are usually triggered by episodes that defeat rational control – moments of surprise, shock, accident, chance, and mischance'. [18] Her masterful reading of Wordsworth's shifts in register and vocabulary mentions punctuation only in passing. Here I want to suggest that the issue of parenthesis elucidates in which way the recording of the Esthwaite incident tells the reader how the unstable sources of Wordsworth's 'powerful imaginative efforts' find a grammatical reflection in his poetical composition. The poet recalls how his experiences in Hawkshead are – seemingly accidentally – crucial from the very beginning:

> Seeking I knew not what, I chanced to cross
> One of those open fields, which, shaped like ears,
> Make green peninsulas on Esthwaite's Lake.
> Twilight was coming on; yet through the gloom
> I saw distinctly on the opposite Shore
> A heap of garments; left as I suppos'd
> By one who was there bathing: long I watch'd,
> But no one own'd them: meanwhile, the calm Lake
> Grew dark, with all the shadows on its breast,
> And, now and then, a fish, upleaping snapp'd
> The breathless stillness.   (*1805*, 5. 456–66)

Half by chance, half guided by his surroundings, the poet crosses an ear-shaped and attentive natural scene. The tension between the natural and the human helps to define the passage. Man invades an inviting, 'open' nature which in turn is also active. The suggestiveness of this particular passage lies deeply embedded in the question of how to negotiate the relation of natural and human agency. The passage's temporal liminality, situated in the break between day and night, emphasises the ambiguity of the terms on which this negotiation has to take place.

Recording nature, and its sometimes human-formed manifestations, the poet is suddenly captured by man. But it is not a living man who demands his attention. Rather, it is a man's trace that the poet notices. The clothes left on the shore are his superficial protective skin, a sign of human civilisation layering itself over nature. Only for solitary and direct contact, such as a swim in the lake, does man leave these layers behind, and usually only for a limited period. But the boy notices that here the usual delimitations and controls of such contact are transgressed. Some of the organising principles which supposedly hold in place the divisions between human 'garments', their owner, and the natural surroundings are unsettled. On the one hand, the garments are 'supposed' to have been 'left' 'By one who was there bathing'. The trace is identifiable, the causal connection unquestioned. On the other hand, the trace has no owner after all – 'long I watch'd, / But no one own'd them'. The destabilisation is economic in nature: the 'unclaimed' garments, somebody's clothes, suddenly are no one's; they do not belong to anybody. The subjective element of property, of ownership, disappears. At the same time, nature's contrasting role seems more ambiguous than we might have expected. In effect, the imagery lets nature herself accompany and foreshadow the circumstances and consequences of such a disruption.

The drowning of the man occurs unseen, off-stage, while the surroundings grow 'dark'. The 'breathless stillness' that forebodes the dead schoolteacher, quiet and not respiring anymore, also resembles the fish that snaps in the air without actually breathing ('a fish, upleaping snapp'd / The breathless stillness'). It is instructive to return to the role of the human garments in the light of this death foreshadowed. The loss of ownership turns this trace into an anticipation of the drowned man's death. More so, the trace itself, this 'heap' of clothes, takes on a metonymic role; it becomes the first monument and memorial to the dead schoolteacher. The heap gains the power of an epitaph, a poem:

> The succeeding day,
> (Those unclaimed garments telling a plain Tale)
> Went there a Company, and, in their Boat,
> Sounded with grappling-irons and long poles.
> At length, the dead Man, 'mid that beauteous scene
> Of trees, and hills, and water, bolt upright
> Rose with his ghastly face; a spectre-shape
> Of terror even!   (*1805*, 5. 466–73)

These garments tell a 'Tale' which helps the story in *The Prelude* along, while simultaneously suggesting how the poem itself will function as an epitaph to its author. The garments' epitaphic quality also serves as an example in *The Prelude* of how one 'reads' one's surroundings.[19] In this passage, the material epitaph becomes a sign to be read, a tale to be interpreted. Because there is no human claim to the material ('unclaimed garments'), the scene can be read as primarily epitaphic. The 'heap' becomes a marker for death, which only later, 'the succeeding day', can be read as such. The deeply textual nature of this interpretation is not diminished by the plainness of the 'Tale'.

Understanding our surroundings along textual lines results in the image of biography as a process akin to hermeneutics. In Wordsworth's text this dynamic is defined through a parenthetical break in the text. The lunulae intertwine the textual and epitaphic within the passage itself: '(Those unclaimed garments telling a plain Tale)'. The garments stating the textual nature of the world, and their epitaphic function, are themselves bracketed. The parenthetical quality of this line again introduces a temporally complex element into the narrative. However, it suggests a much larger dynamic. If it is inherent in the linguistic construct that it always contains several temporal layers that collide, and if nature herself can be described as akin to text, then that much larger text is susceptible to the same type of disruptive pattern. The implication of these claims is that the 'Tale' itself fractures the narratives which such lives produce about themselves. The parenthetical nature of this moment, then, mirrors the entire incident and suggests that it is an ungraspable event. But, at the same time, it helps the poet to reach his *telos*, the result of the mind's growth (*The Prelude*): after all, the tale gets told. The break within the narrative insists on the textual nature of our world and, by the same token, points towards its brokenness. Relocating the same lunulae in the book on 'Books' of the 1805 and the 1850 *Prelude* gives the episode a further spin, in a context where poetry, writing, and books are central to Wordsworth's text. Consider that the drowned man episode in the 1799 version leads directly into the 'spots of time' passage, whereas it moves into Book 4 in *The Five-Book Prelude* and shifts again into Book 5 in the 1805/50 versions of the text. The ungraspable nature of the event makes it difficult to locate the appropriate place for its representation in the construction of an autobiographical narrative.

In all of these versions, however, the poet's own interpretation maintains that his reaction to seeing the disfigured drowned man rise is to be understood in terms of previous reading experiences:

> and yet no vulgar fear,
> Young as I was, a Child not nine years old,
> Possess'd me; for my inner eye had seen
> Such sights before, among the shining streams

Of Fairy Land, the Forests of Romance:
Thence came a spirit, hallowing what I saw
With decoration and ideal grace;
A dignity, a smoothness, like the words
Of Grecian Art, and purest Poesy.   (*1805*, 5. 473–81)

It is not an ordinary shock that impresses the defaced man so deeply on the child's mind. The fear is not of a 'vulgar' nature, and not of the common kind. The child does not succumb to the terror associated with the material appearance of a dead body. He spiritualises the corporeal and elevates the significance of the experience into a primarily internal event. It is the 'inner' eye, specifically bound to a singular personal pronoun ('my'), rather than the openly accessible mass that 'reads' this event. The reason for a successful *Verinnerlichung*, 'internalisation' or 'spiritualisation', of seeing the drowned man is the previous experience of similar 'sights'. Inner seeing prepares the poet for dealing with the outer sights; the two are almost equivalent in their importance for the development of the mind. And let us not forget that in Book 5, 'seeing' can be approximate to reading, or what that reading produced in the imagination. The child has 'seen / Such sights' in the books of 'Fairy Land' and 'the Forests of Romance'. In other words, he assimilates them to texts he has read before. So, at least as far as the ability is concerned to understand an experience textually, the two areas of interpretation described by 'seeing' and 'reading' are akin. Significantly, this slide already includes the important assumption that the textual model *can* be applied to both. Its loose association with the theological tradition of reading the book of nature easily allows Wordsworth to foreground his focus on the aesthetic.

In this passage, *The Prelude* suggests more than just an equivalency between seeing and reading. It is *because* the 'inner eye' encountered comparable theatrical 'scenes' before, namely in the books the boy has read, that the poet escapes 'vulgar fear', and converts what lies before him into a moment of meaning. His 'reading' of the drowned man transforms it into an instance that can be understood via the aesthetic categories of textual construction and its interpretation. The process of rationalising the terror of the natural world into a less 'vulgar' text binds it into an intelligible system of stories and rhetoric that follows a pattern such as fairy-tale, 'Romance', or Classical poetry ('words / Of Grecian Art'). The employment of the imagery of mythology is telling. Mythologising the event allows the narrator to 'read' the 'episode' of the drowned man as a moment of poetical significance in his own biography. The 'spirit' who hallows and mystifies the scene for the boy turns it into an event of mythical proportions. This gives the activity of reading a central status not only regarding Book 5 but also in relation to how the poet understands and interprets the subject matter of reading itself. Reading consequently becomes classifiable (and readable) as such. Mythologising is the counteracting force to the disfiguration represented in the scene, contrasting the defaced human and the myth of smooth 'ideal[s]' of Classical 'decoration' (or decorum, 'grace', and 'dignity', leading to 'purest Poesy'). The figural acts as a compensatory dynamic, providing the tools to construct a textual experience that the boy can read and assimilate. As Cynthia Chase points out, this is a poetologically charged move, which puts the passage itself in a particular literary tradition: 'In making such a comparison, the poet invokes a classic strategy for relating loss to value, or effacement to intensity; within a certain long-lasting and historical tradition, the sculpture of classical antiquity is treasured precisely in the condition of defacement or fragmentation in which many such works were found.'[20] In a certain manner, this is the poet's way of aestheticising the text. Just as the boy makes reference to 'Grecian Art', Wordsworth alludes to a poetic tradition of aestheticising that 'Art'. Turning the experience into an instance of aesthetic, or, rather, rhetorical beauty allows the poet to rationalise and mythologise the event retrospectively (in relation both to the original event as well as to a consequent poetic recording of it). That this is a double move, once allegedly performed by the boy, then by the narrator relating this part of *The Prelude*, intensifies the distancing effect of such a manoeuvre. In and through myth, the boy can recover from disfiguration and make his own experience readable. In this way it is a concise presentation of the logical circularity that the text itself performs throughout Book 5: the spot of time can only be designated as such after one has read certain books, which in turn make it a spot of time supposedly independent of these textual sources.

It is not so much the circularity of this move but rather its purported success that is relevant here. Running together textuality, mythologising, and material event, in order to produce a successful representation, can itself only be a fiction. Especially if we are dealing with autobiographical writing, which, as de Man points out, gains its interest not through the fact 'that it reveals reliable self-knowledge – it does not – but [because] it demonstrates in a striking way the impossibility of closure and of totalization' (*RR*, 71). These are also Chase's terms for reading Wordsworth's account. However, they leave no space for a framework where the entity 'textuality' occupies a mythologised position to the degree that *The Prelude* suggests. The interpretation of one's surroundings as analogous to a textual and hermeneutic exercise elevates the linguistic framework to a referent of mythical proportions (both in Wordsworth's poem and in this analysis). Textuality, by its supposed overarching power to serve as a general framework for interpretation, is itself converted into myth that makes rationalisation possible. It becomes the mythologised centre of the analysis. In Wordsworth's text, the continuously unsettling fracture at its middle prevents it becoming an aestheticised piece of 'Grecian Art' in turn. *The Prelude* allows for intertextuality, semiotics, and biblical hermeneutics, to meet without wanting to immediately create a stable basis for interpretation. However, just as it does for the boy and the narrator, the myth ultimately enables 'reading' for the critic. In other words, only through a mythologising of the power of textuality to *act as myth* can rationalisation take place.[21]

In the passage immediately following the drowned man episode, it becomes clearer what it means for the poet, and poem, to be caught in this circular movement in the middle of a book on 'Books':

> I had a precious treasure at that time,
> A little, yellow canvass-cover'd Book,
> A slender abstract of the Arabian Tales [...].   (*1805*, 5. 482–4)

One of the 'Forests of Romance' ('my inner eye had seen / Such sights before, among the shining streams / Of Fairy Land, the Forests of Romance') that the boy has been wandering through is the *Arabian Nights*. These tales are so captivating that the little book containing them becomes itself an oriental 'precious treasure' covered with the 'canvass' of Sinbad's sails. But the limitations of the 'slender abstract' that the boy possesses are immediately apparent. Through an illustration of the treasure's material boundaries, the boy comprehends its position in a wider textual context too:

> And when I learn'd, as now I first did learn,
> From my Companions in this new abode,
> That this dear prize of mine was but a block
> Hewn from a mighty quarry; in a word,
> That there were four large Volumes, laden all
> With kindred matter, 'twas, in truth, to me
> A promise scarcely earthly.   (*1805*, 5. 485–91)

The 'precious treasure' suddenly is understood to be only a fragment from a much larger quarry. This is why the 'abstract' could retrospectively be classed as 'little' and 'slender'. The previously delimited 'abstract' of the *Arabian Nights* is broken up, and its stories spill out into 'four large Volumes' 'laden' with more treasures and secrets. The fundamental insight is that literature, in whatever form it is fixed (such as in a book), is a temporary and limited arrangement of a certain body of language. But we should proceed with caution. To 'learn […], / From [one's] Companions' means to learn from friends and loved ones. These friends, however, can also be companions of a textual nature, books whose reading may emphasise the limitations of their own form. *The Prelude*'s lines suggest a focus on the self-awareness that textual constructions express regarding their own limits within a larger scheme of language. Books (including Book 5) teach the reader about their own fragmentariness. The 'precious treasure' is only a part broken off from a much larger 'quarry'. The 'block' that the volume becomes is a writing block that is hewn from the 'mighty quarry' of literature or language itself. To be able to limit the consequences of this insight to 'a word', or 'four […] Volumes', must be a chimera. The 'mighty quarry' cannot be contained or quantified in a specific 'Volume'. The fragmentariness of the 'slender abstract' applies to the *Arabian Nights* just as it does to 'the Forests of Romance', the regions of 'Fairy Land', or 'Grecian Art, and purest Poesy'.[22] All of these are 'Hewn from a mighty quarry', fragments of a much wider bibliographic body. The self-referentiality of the book 'On Books' here already foreshadows the broken character of *The Prelude* as Romantic autobiography. The book's position as a 'block' within the larger construction of the narrative is paralleled by understanding *The Prelude* as an unfinished 'antechapel' to the fragmentary *Recluse*. Suddenly, *The Prelude*, and its different versions, emerge as necessarily parenthetical works.

The 'block' also acts as an obstacle, a block that is in the way – very much in opposition to the 'Passage' that was discussed earlier. Immediately after his parenthetical remarks, the poet admits the devastating dimension of 'the promise' that this obstacle reveals. The block makes him understand the fragmentary nature of textual constructions and reveals 'a promise scarcely earthly'. This promise will hold true; it is directed to the future, yet marks another temporal break. The announcement of something 'scarcely earthly' opens up an unclassifiable moment. What this block promises constitutes another of those moments full of 'effects as cannot here / Be regularly classed' (*1799*, 1. 255–6). The block is an obstacle for successful classification, like the difficulty of systematising the stories contained in the *Arabian Nights*. In the end, the stumbling block makes the poet fall into an unearthly region, where identification and control are destabilised. With this move the reading directly bears on the drowned man episode. In the earlier passage, the boy, confronted with an unclassifiable situation, aestheticises the scene according to 'Grecian Art, and purest Poesy'. In the second case, a supposedly rationalised situation collapses to leave reader and writer faced with the radical contextualisability of any literary construction. The conclusion to this section concentrates on the ghostly double bind that holds these two scenarios together.

The 'scarcely earthly' promise of intertextuality goes beyond both materiality and text. In the immediate context of *The Prelude*, it is 'scarcely earthly' to reveal the principle that underlies the disfiguration of 'the precious treasure', the 'slender abstract', into a 'block'. The insight surfaces suddenly and cruelly. Like the drowned man, it is 'bolt upright' and surprises the poet with its 'ghastly face', containing a 'promise' that the 'terror' of its power to deface will be felt continuously. The thought of any piece of writing just being a 'block / Hewn from a mighty quarry' disturbs the surface of the boy's, the writer's, and our own, reading experience. The 'promise' becomes the drowned man of this passage, rising over and over again and disquieting the surface with its haunting power. We have seen that these moments of spectrality and potential 'fear' ('vulgar' or not) are counteracted by means of a rationalising aesthetic. The 'ghastly' and ghostly 'spectre-shape', neither material nor entirely immaterial, is converted into 'words' that can be read like a 'plain Tale'. In the second scenario, the boy attempts to lay the ghost to rest by a desire for completion. But this is also futile. The idea that four volumes might be the entire 'quarry' is recognised as illusory, both by the reader (already reading Book 5 of another book) and by the boy. The impossibility of containing and closing off this textual dynamic gives the 'promise' its 'scarcely earthly' quality, making it impossible to police the gates of a domesticating aesthetic. The textual relation between these two forces emerges as the power that helps the boy escape 'vulgar fear': 'Thence came a spirit, hallowing what I saw / With decoration and ideal grace.' It is a *'spirit'* (my emphasis) that makes rationalisation possible. The tension between these two poles illustrates the double movement at work throughout the passage. In switching from the material to the immaterial, and vice versa, the spectral performs a disruptive and productive function. On the one hand, the 'spirit' of this passage helps to aestheticise a moment of unrepresentability. On the other, the spectre is itself the source of such moments – haunting the passages in which they occur, and predicting endless repetition.[23]

The exploration of this tension through the ambiguous frame of the spectral brings us back to more general concerns centred on the figure of the drowned man who continues to surface. His epitaphic garments suddenly become items on which the identity, the biography, of this 'spectre shape' is based. The ambiguity of their 'plain Tale' in relation to the presence of a 'ghastly face' is unsettling. This is only one part of a constant double movement between epitaphic body and faceless spectre. If we take seriously the idea of the Romantic poem as an epitaphic text that also can be thought of in terms of a body or a corpus (a dynamic that is of importance in the following chapter on John Keats), *The Prelude* becomes both Wordsworth's 'heap of garments', standing in for his body, and the story of his life. Simultaneously, the poem exposes its own textual workings, exemplifying the sense in which it is a gravestone, a 'block / Hewn from a mighty quarry'. *The Prelude* is subject to the same dynamic. The double movement, a repeated aestheticising that constantly undercuts itself, connects and parallels the 'block' and the 'garments', the experience of the 'ghastly face' of a 'spectre shape' and the 'promise scarcely earthly'.

BREACHING *THE PRELUDE*

Parenthesis concentrates certain disruptive textual patterns, but it also points towards a fracturing element beyond the grammatical and rhetorical. The remainder of this chapter will follow a more general consideration of the parenthetical in *The Prelude*, especially how it conditions Wordsworth's representation of the sublime. Much has been written on Wordsworth and the sublime (egotistical and otherwise). It has been the subject of literary criticism from Bradley's chapter on Wordsworth in his *Lectures on Poetry* (1909) to numerous contemporary commentaries. Depending on their wider projects, critics emphasise the philosophical, psychoanalytical, or historical factor in the Wordsworthian sublime.[24] Sometimes these accounts also stress the importance of traditional rhetorical gestures associated with the sublime. Building on this work, I want to illustrate how moments of parenthesis, or the parenthetical, supposedly minute breaks, are important in the conceptualisation and description of moments that are often associated with the sublime, such as the spots of time. My argument is that the Wordsworthian natural sublime, seemingly so distant from anything parenthetical, carries a disruptive bracketing at its centre. The disruption at the heart of Wordsworthian sublimity in *The Prelude* is quite different from the broken basis for the aesthetic category as described in chapter 3. There, the centre of attention was how a category of the seemingly grandiose (which aesthetic discourse has inherited) relies on a shattering principle. Here, the focus is much smaller: it analyses how a specific linguistic fracture becomes important to *The Prelude*'s representation of the sublime. Tellingly, this disruption occurs when the inception of the whole poem is openly thematised and linked to the imagination during the ascent of Mount Snowdon in Book 13:

> With forehead bent
> Earthward, as if in opposition set
> Against an enemy, I panted up
> With eager pace, and no less eager thoughts.
> Thus might we wear perhaps an hour away,
> Ascending at loose distance each from each,
> And I, as chanced, the foremost of the Band,
> When at my feet the ground appear'd to brighten,
> And with a step or two seem'd brighter still;
> Nor had I time to ask the cause of this,
> For instantly a Light upon the turf
> Fell like a flash: I look'd about, and lo!
> The Moon stood naked in the Heavens, at height
> Immense above my head, and on the shore
> I found myself of a huge sea of mist,
> Which meek and silent, rested at my feet:
> A hundred hills their dusky backs upheaved
> All over this still Ocean, and beyond,
> Far, far beyond, the vapours shot themselves,
> In headlands, tongues, and promontory shapes
> Into the Sea, the real Sea, that seem'd
> To dwindle and give up its majesty,
> Usurp'd upon as far as sight could reach.
> Meanwhile, the Moon look'd down upon this shew
> In single glory, and we stood, the mist
> Touching our very feet: and from the shore
> At distance not the third part of a mile
> Was a blue chasm, a fracture in the vapour,
> A deep and gloomy breathing-place, thro' which
> Mounted the roar of waters, torrents, streams
> Innumerable, roaring with one voice.
> The universal spectacle throughout
> Was shaped for admiration and delight,
> Grand in itself alone, but in that breach
> Through which the homeless voice of waters rose,
> That dark deep thorough-fare, had Nature lodg'd
> The Soul, the Imagination of the whole.   (*1805*, 13. 29–65)

The narrator, ascending the mountain, accidentally ('as chanced') 'the foremost of the Band', notices that the ground at his feet is brightening. The flash of illumination is not, however, an experience of certainty; the ground only '*appear'd* to brighten' and even after 'a step or two' only '*seem'd* brighter still' (my emphases). Suddenly, the 'flash' falls to the ground, leaving the narrator to turn towards its origin, rather than trying to understand the unsettling reflection. This is not the first time that Wordsworth has suggested this possibility. In the fragment 'A Night-Piece' (1815), for instance, the traveller,

> the musing [man]
> Who walks along with his eyes bent to earth
> Is startled. He looks about, the clouds are split
> Asunder, and above his head, he views
> The clear moon, and the glory of the heavens. (lines 7–11)[25]

It is as if the breaking rays of light frame the sublime spectacle. The moment of fracture is recuperated as a creative and productive moment.

Although the clear moon illuminates the scene, the narrator's experience itself remains ambiguous. It takes place in a 'huge […] mist', consisting neither of water nor of air, without transparency or clarity. This mist forms a 'sea' but not 'the real Sea'. The silent and 'still Ocean' is bound to human perception while the distinction between the figural and the real is questioned. The alternative description of this 'Ocean' as 'vapours' reflects its ambiguity. A vapour is an 'exhalation' or 'emanation consisting of imperceptible particles' (*OED*). It is neither gas nor solid, neither material nor immaterial. Its constituting particles cannot be seen, though the emanation is visible. The narrator cannot see its parts, and seeing it, in turn, impedes his view: he cannot ascertain on what ground he stands. But although everything appears 'Usurp'd', it only '*seem[s]* / To dwindle and give up its majesty' (my emphasis). A cut finally opens up, defining this scene as a revelation of a different kind. While the moon watches with 'single glory', the poet identifies a fracture beneath: a blue chasm. This break, disrupting the division between different levels of reality (the sea of mist and of water), is surveyed by the narrator from a vantage point:

> and from the shore
> At distance not the third part of a mile
> Was a blue chasm, a fracture in the vapour,
> A deep and gloomy breathing-place, thro' which
> Mounted the roar of waters, torrents, streams
> Innumerable, roaring with one voice. (*1805*, 13. 54–9)

This blue chasm – signalling one of the defining episodes of *The Prelude*'s journey – is indicative of a larger dynamic in the poem. The poet himself assigns to the scene a deeply representational character, when he calls it a 'universal spectacle' which 'throughout / Was shaped for admiration and delight'. But it is the fracture itself that provokes the most explicit and elaborate description. The sublime scene, 'Grand in itself alone', merely provides the setting for the chasm where the ultimate source of power is mysteriously located:

> in that breach
> Through which the homeless voice of waters rose,
> That dark deep thorough-fare, had Nature lodg'd
> The Soul, the Imagination of the whole.   (*1805*, 13. 62–5)

In the sublime scene, the breach or break first appears as a disruptive moment. However, we realise that the entire arrangement of the sea depends on nature's fractures – its self-division – and that the chasm represents an inspirational moment where 'the Soul, the Imagination of the whole', manifests itself. The gulf that opens up before the narrator will ultimately provide the source for the scene it inspires. A creative principle is lodged in the fracture.

The tension between sublime grandeur and its unstable foundations permeates the scene at Snowdon. This reading is at odds with recent very influential interpretations which often prefer to foreground the political aspect of the passage as overwhelmingly important. Alan Liu's reading in his important *Wordsworth: The Sense of History* (1989) is a case in point. After quoting selections from Book 13, Liu argues: 'What a historical reading of the end of *The Prelude* shows with conviction […] is that the aesthetics of closure constructed at Snowdon is one with Wordsworth's politics of patriotism.'[26] Liu is sensitive to dialectical movements both in the text and in his own procedure; he also explicitly draws attention to his agency in selecting the passage. He quotes the passage including the reflection of the moon, and then switches to Wordsworth's meditation upon the scene (which I have omitted in turn here). Considering the larger aims of his reading, this betrays a certain knowing anxiety. Liu silences Wordsworth's counterpart to the experience of the moonbeam, and cuts the text from 'Meanwhile' onwards. The omission of the whole second part of the passage leads him to ignore how the text thematises the uncertainty of its own creation. Thus it centres on the first experience of glimpsing the moon, and links it to the later reflections on the scene. Liu finally believes Snowdon to be 'Wordsworth's moment of Absolute Knowledge'.[27] This reading of Snowdon, for all its persuasiveness in other areas, seems to me to underestimate how the passage also shows precisely the dangers, sometimes impossibility, of trying to illustrate things with conviction and closure, let alone 'Absolute Knowledge'. The passage suggests that if there is a 'whole' it rests, is constructed, on a 'chasm', a break. Rather than affirming a particular form of closure, the text is torn about its own origins, ultimately showing them to be broken.

The 'chasm', visible from Snowdon, divides the plane and focuses attention away from the surface onto the hidden, darker, but nevertheless active properties that underlie the 'hundred hills' protruding from the sea of mist. The break itself is described as 'gloomy', even melancholic. At the same time, it is 'breathing', thus life-giving and rhythmically structured, becoming what Hartman terms 'a trait between two worlds'.[28] The breathing suggests a dialectic or double movement. Within the fracture lies the 'roar of waters, torrents, streams' – a wild confusion of forces. Although we are assured that these are 'Innumerable' and that different elements roar with 'one voice', they do not add up to an intelligible utterance. The repeated 'roaring' is non-linguistic. The 'homeless voice' is missing a referent, something or somebody that it can identify with or be identified as. Its origins and inhabitants, its 'home', are absent and obscure. This 'voice of waters' never rests within a singular source. Thus, the 'lodging' of 'The Soul, the Imagination of the whole', in the breach is not as straightforward as it seems. We are caught, with the poet, between oscillating understandings of the scene: on the one hand, this is a paradigmatic instance of a rationalised experience of sublimity, firmly located in the parameters of aesthetics. On the other, the experience is unsettled by a power that radically negates the process of rationalisation and controlled representation.[29]

The ascent of Snowdon, like the drowned man episode, is a structuring moment in *The Prelude*. But it is not simply their function as structuring principles that gives these 'spots' their importance. As David Simpson writes punningly: 'That wholeness should emanate from the hole is itself notable.'[30] These crucial moments mirror and repeat a double movement *within themselves* which exemplifies a central aspect of *The Prelude*'s construction. The language and imagery of such passages insist on a double-sided nature: they are both destructive, uncontrollable moments of rupture and *at the same time* structuring and rationalising events which help to aestheticise and narrativise experience. The breaks are elevated to a creative principle. Thus, not only are they spots of time around which *The Prelude* is organised; they are also, and more fundamentally, instances which allow the production of *The Prelude* in the first place. Fracture becomes the principle by which the poem hangs together, making its aesthetic representation possible. Anxiety about the ultimately negative qualities and breaks within the self-construction is reflected in the language used to represent that subject. The project of *The Prelude* is fractured at the heart of its composition and construction.

This conclusion brings us back to the beginning of the chapter. *The Prelude* insists that its severing moments feed subsequent aestheticisation.

The very last lines of the poem again illustrate how parenthesis can be a marker for contradictory tensions. Musing on its possible influence on future readers, the narrator closes the poem by invoking

> how the mind of man becomes
> A thousand times more beautiful than the earth
> On which he dwells, above this Frame of things
> (Which, 'mid all revolutions in the hopes
> And fears of men, doth still remain unchanged)
> In beauty exalted, as it is itself
> Of substance and of fabric more divine.   (*1805*, 13. 446–52)

After thirteen books, the 'growth' of the poet's mind still has to be described parenthetically. The lunulae become the temporal framing instances for the qualities of the earth on which man 'dwells'. How the 'frame of things' relates to our construction of it has been the subject of the entire poem. The last parenthesis, two lines from the end, is a reminder of how this rhetorical figure haunts the poem. Even here, at the very end-point of a triumphant self-celebration, the poem breaks self-consciously, with a marker that is also the figure of fracture.

CHAPTER 5

Letters from the grave: John Keats's fragmented corpus

A dialogue is a chain or a garland of fragments. An exchange of letters is a dialogue on an enlarged scale, and memorabilia are a system of fragments.[1]

LETTERS AS LITERATURE

This chapter is on John Keats and fragmentation. Its main body and argument will show that the rhetoric of Keats's letters reveals how his epistolary poetics relies on an economy of fracture and reciprocal movement. I will attempt to explain how this dynamic of exchange parallels the condition of a linguistic predicament of brokenness. Finally, the analysis will illustrate how the letter in Keats's work becomes a fragmentary principle around which his posthumous corpus is constructed. Keats's grave, containing an unopened letter addressed to him, and marked by a broken lyre, offers a powerful image for the way his corpus relies on fragmentariness. Fragmentation becomes the point around which his archival body, dominated by the rhetoric of brokenness, is assembled and understood. The discussion thus locates a fracture at the point of supposed origin. As its title indicates, the chapter will focus mostly on Keats's letters and their reception. While this is not a canonical straitjacket, I have mostly omitted references to, and discussions of, his poetry. This is a directed and critically deliberate decision. As will transpire, I believe that the formal status of the letter is especially powerful in illustrating the link between fragmentation and Romanticism. It goes without saying that it is not a qualitative judgement à la T. S. Eliot, somehow thinking the letters superior to the poetry. They simply illustrate what I want to say better, and in a more original way.

Nevertheless, it should be mentioned that to view John Keats's letters as fragmentary productions of literature challenges some widely held critical assumptions. Most importantly, it questions a strict division between the poetical corpus and the epistolary work which generally understands the latter as a supplement to the former. Many commentators either openly or implicitly adopt this received position. Generally, these accounts take the superiority of the poetry over the letters as a given.[2] Robin Mayhead, for instance, comments that 'With the exception of the verse-epistles, Keats's letters were simply written *as* letters, not as works of art', and concludes with his suggestion that they should be read simply as comments on the poems.[3] Following this line of thought, the letter becomes a supplementary text to the poem, or else provides the biographical basis for its interpretation or a retelling of the poet's life. Fortunately, this critical view has changed somewhat in recent years. Susan Wolfson's stress on the spontaneity of Keats's letters and Timothy Webb's insistence on their interest in pushing the limits of language both take seriously the letters' literary qualities.[4] However, often enough one can still detect at least a residue of their treatment as secondary material. Even a highly acute account such as John Barnard's recent contribution 'Keats's Letters', admirably receptive to the literary aspects of the epistles (which he wants to read 'in their own right'), defines them as an 'invaluable supplement' to the work of the Keatsian critic.[5]

The continuity of these classifications is primarily due to an investment in the sharp division between Keats's letters and his poetry. Apart from a number of theoretical difficulties, this position ignores the way in which the production of Keats's letters and poems is often closely intertwined (a poem is written in a letter) or linked through citation (a poem is quoted in a letter) and in some cases simply identical (his verse epistles). The rhetorical dynamics of the letters often reveal how such a divide is critically restricting. The same applies to the related way of approaching the letters through the framework of a rigid distinction between public and private discourses. This division is particularly emphasised by sociological and aesthetic accounts of the epistles, such as Jürgen Habermas's and Karl-Heinz Bohrer's famous discussions. Especially the work of Habermas informs much of the extensive scholarship that has been done on the gendering of epistles in eighteenth- and nineteenth-century discourse (the letter is often characterised as a peculiarly female form).[6]

By contrast, I will argue for an approach that primarily highlights the literary aspect of Keats's letters, reading them as literary constructs. This is to follow their own self-reflexive emphasis on their status as writing which combines with numerous allusions accentuating their specifically literary status. Such references go beyond Keats's well-known joke on handing his correspondence to Murray for publication ('our [Fanny Brawne's and his] correspondence (which at some future time I propose offering to Murray)

[…]' [*L*, 2. 282]). Literature invades the letters via figures who are immediately associated with the epistle's poetic power. The ocasionally light and
passing manner of these remarks does not erase Keats's evident awareness of
the letter as a literary object in its own right. His first known letter to Fanny
Brawne begins:

I am glad I had not an opportunity of sending off a Letter which I wrote for you on
Tuesday night – 'twas too much like one out of Ro[u]sseau's Heloise. I am more
reasonable this morning. (*L*, 2. 122)

Although apparently wanting to resist a literary tone, Keats's language
betrays his arch awareness of the relation between letter-writing, publication, and literature. His resistance to Rousseau's epistolary novel is tellingly
'reasonable'. Keats is acutely aware of the danger of the letter as a literary
witness to over-passionate feeling. A letter that reads like 'one out of
Ro[u]sseau's Heloise' succumbs to an effeminising style, for which *La
Nouvelle Heloïse* (1761) becomes a shorthand. Keats wishes to be 'more
reasonable', to compose his literary epistle soberly 'in the morning', and
does not want to yield to the uncontrollable emotions that the 'night' seems
to hold. The reference to Rousseau's *La Nouvelle Heloïse* is a sign of Keats's
intense awareness of the literary dimension of his own writing. This self-
conscious moment shows how much the letters suggest a constant
re-examination and meditation on the conditions of epistolary writing.

A year later, Keats once again uses Rousseau as an example in his
correspondence with Fanny Brawne. After reporting that he has been
reading the Frenchman's epistolary works ('I have been turning over two
volumes of Letters written between Rousseau and two Ladies') he fantasises
about the reversal of this reading:

What would Rousseau have said at seeing our little correspondence! What would
the Ladies have said! I don't care much – I would sooner have Shakespeare's
opinion about the matter. (*L*, 2. 266)

For all his disclaimers, Keats thinks of the correspondence as something that
is positioned in a literary realm – to be read, if not by Rousseau or his literary
characters, then by Shakespeare, the favourite judge of Romanticism. When
it comes to his epistles, Keats does not want to rely on 'the Ladies'.[7] Neither
does he want to be judged by the standards of *La Nouvelle Heloïse* and
sentimental epistolary fiction. Both statements betray an anxiety about the
kind of fictionalisation that Keats's own correspondence represents or will
be subject to. He wants to resist falling into the patterns of Rousseau's
characters or of Rousseau as a character. This is the main reason behind his

wish to find different terms for his and Fanny's letters. Keats's relief at not having either to 'be' Rousseau or to behave like a character in one of his novels makes him write: 'Thank god that you [Fanny] are fair and can love me without being Letter-written and sentimentaliz'd into it' (*L*, 2. 267). Keats wants to be loved without a novel's epistolary sentimentalism. Hence he does not 'care much' for Rousseau as imagined reader of his correspondence with Fanny. Apart from suggesting a complicated relationship between Keats and Rousseau, his letters reveal a highly self-conscious awareness of the epistle's literary dimension and potential for 'sentimentaliz[ing]'. Keats's letters are not simply a way of illuminating his poetry or constructing his biography. Their literary qualities also invite us to explore their rhetoric – their poetics – on their own terms.[8]

A DISSERTATION ON LETTER-WRITING

One of the first and most basic moments of any phenomenology of letter-writing is the division within oneself, and in relation to the addressee. As Gilles Deleuze and Félix Guattari write on another canonical letter-writer, Kafka, 'because of their genre, they [letters] maintain the duality of the two subjects […]'.[9] First and foremost, the letter is linked to displacement: displacement of oneself, the writer, the reader, and, in the act of writing, a displacement of time. Frances Ferguson points out that 'Another letter and another and another will be necessary not just to explain, interpret, and clarify for the reader but also to resurrect, if only temporarily, the letter writer's sense of having a self to express – which will appear in the next letter.'[10] The vocabulary of the 'echo' in Keats's letters points towards the self-doubling voice of the letter, while at the same time alluding to its dialogic character. Assuring his sister that her 'letter shall be answered like an echo –' (*L*, 2. 42), Keats hints at the self-doubling activity of epistolary writing. But by making the voice Fanny's, and the echo his own, he also includes the more obvious connotations of dialogue that the letter usually carries. This double movement is retained in the verse epistle 'To G. F. Matthew' (1815), where Keats writes, 'Fain would I echo back each pleasant note' (*L*, 1. 101). Writing to his brother Tom, Keats further connects echo and division when describing his walk to Nevis and speaking of scenes reminiscent of Wordsworth's Snowdon passage:

Talking of chasms they are the finest wonder of the whole – the[y] appear great rents in the very heart of the mountain though they are not, being at the side of it, but other huge crags arising round it give the appearance to Nevis of a shattered heart or Core in itself. […] We tumbled in large stones and set the echoes at work in fine style. (*L*, 1. 353)

Keats locates the 'chasms' at the centre of this ostensibly organic natural 'whole'; the 'rents' appear 'in the very heart of the mountain'. Although they are actually located at the margins, in their sum ('other huge crags arising round it'), they make the mountainous source of the sublime appear 'a shattered heart or Core'. The break within nature lies at its centre. This 'shattered heart' is the scene for Keats to 'set the echoes at work in fine style'. He doubles the breaks and rents around him with his own work. The 'shattered heart' of Nevis becomes an enactment of his own division. The letter is a place where Keats also sets this doubling to work. Like the echo on Nevis, the letter will repeat self-division 'in fine style'. Both written and spoken echoes are subject to the divisions and rifts that they reproduce.

Despite, and because of, its strongly dialogic character, the letter always labours under a fundamental tension.[11] The repetition of making the other and oneself simultaneously present through the activity of writing (and sending) a letter reinforces the gap that exists between the interlocutors. Keats attempts to overcome the distance (that leads him to write the letter in the first place) by creating a geographical and temporal virtual 'space' in which the contradictions necessitating this illusion are supposedly resolved. Writing to his sister-in-law, recently emigrated to North America, he imagines such a space:

Now the reason why I do not feel at the present moment so far from you is that I rememb{er} your Ways and Manners and actions; […] You will rem{em}ber me in the same manner – and the more when I tell you that I shall read a passage of Shakspeare [*sic*] every Sunday at ten o Clock – you read one {a}t the same time and we shall be as near each other as blind bodies can be in the same room […]. (*L*, 2. 5)

Apart from the immediate charm of Keats's idea, the language describing his vision succinctly illustrates the difficulties encountered by any attempt to bridge the insurmountable gap between writer and addressee. The predicament of distance, in its various forms, does not loosen its grip on the text. Although Keats does not feel 'so' far away from Georgiana Keats, he is nevertheless 'far away'. Keats's uncertain use of tenses is the temporal equivalent of this uncomfortable shifting. The insistence of the switching of tenses is remarkable ('Now […] at the present moment […] You will remember me […] I tell you […] I shall read […] you read one […] we shall be […]'). The continuous movement between present and future is a linguistic witness to the contradictions inherent and typical for Keats's position.[12] Keats's language betrays that reading (another linguistic activity) – advocated here as the medium through which the gap is to be bridged – is not a solution to the ultimate division between two 'blind bodies'. The letter describes reading (at an agreed time) as the force that catapults the subjects into an imaginary psychic space in which they will be 'as near each other as blind bodies can be in the same room'. But the image of blindness in relation to reading already indicates how this strategy is doomed to fail. The virtual space of encounter is ridden with contradictions: the blind bodies cannot read; neither can they find one another in a room. The heightened tactile sensuousness of a blind body is not the only Keatsian theme here: the price to be paid for this sensitivity is the loss of sight, just as sensuous as touch. The fantasy that allegedly bridges the geographical gap between reader and writer only reproduces the distance between them. Reading might be advocated as a strategy for transcending geographical space. However, as performed by 'blind bodies', it evokes the unbridgeable division between the two. The space remains invisible for its blind creators.

By reconfirming its dialogic status, the letter simultaneously marks the fundamental gap within and between subjects. This dynamic is constitutive of the letter's form. Beginning a correspondence is like starting a conversation. Keats starts his first letter to his sister: 'Let us now begin a regular question and answer – a little pro and con' (*L*, 1. 153). In another place he again likens the exchange of epistles to a 'proing and conning' (*L*, 1. 156). And, like a conversation, this written dialogue is continued. Once the dialogue has begun, it will form a 'brace of letters, very highly to be estimated' (*L*, 2. 166). Keats's image is curiously similar to Schlegel's comparison (cited in the epigraph) of the enlarged 'dialogue' of a correspondence to 'a chain or garland of fragments'. Keats varies the dialogic imagery by making reference to his own writing: the 'brace' of letters finds its correspondence in the remark that 'there can be nothing so remembrancing and enchaining as a good long letter' (*L*, 2. 208). The links of the dialogic fragments connect one letter to the next, making them, as we shall see, into a 'system of memorabilia'. However, this image also allows for a reading of a slightly more restrictive nature. The 'enchaining' letter is part of a system which organises the pros and cons of the epistolary dialogue.

To produce a gripping and 'enchaining' contribution to such a conversation is not an easy task. As George Keats maintains,

[T]he giving the fragments of thoughts with a few dashes of the pen, can only be done by one in 10,000, and <the> ordinary conversation, on paper is mere drivelling; only those who have very *much* to say can write an interesting letter, the essence of which is to condense *much* into a small and piquant form: which I have not the art to do as this page testifies. (*KC*, 2. 45)[13]

The dialogic 'giving' of 'fragments', which can itself never be complete, is highly self-conscious. George already points towards his (in)ability to cope with the letter form elegantly and to maintain an adequate dialogue. In a related instance, John Keats invokes the very materiality of the medium to insist on the difficulties of the form and its requirements: 'So how can I with any face begin [the letter] without a dissertation on letter writing – Yet when I consider that a sheet of paper contains room only for three pages, and a half how can I do justice to such a pregnant subject?' (*L*, 1. 367). The 'subject' of the epistolary is too pregnant for its own body. It cannot give birth on the page of Keats's letter. This implies that the fragment of the 'garland' always carries the possibility of finding itself aborted as soon as Keats ends his 'dissertation'. The dialogue, rather than being a harmonious meeting point, is always a reminder of the unbridgeable gap between the interlocutors. The form of the letter itself is caught in this tension. With each attempt to close this gap, the division is reinforced. The next section presents a particular aspect of the epistolary dynamic that illustrates how this tension finds its way into the rhetoric of Keats's letters.

EXCHANGING LETTERS

One of the reasons for the importance of the quality and character of Keats's epistolary 'fragments' is that their 'giving' is involved in a much wider context. The letter is part of an exchange and will be the trigger for another letter, seemingly subject to the same criteria. We have already seen that the dialogue whose dynamic and quality are at stake here is not at all straightforward. One way of understanding better what kind of exchange occurs here is to introduce into our reading an aspect of the well-known framework of gift-theory. The literature on the topic of the gift is vast and has received continuous attention from scholars in anthropology, philosophy, theology, and literary criticism. Some commentators trace gift-theory, as we understand it today, back to Classical authors such as Seneca. However, most writers take Marcel Mauss's highly influential *Essai sur le don* (1925) as their real or imagined point of departure.[14] Without attempting to outline gift-theory as a whole, I will briefly explain the importance of one of its aspects for my readings of the *Letters*, items of an exchange that obeys what Mauss in the *Essai* terms 'l'obligation de rendre'.

The reception of Mauss's essay in philosophy and literary theory has mostly focused on two main issues, both of which stand in relation to obligation and reciprocity. The first question concerns the intrinsic (im)-possibility of a completely disinterested gift. Secondly, the related issue interrogates the dynamic of reciprocity perpetuated by a continuous imbalance of the positions of giver and receiver. From Marilyn Strathern to Jacques Derrida, from George Bataille to Pierre Klossowski and Pierre Bourdieu, all these aspects have been discussed at great length. This is not the place to expand analytically on these larger questions of the gift as part of, or removed entirely from, the circle of exchange. It is more effective to contextualise the present discussion by way of a challenge that Jonathan Perry mounts against some received receptions of Mauss's work. He convincingly argues that the discussions equating the 'free' and 'disinterested' gift (which then is problematised) in fact rely on a canonical but mistaken reading of Mauss's essay. According to Parry, Mauss's *Essai* is not so much an exposition about the impossibility of a gift, but rather a meditation on the conditions that lead us to think about the gift in such a way. As he points out, 'The whole ideology of the gift, and conversely the whole idea of "economic self-interest", are *our* invention; and the text [Mauss's *Essai*] explicitly acknowledges the difficulty of using these terms [...] So while Mauss is generally represented as telling us how *in fact* the gift is *never* free, what I think he is really telling us is how *we* have acquired a *theory* that it should be.'[15]

Significantly, large parts of Parry's argument, just as Mauss's, rely on linguistic analysis. Language illustrates how the assumed contrast of self-interest and the selfless gift is in fact better understood as an interdependence. This link of language and reciprocity is central to my argument regarding Keats. Linguistic exchange, specifically in its epistolary dimension, helps to reconsider the 'forms' an economy of language and aesthetics can take. Keats's epistles are one such form. Their rhetoric allows us to uncover the linguistic dimension of reciprocity as deeply connected to fracture. The epistolary obligation to reciprocate is a symptom of the fragmentariness of language. The rhetoric of Keats's letters continuously thematises this brokenness and its subsequent imbalance. These epistles negotiate a linguistic condition which they diagnose via their obligation to reciprocate. Keats develops various impossible fantasies regarding the possibility of escaping this predicament. Ultimately, it transpires that the predicament is not necessarily as negative as might be assumed at first. In fact, the letter becomes a form that can archive this contradiction in itself and make it part of the Romantic corpus it comes to represent. As Michael Wetzel points out in a different context:

Romanticism rediscovered the *letter* as a medium of this *gift from a distance*. As genre of the love-gift it unites in its technical aspects of bestowing writing, addressing, dating, and transport, all the preconditions to make the desire of the other an event, to invent the other through imaginative excitement. The letter gives, but simultaneously, in its presence as gift, is already absence again, i.e. memory of that which is given, and it tells, like a scar, simultaneously of injury and healing.[16]

Just as 'The concept of interestedness relies on the concept of disinterestedness for its very intelligibility',[17] we realise that it is the epistolary economy of fragmentation that helps to keep Keats's corpus alive. Thus my discussion should not be misunderstood as a blinkered 'application' of a model of gift-theory to Keats's *Letters*. This is not simply a chapter about Keats's desire to have his correspondence answered. Rather, it attempts to illustrate how the *Letters* are an intriguing and good example of an epistolary economics that both rests on a linguistic predicament of lack and, simultaneously, allows the construction of a literary corpus. The notion of fragmentation offers a productive reading of this double-edged form. To theorise the form and dynamic of the Romantic letter through the lens of fragmentation accommodates their internal poetics, and its linguistic presuppositions, in a specifically relevant way. It tells us something very particular about the formation of Keats's corpus – a canonical body of writing of Romanticism.

Through the dynamic of exchange, the letter becomes an item charged with significance and value. The 'dialogue', as a sequence of reciprocal acts, is not just an 'innocent swapping'. The nature of the organisation of epistolary exchange includes the obligation to respond. The other has placed one in a position where it is necessary to reciprocate, by returning this obligation. By receiving a letter, a fragment of dialogue, one is under pressure to abide by the laws of this exchange and produce an adequate response: another fragment. Stepping outside this reciprocal system belongs to the world of fantasy. As Keats writes, 'To give me credit for constancy and at the same time wave [*sic*] letter writing will be the highest indulgence I can think of' (*L*, 2. 147). The impossibility of gratifying such 'indulgence' is clear enough. Keats himself polices the epistolary dynamic of his circle. Woodhouse reports in a letter to Taylor: 'He [Keats] very kindly reproach'd me with never writing to him. You may suppose I promised amendment, & stipulated (as Paddy says) "that all the reciprocity should not be on one side"' (*L*, 2. 165). Keats insists that continuous disregard for the rules of the system ultimately leads to an exclusion from it: 'Mr B.[rown] wrote two Letters to Mr Abbey concerning me – Mr. A. took no notice and of course

Mr. B. must give up such a correspondence when as the man said all the Letters are on one side –' (*L*, 2. 284). Mr. A. and Mr. B., shorthand for any two entities communicating by letter, are disconnected if one of the parties takes 'no notice' and the dialogue breaks down. If there is no connection between the first two letters, the differential and metonymic sequence of the alphabet will not get going either.

The necessity for exchange reinforces the fundamental gap both within the subject and in its relation to other subjects in a variety of ways. I want to concentrate my focus on the linguistic negotiation of a particular aspect of this fundamental split. A prime example of such a linguistic negotiation in the *Letters* occurs in Keats's letter of 31 August 1819:

My dear Taylor,
   Brown and I have been employed for these three weeks past from time to time in writing to our different friends: a dead silence is our ownly answer: we wait morning after morning and nothing: tuesday is the day for the Examiner to arrive; this is the second Tuesday which has been barren even of a news paper – Men should be in imitation of Spirits 'responsive to each others note' – Instead of that I pipe and no one hath danced – We have been cursing this morning like Mandeville and Lisle – With this I shall send by the same Post a third letter to a friend of mine – who though it is of consequence has neither answerd right or left […]. (*L*, 2. 153)

Answering 'neither […] right or left' leaves the exchange with nowhere to go. Keats is faced with 'a dead silence'; the dialogue is about to collapse. It is quite clear where the problem lies. Ideally, the participants of the exchange 'should be in the imitation of spirits "responsive to each others note"'. These 'notes', musical and epistolary, are fragmentary writings inviting the other to dance or to respond. Keats's musical pun refers to Milton's spirits, 'singing their great Creator' with their 'celestial voices', thereby dividing 'the night, and lift[ing] our thoughts to Heaven' (*Paradise Lost*, 4. 684–8). In contrast with this divine scenario, Keats's powers as a creator are ignored: he 'pipe[s] and no one hath danced'. Despite producing the notes – writing the fragments and piping them – he finds no dancing movement, no reciprocal exchange or response. Instead of a lively movement there is only 'dead silence'.

The 'notes' are simultaneously caught up in yet another system of exchange; they become economic notes, banknotes, with which one pays and repays one's attention by corresponding, thereby creating an economy of the letter. This economic quality of the letter is a means of asking for money in a short and economic way: Keats, only a few lines later, asks for a loan from 'dear' Taylor. More importantly, it also adopts the metaphors and concepts of monetary reciprocity – not least because in 1819 Taylor, as recipient, has to pay the postage. Keats's fantasy about 'credit for constancy' indicates how far the rhetoric of credit, as well as of economy, influences Keats's negotiation of the epistolary exchange. More generally, this economy also points to a fundamental gap between language and subject. This is the precondition for the dynamic of exchange, suggesting how language, in the process of attempting to bridge it, cannot but repeat and reinforce the divide.

Keats tells Dilke: 'You must give me credit, now, for a free Letter when it is in realty [*sic*] an interested one, on two points, the one requestive, the other verging to the pros and cons –' (*L*, 2. 178). Although the letter pretends to be 'free', it immediately admits that, as far as 'realty' is concerned, this cannot be the case. The fundamentally problematic, even paradoxical, nature of the exchange is here translated into the monetary terms of epistolary notes. There is no letter 'free' of interest, an interest both personal and monetary. Hence asking for 'credit' in exchange for the supposed gift (the 'free' letter) intensifies and reinforces the point that this desire cannot be fulfilled. Keats's debt is the result of interest built up on Keats's side, which he has to repay. A 'free' letter to Dilke would do more than that. What is most in Keats's interest is to give Dilke a free letter. The more self-disinterested that letter appears, the more repayment it will ultimately be able to expect. As soon as Dilke receives the note, he will be owing interest until he repays his correspondent. The rhetoric of economics haunts not only Keats's epistolary dynamics but also the aesthetic production within them. Keats's verse-epistle, 'To Charles Cowden Clarke', in the *1817* volume makes this evident:

> And can I e'er these benefits forget?
> And can I e'er repay the friendly debt?
> No, doubly no; – yet should these rhymings please,
> I shall roll on the grass with two-fold ease [...].[18]   (lines 76–9)

The 'benefits' Clarke gave to Keats were not purely charitable and free of interest. It is impossible to forget them. They can never be returned, and thus turn from 'benefits' into straightforward 'debt'. The more 'friendly' the debt, the harder it is to 'repay' it. The verse-epistle insists that this is impossible by denying the chance for repayment twice over ('doubly no'). And after pondering possible alternatives, creating a moment's mental space through the parenthesis, the poem's only answer is to attempt an escape into another system. The 'rhymings' are offered as an alternative payment for a debt that is impossible to amortise. However, this offer relies on a circular logic whose movement is betrayed by Keats's 'roll[ing]'. Keats wants to ease his interest by escaping the system in which he is a debtor and, at the same time, step into a new one in which he can take the reciprocal initiative. The friendly debt and benefits can be forgotten, so goes the fantasy, once Clarke accepts the aesthetic offerings of Keats's 'rhymings'. The pleasure that these potentially entail would make Keats 'roll on the grass' and thereby enact his and his debt's easement in a 'two-fold' manner. However, the excessive doubling-up on each side ('doubly no' and 'two-fold') indicates that a transition from one system to the other, so wished-for in Keats's fantasy, is impossible. Keats's debts relate to the economy of reading in whose system Clarke saved Keats time and effort by giving friendly and beneficial advice. However, this does not translate and repay in the economy of writing and 'rhymings'.

The rhetoric of monetary interchange in these letters becomes a short-hand for negotiating the reciprocal dynamics of epistolarity. The monetary sense of 'the brace of letters, very highly to be estimated' concentrates the broader problematic of any exchange, which resembles the fundamental fracture between language and subject. In a different context Georg Hamann cryptically refers to this much larger issue:

Money and language are two things whose interrogation is as deep and abstract as their use is common. Both stand in closer relation than one would surmise. The theory of the one explains the theory of the other; they therefore seem to flow from common causes.[19]

To put it in the words of the first chapter of this book: the 'obligation to reciprocate' is a thoroughly post-Babelian condition, a lapsed linguistics. The systems for the exchange of words and money, including the value that the items have in them, are parallel in both their dynamic and their origin. The implicit assumption about a necessary break at the origin of each system is important here. Taking his cue from Hamann, Jochen Hörisch attends acutely to this dynamic when he points out that both money and language 'share' a fallen origin. They are only necessary in a world in which exchange is inevitable because reciprocal relations are imbalanced and must be negotiated. He argues:

Only in a world of want, i.e. in a wanting world, do human language and money have common reasons to exist. […] Language and money share their precondition and their threat: they only make sense in a sinful world of want and never-ending problems. […] However, not only the conditions of possibility but also the questioning of language and money 'flow' from the same 'reasons'. Language is – at least since the tower of Babel – as unstable as that tower.[20]

The broken condition of language and its currency is reinforced and illustrated with each exchange, be it monetary or linguistic. Both the monetary and the linguistic exchange follow the same structure of imbalance that cannot be settled. The continuous perpetuation of the system of imbalance, through monetary or linguistic 'notes', is an ever-present reminder of the fundamental rupture that lies at the origin of our exchanges.

During his discussion of Wordsworth, Simon Jarvis points out that 'When knowing, or feeling, or imagination, or writing poetry are discussed in the language of exchange we are not simply in the presence of "metaphors".' He rejects a separation of 'ontological and political-economic languages' that corresponds to a separation between literal and metaphorical exchange. In contrast, 'it can hardly be determined which comes "first", but it can be affirmed that metaphysics, ontology, and epistemology have never succeeded in getting rid of the language of exchange, right down to Kant's use of the word "reciprocity" to explain one of his twelve logical categories'.[21] Although Hörisch and Jarvis differ in their approaches, their accounts converge in stressing the importance of the 'logical' intersection of exchange and linguistics as a moment of origin. For the present concern it makes no difference that most analyses locate this question in the field of epistemology. Despite the different inflections of these narratives, the presence of economic vocabulary in the context of exchange is not simply a negative reminder of the supposed juxtaposition between different 'kinds' of languages or spheres. The issue here, then, is not a supposedly 'disinterested' vocabulary of aesthetics (whatever that might be) as opposed to an 'interested' vocabulary of economy. Rather, the question revolves around a marker of the predicament of any linguistic utterance and its links to the fractures that any exchange necessitates. Hence, their original convergence – their broken origin – is localised at a logical rather than a historical point.

ARCHIVING LETTERS

The history and mode of Keats's survival is part of the construction of British Romanticism. From Shelley's 'Adonais' (1821) to Susan Wolfson's 'Keats Enters History' (1995), the way that Keats's ouevre thematises its own survival has been at the centre of its understanding. Especially in recent scholarship, a number of powerful readings of Keats's poetry along these lines have emerged. In a general survey Nicholas Roe points out that 'Keats had anticipated the aesthetic view of his poetry which was adopted by generations of nineteenth- and twentieth-century readers.'[22] It is a theme that underwrites nearly all the contributions of the collection *Keats and History* (1995), published in Keats's bicentennial.[23] Paul Hamilton shrewdly comments on the economic dimension of Keats's poetic and historical legacy when he calls him a 'poetic inflationist'.[24] Andrew Bennett has masterfully explored Keats's obsession with his own afterlife in particular as a specifically Romantic concern. The entity 'Keats' has become a representative figure of Romanticism's worry about posthumousness. Bennett formulates perceptively one of the contradictions on which a construction of this posthumous aspect of Keats's fame relies: 'If immortality for Keats is associated with a failure of the body, a corporeal fading or dissolution, this failing body is precisely the condition of Keats's success in his afterlife, the necessary correlate of his afterfame.'[25] Extending these critical observations to his letters reveals how this 'corporeal fading' is linked to the epistolary and its subsequent role in the construction of a posthumous body.[26] The conclusion of this chapter will show how the preoccupation with exchange and language in Keats's letters allows us to understand how a continuous and reciprocal movement forms one of the cornerstones of Keats's survival.

The notion of an exchange or correspondence of letters implies the assumption that epistolary writings can be classified and preserved in a meaningful way. In other words, the letter is subject to archivisation. In the construction of the figure 'Keats', known through biographies for example, the letters form part of an archive that is used to represent this figure (or his oeuvre) in a certain way. It is not only the text of the letter that comes into play. The letters are items in an entire 'system of memorabilia' that constitutes a material archive. The fragmented text of the letter forms part of a record that informs our representation and understanding of the entity 'Keats'. But the archive is always necessarily fragmented. No archive is complete. One does not, nor can one ever, have the entirety of Keats and his oeuvre represented in an archive. Keats's fragmented text forms part of the incomplete assemblage of memorabilia that is responsible for his representation as a Romantic poet. It is important to understand how this assemblage of memorabilia is collected and why fragmentation is central to it.

Keats's own construction of the archive of a figure who 'will be amongst the English poets' after his death (*L*, 1. 394) is already under way when he writes to his sister in 1817:

My dear Fanny,
   Let us now begin a regular question and answer – a little pro and con [...] You will preserve all my Letters and I will secure yours – and thus in the course of time we shall each of us have a good Bundle – which, hereafter, when things may have strangely altered and god knows what happened, we may read over together and look with pleasures on times past – that now are to come. (*L*, 1. 153–6)

Keats begins his dialogue with Fanny expecting it to last until after the moment of separation that necessitates this form of communication. His insistence that the items constituting this dialogue shall be 'preserved' and 'secured' still alerts us, until today, to his archival concern. And, indeed, the pieces of correspondence still document the development of the 'question and answer'. In this sense Keats's 'now' is, like the rest of the correspondence, simultaneously directed into both past and future: into the past, because the letters are something written, fixed; into the future, because they are part of a construction, an archive, which 'in the course of time' will be a representation of 'times past'. Those 'times past' begin at the moment of writing the epistle which Fanny is reading: from 'now' on they 'are to come'. Keats's acute awareness of the temporal status of letter-writing is reinforced when he describes the 'course of time' as possibly 'strangely' altering things. In fact, only 'god knows' what will happen. The reading of the 'Bundle' will be performed under circumstances that are very different from Keats's present. He and his sister cannot read the letters together while they write to each other. There is no guarantee that the 'Bundle' as an assemblage of past circumstances will come to mean what now it is assumed it will come to mean.[27]

This dynamic is not restricted to Keats's general insistence on the contingency of historical circumstance. It has equally important connotations in relation to a specific problem – the hermeneutic gap of interpretation that any temporal displacement implies. By self-consciously thematising this gap in the very (material) object of future interpretation, the letter, Keats already enacts this movement as he writes. The point gains relevance when we connect the way John and Fanny Keats 'preserve' and 'secure' their 'Bundle' with how a reader today understands how 'in the course of time [...] things may have strangely altered'. The unpredictability of the dialogue is matched in a double sense by Keats's 'god knows'. It is not clear how the future archive is going to develop – the fate of the letters is uncertain. In addition, the way this process will be interpreted is unpredictable. How are these letters going to be read in the future? This point gains its full power if we attend to the way in which the literary 'body' of Keats is constructed in archival fashion. His 'body' is at least partly constituted by the 'Bundle' we have 'secured' and 'preserved'. And this body is also constituted in ways that are crucially formed by fragmentation. More specifically, two fundamental levels link the constitutive parts of Keats's corpus, and their organising force, to the rupturing dynamic. First, the particular items of this archive, the letters, are fragmentary. As fragments, the letters *in themselves* already embody the incompleteness of the archive. Secondly, their own rhetoric, together with the vocabulary of their first archivists, reveals that the organ-ising principle of their classification is inextricably tied to fragmentation.

As we have seen, Keats himself insists on the materiality of the objects that will come to represent the past. The 'Bundle' consists of material objects and is to be understood as such. He emphasises the texture of the items that will constitute the archive. They are part of a whole host of other objects of memorabilia. In relation to Keats's obsession with the decay of the material, and the notion of fragmentation through time (think of the Elgin Marbles), this becomes an important image in his correspondence. It goes far beyond Fanny and Keats rereading their epistles together. It begins to form part of a wider concern which permeates his writing as a whole. The letters become markers for a decaying archive of physical objects whose meaning may be lost. This is important when these objects, as items of a body of writing, are consciously constructed to stand in for a dead subject. To understand how this construction takes place is to comprehend the corpus of Keats as an assembly of memorabilia to come.

Writing to Sarah Jeffrey, Keats inscribes the importance of the archival process onto one of its parts:

I was making a day or two ago a general conflagration of all old Letters and Memorandums, which had become of no interest to me – I made however, like the Barber-inquisitor in Don Quixote some reservations – among the rest your and your Sister's Letters. I assure you you had not entirely vanished from my Mind, or even become shadows in my remembrance: it only needed such a memento as your Letters to bring you back to me […]. (*L*, 2. 112)

This description provides a direct insight into how Keats's own archive is constructed. Notes with 'no interest' suffer a 'conflagration'. Sarah Jeffrey's letters, however, are not destroyed in the fire, preserving her in Keats's memory. The reason for the preservation is circular. She will form part of the archive because her letters are manifestly successful in producing the illusion that such 'memento[s]' are not necessary, and they 'bring [her] back to me [Keats]'. Keats's phrasing indicates the tension between having to construct a textual body by which we remember a person, and, at the same time, maintaining that the most representative aspects of that body make it seem unnecessary to create it in the first place. That this is a fundamentally textual problem is suggested by Keats's literary reference to *Don Quixote*. Keats's fantasy makes him the barber in Cervantes's novel (in volume 1, chapter 6). That figure is responsible for preserving some select items of literature to be spared from the mass of writings condemned by the 'inquisitor' priest to the flames. It is thus the literary value that is responsible both for the successful creation of the virtual space triggered by the letter and for securing its place in the archive. Keats's allusion invites us to read these criteria of, and for, classification back into his own textual productions. It is not only because Sarah Jeffrey's letters still have the power to displace ('to bring you back to me') that they remain interesting. If Keats's own letters have a similar power, and his correspondents similar criteria, they will also survive a 'general conflagration'. His epistolary writing will become part of the corpus constructed to represent the poetic entity 'Keats'. And, through a generous self-referential twist, Keats also incorporates Sarah Jeffrey into this body of writing. It is evident that the references to the preservation and destruction of letters are far from innocent, especially for a figure as concerned with immortality as Keats. Keats's archival preoccupation here focuses the wider Romantic concern of posthumousness and posterity mentioned earlier. Another vivid example of this dynamic in Keats is a correspondence that ultimately fails and also ends Keats's epistolary existence – his exchange with Fanny Brawne.

Keats feels his letters with every nerve. His reasons for leaving Leigh Hunt's house in 1820 are of an epistolary nature: one of Hunt's servants breaks the seal of a letter addressed to Keats. It turns out to be a note by Fanny Brawne. On understanding that the note may have been opened before it reached him, Keats weeps for several hours, wanders sobbing around Hampstead, and finally ends up at the Brawnes' where he remains until going to Italy.[28] This pronounced oversensitivity to love letters (undoubtedly heightened by his tuberculosis) persists in an even more poignant fashion once he leaves London and the physical distance between the correspondents grows. Writing from Rome, Joseph Severn reports Keats's reaction to receiving a letter from Fanny: 'Such a letter has come! I gave it to Keats supposing it to be one of yours, but it proved sadly otherwise. The glance at that letter tore him to pieces; the effects were on him for many days. He did not read it – he could not –.'[29] Keats is 'torn to pieces'; the affective power of the letter as object prevents it from being read, let alone answered. In the face of such an event, the exchange begins to disintegrate. Keats's deterioration correlates with his emotional fragility when faced with Fanny's living hand. He himself admits as much when he writes that:

I am afraid to write to her – to receive a letter from her – to see her hand writing would break my heart – even to hear of her any how, to see her name written would be more than I can bear. (*Life*, 2. 352)

Keats, torn to pieces, is unable to bear seeing Fanny's handwriting or even her written name. The exchange finally ends with Keats's death in the face of the unreadability of the letter. For all the melodrama that frames many accounts of Keats's death, their pronouncements are instructive when they are followed to their logical outcome. Severn gives details about how Keats 'requested me to place it [Fanny Brawne's letter] in his coffin, together with a purse and a letter (unopened) of his sister's' (*Life*, 2. 91). By repeatedly quoting Severn, Richard Milnes, the first 'editor' of the letters, anxiously assures his readers that these letters are lost: 'The letters I placed in the coffin with my own hand' (*Life*, 2. 94). They remain unread by us, as by Keats. His coffin becomes a grave for unreadable letters, placed here, impossibly, by Keats's living hand.

Simultaneously, Keats's coffin also becomes the basis for the posthumous construction of his literary corpus. The unopened letter is an image for the oblique moment on which the archive that constructs this body rests. The creation of the posthumous corpus of Keats is fuelled by a force that is deeply fragmentary. The coherence of the body 'Keats' relies on the linguistic fragments that constitute his correspondence. In addition, these fragments form part of an exchange that has already been shown to depend on the fundamental brokenness of language. Some of the earliest instances of archivisation of Keats's corpus indicate this dynamic. Richard Milnes's *Life, Letters and Literary Remains of John Keats* (1848) already understands the figure of Keats through the lens of a premature failing of the body. It thereby implicitly stresses the importance of the corpus that Milnes is constructing as a memorial. Milnes is a central example for understanding how the fashioning of Keats's posthumous body is performed. The *Life, Letters and Literary Remains* is one of the first and most explicit attempts to create the full and complete poetical figure of 'Keats' by using his epistolary writings. It does so in an unprecedented way. Milnes's anxiety about how far a fragmentation of this corpus is necessary, inevitable, lamentable, or positive, is illuminating. All these aspects form part of Milnes's self-appointed task of creating Keats's body through and within the *Remains*.

The title of Milnes's work already indicates how these specific concerns are intertwined with the epistolary. At the very beginning of Milnes's archive he states that:

It is thus no more than the beginning of a Life which can here be written, and nothing but a conviction of the singularity and the greatness of the fragment would justify any one in attempting to draw general attention to its shape and substance. (*Life*, 1. 2)

The beginning of the *Life, Letters and Literary Remains* insists that the life it describes ended prematurely. It follows that it is a fragmented, incomplete, and partial representation of a poetic corpus. This, in itself, would not be so remarkable. However, it is followed by a peculiar justification for representing such an unfinished corpus. Milnes's apologetic tone repays attention. He states his conviction of the 'singularity and the greatness of the fragment'. Milnes accepts that his own *Remains*, too, can only remain fragmentary. The rhetoric with which the *Life, Letters and Literary Remains* presents itself makes it clear that, as a work of criticism and classification, it is only a beginning. Keats's afterlife finds an epistolary genesis in the attention Milnes draws to the fragmentariness of Keats's entire corpus and the letters that constitute the archive. It also points towards one of the major problems Milnes's account has to negotiate. What the *Life, Letters and Literary Remains* represents was never complete to begin with. Milnes attempts to resolve this difficulty by elevating the fragmentary to a more representative status:

> The following pieces are so fragmentary as more becomingly to take their place in the narrative of the author's life, than to show as substantive productions. Yet it is, perhaps, just in verses like these that the individual character pronounces itself most distinctly, and confers a general interest which more care of art at once elevates and diminishes. (*Life*, 1. 282)

The familiar contrast between the lyrical 'substantive productions' and the biographical 'narrative' of letters and fragmentary poems begins to emerge.

Together with the argument that the fragmentary 'pronounces […] most distinctly' the 'character' of the poet, the scene is set for a negotiation of how these two spheres interact. These fragments, according to Milnes, are best understood as part of the 'narrative of the author's life'. In other words: within the *Life*'s constructed status (as narrative), fragmentary poems are more typical than those which are complete. This means that they have a more representative value than items that are ordinarily supposed to compose that corpus (the 'more substantive productions'). The difficulties of this move describe the conditions of Milnes's project. He openly states that the fragmentary is the basis of his narration. This fragmentariness unites the life and its remains, so much so that it becomes the instance that 'most distinctly' characterises the narrative force binding the *Life, Letters and Literary Remains* together. Fragmentation becomes the lens through which we focus and construct the body of Keats. His 'untimely death' has become a commonplace; his biography is presented as a narrative of a literary life broken off, rather than 'complete'. Joseph Severn's letter to William Haslam already rehearses this posthumous construction:

Poor Keatss [*sic*] grave is still covered with daisies – and if I do not have answers with the inscription by the next Post – why I will proceed with the Stone – the design I made is this – A delicate Greek Lyre with half the strings broken – signifying his Classical <Genius and> Genius – left unfinished by his early death –. (*KC*, 1. 252)

The 'strings' of Keats's life are fractured, his poetical genius left unfinished. The broken lyre provides the basis for his posthumous representation. It comes not only to 'signify' his poetic talent and untimely death but also to form the basis for a subsequent construction of his posthumous literary body. The corpus rests on a monument to fragmentation. It is only fitting that, alongside Keats's body, '*Our* Keats Tomb' (*KC*, 1. 273; my emphasis) should enclose parts of an incomplete epistolary correspondence.

Keats's grave is the nexus of a difficult negotiation between language, exchange, and preservation in yet another way. His epitaph, 'Here lies one whose name was writ in water', concentrates this relation in a neatly condensed form. The image of writing in water (or air) is a metaphor with a long history.[30] The scholarship is divided on what Keats's particular source of the image might have been (the most commonly cited one is Beaumont and Fletcher's *Philaster*).[31] Be that as it may, for the present context the immediately Heraclitean connotations of the image – irrespective of Keats's doubtful familiarity with the pre-Socratic – are most appealing. Famously, water, often figured as a river, is a central metaphor in Heraclitus's work. His fragment 'It is not possible to step into the same river twice' has become a shorthand for theories of flux and change.[32] In Keats's context the 'name writ in water' also invokes constant change and erasure. It insists on the double-edged construction of his corpus to live among the English poets. Even the name, around which this corpus is created, is affected. The systems of reciprocity and exchange, which refine and consolidate this name, are also unstable by definition. They presuppose movement and flux, denying the fixity with which a successful posthumous existence is normally associated. However, it transpires that precisely these reciprocal systems are essential in creating the corpus that we come to know as 'Keats'. Keats's survival relies on the flux and lack of an economy of brokenness. The regeneration of the name via the change becomes its strength: the stony epitaph survives until today. Its history exemplifies that the economy of flux is dependent on a receiver (just as in a Wordsworthian epitaph). After all, Keats never wrote down his own epitaphic line; it only survives through Severn's reports, and the discussions between him, Brown, and Taylor, that finally led to the unfortunate additions that still 'embellish' the tomb.[33]

The invocation of Heraclitus is not purely impressionistic here. His role in the theorisation of economy and language has been pointed out by thinkers from Aristotle to Karl Marx and beyond.[34] Keats's epitaph, thus, provides a link to the particular forms that the deep connection of systems of exchange (be they monetary, sensual, or archival) and language takes in his writing. As Marc Shell in his landmark study *The Economy of Literature* (1978) points out: 'The Greek concept of exchange includes not only commercial transactions and physical sequences but also such transfers as metaphor and dialectic.'[35] He singles out Heraclitus as one of the most important theoreticians of exchange:

Some thinkers, moreover, came to recognize interactions between economic and intellectual exchange, or money and language. (*Seme* means 'word' as well as 'coin.') Heraclitus, for example, described the monetary exchange of commodities in a complex simile and series of metaphors whose logical exchanges of meaning define the unique form of simultaneous purchase and sale of wares that obtains in monetary transfer.[36]

It is the movement of the system which allows for the most important insights: 'We both step and do not step into the same rivers; we both are and are not.'[37] Famously, Plato, one of Heraclitus's most important critics, provides a counter-model to the theory of flux. He denies the sustaining powers of change by insisting on stability. Without going into the question of pre- versus post-Socratic philosophy, it is useful to take up Shell's suggestion which presents Plato and Heraclitus as two antagonists in thinking about exchange, both monetary and linguistic:

Heraclitus was a master of the kind of linguistic exchange Plato most disliked. The Platonic attack on Heraclitus usually takes the form of mocking the Heraclitean doctrine of motion and exchange. [...] What Plato most dislikes in Heraclitus's philosophy is the lack of a concept of metaphysical stillness and of a concept of justice above the supposedly escapable movements of commodities.[38]

Linguistically speaking, 'Heraclitus internalized the money form into his thoughts differently [from Plato], focusing on metaphorization and symbol-ization themselves. If Plato studies the metaphor of still Being, Heraclitus studies the activity of metaphorization itself.'[39] Movement, and the asso-ciated change with the passing of time, including the assumed erasure of the visible – such as writing in water – are thus central themes in a Heraclitean economy.

The contrast between the models of exchange that favour, respectively, flux or stasis clarifies why such accounts can illuminate certain aspects of Keats's inscription and its reception. It is suggestive to think of Keats as a poet whose fame relies on the constancy of change. He is remembered through an epitaph that erases the fixity of his name. The basis for Keats's grave and fame is an unreciprocated, and therefore still active, item in a system of exchange: an unopened letter. As we have seen, the association of the economy of the name with a reciprocal system of continuous imbalance is crucial in the construction of his corpus. A fixed, completely balanced, healthy, and unbroken system would mean death to Keats. As Johann Wilhelm Ritter so brilliantly writes in the neglected *Fragments from a Young Physicist's Nachlass* (1810):

In *complete* health, we would, most likely, not be alive, but dead. It would be absolute unity, nothing to compare, nothing limited, but only ideal activity. Thus one can also die from too great a health, and life always includes an illness.[40]

In the unhealthy exchange of letters that keeps Keats alive, motion is just as important as the items that change hands. At the centre of that exchange lies an unanswered epistle. The premature and posthumous Keats of our Romanticism is kept alive by a fragmentary piece of writing, never to be answered. His letters and poetry condense the vocabulary of exchange as a concern directly related to the form of language and its preservation in writing. They put fragmentation and the continuously unsuccessful attempt to overcome it at its centre. In their brokenness and failure they ensure his survival.

CHAPTER 6

The doubling force of citation: De Quincey's Wordsworthian archive

Over many citations oneself becomes a citation.[1]

Ralph Waldo Emerson considered the status and problem of citation as both fundamental and deeply troubling. In his essay 'Quotation and Originality' (1876), he writes: 'We quote not only books and proverbs, but arts, sciences, religion, customs and laws; nay, we quote temples and houses, tables and chairs by imitation. [...] The originals are not original.'[2] Knowing of our inability to produce outside the chain of quotations, however, still does not lead us to renounce ownership of our creations. As Emerson recounts in the same essay: 'Wordsworth, as soon as he heard a good thing, caught it up, meditated upon it, and very soon reproduced it in his conversation and writing. If De Quincey said, "That is what I told you," he replied, "No: that is mine, – mine, and not yours".'[3]

Emerson's conceptualisation of the power of citation and its metaphorical force through the figure of originals and precursors sounds almost like a prefiguration of a Bloomian anxiety of influence, or even a post-modern insistence on pastiche. Rather than reading this curious Emersonian fantasy in these psychoanalytical or intertextual terms, however, this chapter wants to suggest that its less obvious reverse – De Quincey's archiving of whatever Wordsworth claims for himself – is more revealing. It sheds light on how the rhetoric and language of criticism have to deal with the tensions that are produced through the practice of citation. One textual complexity that citation produces is the dynamic of fracture. A citation breaks the text it is in, and the one it is taken from. My readings will attempt to show how fracture and citation are connected, and how the former, via the latter, plays an important part in the construction of Romanticism as it has been presented here. Evidently, citation fractures any text, irrespective of its period. However, if fracture is part of our definition of Romanticism, it becomes a matter of concern for our historical and conceptual analysis to understand how a critical practice that contributes to construct this definition also *enacts* the fracture (by citing). The particular way De Quincey cites – that he cites what he cites when he cites it – reveals and records that for his Romanticism, and its legacy, fracture is of central importance. Unsurprisingly, the repetition and enactment in the recording process illustrate the Romantic quality of De Quincey's own critical construction. This does not weaken the status of his work as a representative instance of Romanticism's first recording or archivisation. In fact, insofar as we can recognise a Romanticism that is still powerful, De Quincey presents another instance of how the origin of this Romanticism feeds off broken structures.

The discussion in this chapter will proceed from an explanation of the link between citation and fracture to a specific textual analysis of why and how it is fruitful to read some of De Quincey's writings (especially his critical essays and autobiographical fiction) in this light. The first section will discuss briefly, in a theoretical manner, why and how the notion of fracture is linked to citation. The chapter will then proceed to explain in three separate sections how this practice is important in De Quincey's authorship. They will present the contradictory force of citation, and illustrate how it becomes central to the definition, as well as the archivisation, of Romanticism in De Quincey.

THE FRACTURING FORCE OF CITATION

Citation is a wide and heterogeneous topic whose history has invited a variety of critical approaches and responses. Especially in literary criticism, it is often treated as identical to or coextensive with its linguistic instance, quotation. The following readings want to avoid this collapse, and include the philosophical and jurisprudential connotations of the term in its linguistic analysis. These wider meanings are central to the strategy of citation as a critical tool and their mirroring in its deployment of language. Thus the readings treat quotation as a subset of citation and stress that the practice of quotation always implies a wider citational dimension. It includes the idea of the call or the summons, in the sense that citing means 'to summon officially in court of law' (*OED*). To be consistent, I will use the term 'citation' throughout.

Understood in its wider sense, citation is a multifaceted subject. Depending on the focus and disciplinary approach, its theorisation highlights questions of philosophy, authority, iterability, history, and intertextuality. Jacques Ehrmann's polemical intervention that 'To write would be first of all to quote' has become a cornerstone of intertextual criticism.[4]

Similarly, Mikhael Bakhtin – a reference-point for most intertextual analyses – assigns citation an important role in literary composition and interpretation. His Emersonian claim is that most of the time we do not utter 'original' ideas, but, rather, rely on references found in discourses anchored in the public: '[I]n the everyday speech of any person living in society, no less than half (on the average) of all the words uttered by him will be someone else's words (consciously someone else's), transmitted with varying degrees of precision and impartiality (or more precisely partiality).'[5] While Bakhtin here does not describe citation in the strict sense, the same essay makes a convincing claim that the continuous reference to different discourses determines the composition and analysis of fictional prose, especially the novel:

> We have in mind first of all those instances of powerful influence exercised by another's discourse on a given author. When such influences are laid bare, the half-concealed life lived by another's discourse is revealed within a new context of the given author. When such an influence is deep and productive, there is no external imitation, no simple act of reproduction, but rather a further creative development of another's (more precisely, half-other) discourse in a new context and under new conditions.[6]

Bakhtin here gestures towards quotation understood in its most general and generously productive form. On the other side of the spectrum lie Coleridge's and De Quincey's plagiarism, abusing the discourse of another and appropriating it by repeating, citing, without quotation marks. Plagiarism haunts Coleridge and De Quincey all through their careers, both individually and in relation to one another. Nigel Leask remarks on this when he classifies De Quincey's *Confessions of an English Opium Eater* (1821; 1856) as 'parasitic' on Coleridge's *Biographia Literaria* (1817).[7] This is especially relevant as it is De Quincey who publicly uncovers Coleridge's plagiarism of Schelling in the *Biographia*. Leask attributes many of the similarities between the two books to De Quincey's 'paradoxical "plagiarism of the plagiarist," although at the narrative level these parallels are often deliberately crafted'.[8] The high profile of Coleridge's and De Quincey's case (along with others such as the Ossian controversy) shows that the obsession with citation, literary history, and originality are all important subjects for Romantic criticism.

Despite the continuous interest in editorial matters relating to De Quincey's work, not least in connection with issues of plagiarism, there are very few studies that consider the role of citation in his oeuvre. Apart from a short article by Grevel Lindop in 1995, there is no secondary literature on how citation forms an integral part of De Quincey's writerly practice. Lindop's short piece 'examine[s] specifically the use of quotation from Wordsworth in De Quincey's text'.[9] The work Lindop has in mind is the *Confessions* and, while presenting a detailed intertextual analysis of this case, he is not really concerned with the theoretical ramifications of De Quincey's practice. Thus it seems appropriate to cast the net slightly wider and include a number of De Quincey's critical works. As a result, the attention will predominantly focus on his critical essays but also make recourse to his autobiographical writing, such as the pieces that have become known as *Recollections of the Lakes and the Lake Poets* (1834–39) or *Suspiria de Profundis* (1845).

The conceptual connection between citation and creation, and their role in criticism, is historically established. In a structuralist vein, Antoine Compagnon attempts to map and analyse the most important interventions of this development in *La seconde main, ou le travail de la citation* (1979).[10] While he distinguishes between different fields of citation, such as its phenomenology and semiotics, Compagnon's title also alludes to a theme that has often been associated with citation, namely iterability and repetition. Iterability, in turn, especially in its philosophical and theological dimensions, is a topic of central importance, most notably in contemporary philosophy of language. Famously, Derrida's notorious exchange with John Searle in *Limited Inc* (1988) centres on this theme. Balfour's recent account of the interrelation of citation, iterability, and prophecy shows how some of these aspects are directly linked in a Romantic literary context too. Speaking of the prophetic – a deeply Romantic concern – as a form of citation, he writes that 'Even if the prophet's word seems originary, it is always already a repetition of the divine one, a quotation with or without quotation marks. In general the Romantics demonstrate an implicit and sometimes explicit awareness of this predicament, which is at the same time a potential resource for poetry.'[11] Taking Balfour's brilliant analysis into a slightly different direction, I want to suggest that the predicament of which he speaks is also a potential resource for criticism.

Citation fractures both text and page on the most immediate and apparent level. Some writers throughout the nineteenth century are deeply aware of this. For example, the title of the pamphlet *Force of Contrast* (1801), attributed to Thomas Drewitt, already intimates this dynamic.[12] Here the page is split, *Glas*-like, into two columns, one competing with the other for authority. On one side of the page, the author cites a pamphlet that attacked the 'original' text, which the author wants to defend. This visible severing also points towards a more inherently linguistic or textual break performed by citation. A particularly striking example of a work openly thematising this aspect is Thomas Lynch's *The Ethics of Quotation* (1856). Here the image of the corpus as a textual body is employed to insist melodramatically on the disruptive power of citation: 'Tearing the verse limb from limb, he [the author's misquoting adversary] holds forth the fragments quivering and bleeding: and having, with far less skill than a butcher's, divided the poetic word; with the assumed wisdom of the anatomist, he proceeds to lecture thereupon.'[13] The quivering poetical body is ripped apart by being analytically and critically cut into pieces. However, not with a skill that might promise textual survival or accuracy. Rather, language is attacked, with even less anatomical ability than a butcher might display (an odd image, considering that a butcher, in fact, knows rather a lot about anatomy). The interpretative faculties of Lynch's adversary are, predictably, equally brutal. Posing as the clinically dissecting anatomist, this critic has only an 'assumed wisdom' in relation to the body that he is working on. Citation assaults writing in even more complex ways than Lynch's shrill anxiety suggests. It divides the page, both rhetorically and conceptually, reminding the reader that citation breaks up the very text it forms a part of. Within the citation one is reading and not reading a text in its particularity (that is, reading a piece by x and not by x at the same time). Simultaneously, however, it also severs the text that it is taken from. The cited passage fractures both constructs at once. A fragment of language is presented out of context or in a new context altogether. The disruptive force of citation works in two directions.

A citation is both a part and not a part of the 'new' text. It still forms part of the 'original' in which it was not a citation at all but which it now represents in fragmentary form. Sometimes the citation can gain a powerful momentum in itself, 'ceasing' to be a citation altogether, becoming irreducible. Maurice Blanchot suggests in *The Writing of the Disaster* (first published 1980): 'If quotations, in their fragmenting force, destroy in advance the texts from which they are not only severed but which they exalt till these texts become nothing but severance, then the fragment without a text, or any context, is radically unquotable.'[14] Blanchot reformulates the double-sided break that citation introduces, while also hinting at the deeply problematic status of a 'representational' citation as textual fragment. He intimates what might occur when this status is altered, suggesting that once the fragmentary citation becomes 'representational' it turns into a separate entity.

The conceptual implications of the citational process point towards another central aspect of its fracturing power. Citation not only fragments particular texts. It has a much wider and deeper dimension connecting it to both thought and language in general. To uncover this connection it is helpful to think about the philosophical and jurisprudential connotations revealed by the activity of citing. Any type of citation – including its linguistic form – is inextricably linked to the idea of the juridical summons. In citation, language both summons and is summoned in a number of ways. When De Quincey 'cites' Wordsworth, he uses him as an advocate. But, at the same time, he calls on Wordsworth's text to present itself to the reader: he summons the figure of 'Wordsworth' (a unique poetic identity). In doing so he also summons language itself, including his own. Benjamin forcefully articulates the implication of this position in his essay on Karl Kraus (1931):

From within the linguistic circle of the name, and only from within it, Kraus's polemical basic procedure reveals itself: to cite. To cite a word means to call it by the name. In the saving and punishing citation; Language proves itself to be the matrix [Mater] of justice.[15]

Benjamin intimates that the philosophical and legal connotations involved in citation can reach a level that encompasses 'Language' as such. The framework for this theorisation of the linguistic harks back to the ideas of Benjamin's earlier writings on language, discussed in the first chapter of this book. Benjamin's assumption remains that there is a fundamental rift, but also a deep link, between a prelapsarian *Ursprache*, a Language of plenitude, and fallen human or natural languages. The moment of citation in language, its breaking power, turns out to be structurally related to the fragmentation of Language into languages.

According to Benjamin, to cite a word is to call it by its name. This means not only to call it what one has judged it to be. It also, says Benjamin, reminds us that language, with all its names and words, separates the word from Language. Citation repeats this separation and mirrors it in the fragmentation of language on the page. For Benjamin, citation breaks the word out of its original context by reminding us that every word *has* a name. When this name is cited, called forth, it becomes a marker for the fallenness of the language it is part of – it does not belong to Language anymore. In other words: the name continues to point towards the impossibility of being cited before a court of Language; only the fallen post-Babelian tongue can be its judge. Although Language is still the framework and origin (the German 'Mater' refers to both 'matrix' and 'mother') through which the citation into language becomes possible, the citation itself must always involve a fallen medium. It performs a fracturing process that involves breaking the word out of Language.

Benjamin goes even further in his theorisation of citational power. In his essay he subtly varies the image of the 'calling': 'The citation calls the word by name, breaks it destroyingly out of the context, but through exactly that it also calls the word back to its origin.'[16] Here, citation itself calls and summons the word, rather than somebody or something citing it. Again, whenever citation calls the word by its name, it creates a moment and process of fracture. The call is a destructive power that breaks the word out of its context. Benjamin's image can be understood on two mirroring levels. On the first, citation breaks language; it is a rhetorical marker of fragmentation. On the second, every instance of language is already a citation, an incomplete and fallen version of Language. And every time we come across citation, it is a reminder of this division. However, Benjamin also suggests that there is a reverse side to this division when he insists that citation 'calls the word back to its origin'. While language is exposed as fallen, it simultaneously points towards its origin within a higher plenitude of Language. Whenever citation makes the fragmented character of language explicit, it also reveals Language as the ultimate source of that linguistic system.

In his philologically astute study, Manfred Voigts locates the Romantic sources of the dialectic that Benjamin invokes in his meditations on citation.[17] One of them is Ritter's already mentioned *Fragments from a Young Physicist's Nachlass*. Ritter is one of Benjamin's favourite authors and remains an important figure in the landscape of European Romanticism.[18] In his *Fragments* he describes and links the way an epitaph relates meaning to a citation of life from the region of death: 'Because the monument simply keeps us alive and gives life to to whom it is erected. [...] One cites life here, as Shakespeare and the Ancients cited the ghosts.'[19] Through the epitaph, the citation names (and preserves) the one who has ceased. However, it is not the name that gives the citation meaning, but rather the citation (through calling the word by its name) endows the name on the stone with meaning. Once we take the name on the gravestone to be a shorthand for a much wider 'linguistic circle', we can see how its position vis-à-vis citation is crucial. (The link to Wordsworth's *Essays upon Epitaphs* and the discussion in the first chapter is evident.) The idea of the epitaph as citation suggests a novel way of understanding Romantic poetry as citational.

THE INSOMNIAC'S CITATION

While not quite as metaphysical as Ritter or Benjamin, De Quincey shares with these two thinkers a concern to understand the relation between the mental and the linguistic through citation. In some of his critical essays, De Quincey suggests that an understanding of the relationship between thought and word is fundamental for an appreciation of language (and therefore, presumably, its poetical products). In a general aside in his 1848 review of Alexander Pope's newly published *Works*, De Quincey ponders the double-sided nature of language as a limited medium of representation:

The scale of an alphabet – how narrow is that! Four or six and twenty letters, and all is finished. Syllables range through a wider compass. Words are yet more than syllables. But what are words to thoughts? Every word has a thought corresponding to it, so that not by so much as one solitary counter can the words outrun the thoughts. But every thought has *not* a word corresponding to it: so that the thoughts may outrun the words by many a thousand counters. In a developed nature they *do* so.[20]

This rich passage suggests that there are thoughts that lie too deep for words. Not even the variety of possible combinations of the alphabet can capture the wealth of the conceptual world. The 'scale' of language expands from a linear alphabet, where 'all is finished' after twenty-six letters, to a circular and 'wider compass' through combination of its units, syllables, and, eventually, words. But the jump from the 'narrow' scale to the 'wider' compass is not sufficient to include the sphere of the mental. Although the linguistic relies on the mental, the mental does not rely on the linguistic. The 'race' between words and thoughts will always be 'won' by the thoughts. Evidently, De Quincey's unspoken target here is the widespread idea that words and thoughts are coextensive. The view that the formation of our ideas is bound by specific linguistic units, such as words, is presented as reductive.

For De Quincey, then, thoughts go further than words. Although words are the expression of thoughts, and the two correlate in this way, they are not to be misunderstood as two equal scales. The mental field is more extensive than the linguistic. De Quincey's stance is important for at least two reasons. First, he claims a place in the long history of discussions surrounding the relationship between the mental and linguistic. Secondly, his position has implications for his own writing as well as for his critical assessment of other writers. The passage on Pope illustrates how these two aspects combine in De Quincey's thought. It also suggests that if the analysis of poetry produces literary criticism, this will allow for a particular version of literary history that is not confused about its prime object (language). As a critic, De Quincey is deeply concerned about the status of the category of criticism and its tools. In a strange repetition of these concerns, scholarship has re-enacted a particular version of De Quincey's literary history that classifies him as a singular figure in the narrative of Romanticism.

A surprising amount of the secondary literature surrounding De Quincey's work emphasises his role as a writer at a critical juncture in literary history. After decades of relative neglect, recent years have seen the emergence of a substantial body of commentary on De Quincey. A surprising amount of this claims a singular place for him in literary history. Frederick Burwick, for instance, maintains that 'He [De Quincey] is the first to elucidate Wordsworth's poetry in terms of associationism. He did not invent the subconscious. Nor was he even the first to name it. But he was the first to use the term in literary criticism. In his criticism of Wordsworth's poetry, he identified the subconscious as the arena out of which the conscious mind draws its power.'[21] While not discussing associationism in detail, Alina Clej's important study *A Genealogy of the Modern Self* (1995) refers to De Quincey's sense of subject as crucial for his unique position in the history of literary criticism. She presents a De Quincey who, while indebted to Romanticism, ultimately breaks with it: 'I am interested in the legacy Thomas De Quincey left to modernity [...] De Quincey is one of the first writers, if not the very first, to experience and work out the symptoms of modernity.'[22] Ultimately, Clej believes, De Quincey allows modernity to be so distinctly different that it can be subsequently contrasted with Romanticism. In a different vein, Joel Faflak highlights the period between Romanticism and Modernism as crucial for an understanding of De Quincey's historical development. According to him, it is primarily Victorianism that De Quincey is shaping. Taking the different versions of the *Confessions* (1821 and 1856, respectively) as representative, Faflak reads the changes of De Quincey's self-editing as reflecting a move from a Romantic to a Victorian sensibility, paradoxically 'support[ing] and resist[ing] this distinction'.[23]

One of the most sophisticated and sustained discussions of De Quincey that has appeared in recent years is Margaret Russett's *De Quincey's Romanticism* (1997). As the title suggests, it explains how De Quincey helps to construct (and own) the category that he is often supposed to transcend. While Burwick, Clej, and Faflak take De Quincey to look forward from an already defined period, Russett shows how De Quincey is instrumental in the construction of that period. Her book pays particular attention to the importance of De Quincey in the establishment of Wordsworth as a representative figure of Romantic genius. It unveils the relevance of De Quincey as a critic of Wordsworth, and how their peculiar relationship affects both De Quincey's fiction and his criticism. In this context, Russett succinctly remarks that 'Wordsworth is canonized, then, by stripping away the accretions of his natural life to reinstate an idealized and immutable great decade, incarnated by De Quincey's recollections.'[24] This canonisation, which is an archivisation too, is a difficult process in which the two figures, Wordsworth and De Quincey, cannot be separated entirely. Although Russett offers a rich and highly illuminating reading of this complex development, she assigns little importance to the role of citation. However, it can be instructive to address the significance that citation plays in the *form* of De Quincey's recollections that canonise Wordsworth. Because he records in the way he does, De Quincey's role becomes inextricably linked to the image of Wordsworth and Romanticism that is created. As Russett herself mentions in relation to De Quincey's essay 'Wordsworth': 'The collapse of affiliation, while posing a problem of empirical authority, also suggests that authorship can never be owned singly – that it is always and necessarily a fractured and corporate endeavor.'[25] What I want to focus on here is how De Quincey's use of citation is a significant form of this 'fractured endeavor'. It is a fracture that, in itself, archives and reproduces an image of Romanticism that becomes De Quincey's as well as ours.

Citation is an inevitable part of any writing of criticism that proceeds via sources or examples. Therefore, its fracturing character arises as a central predicament of the possibility of establishing a critic's reading. In De Quincey's writing, textual break and citation, inextricably linked, represent a historically specific instance that connects Romanticism and the notion of fracture. De Quincey's writing also counts as one of the first bodies of texts to create the literary category of Romanticism. It becomes evident that couching the terms of this analysis through Wordsworth and De Quincey, then, is not simply following an Emersonian whim. In effect, it is a specific argument about how citation operates within Romantic literature and its critical reception for the construction of the category of Romanticism itself.

De Quincey's general aside in his review of Pope's *Works*, mentioned above, forms part of a complex set of relations between his Romantic present and future which De Quincey is at pains to clarify. The literary criticism on the Augustan poet also articulates an understanding of the era that follows him. Because Wordsworth is so closely identified with the Lake poets, as well as being an influential critic of Pope, De Quincey's essay indirectly forms part of his continuous project of defining his relationship to Wordsworth. Considering De Quincey's wider work, Wordsworth becomes more than just a mediating figure in De Quincey's statements about the interrelation between language and thought. A look at his texts suggests that the mentor continuously haunts his reader's attempts to negotiate an independent position vis-à-vis the mental and linguistic. De Quincey's strategy of citation is an example of how such a negotiation introduces Wordsworth's writing into the critical text in more ways than one. For instance, De Quincey's image of the race between words and thoughts is best likened to a citation transformed. He can also be much more direct. De Quincey champions a famous Wordsworthian dictum on language by giving a direct citation. Writing 'On Style' (1841) for *Blackwood's Magazine,* he insists that:

His [Wordsworth's] remark was by far the weightiest thing we ever heard on the subject of style; and it was this – that it is in the highest degree unphilosophic to call language or diction 'the *dress* of thoughts;' and what was it then that he would substitute? Why this: he would call it 'the *incarnation* of thoughts.' Never, in one word, was so profound a truth conveyed. […] If language were merely a dress, then you could separate the two: you could lay the thoughts on the left hand, the language on the right. But, generally speaking, you can no more deal thus with poetic thoughts, than you can with soul and body. (*DQ*, 12. 73–4)

De Quincey refers to Wordsworth's claim in the *Essays upon Epitaphs* that it is mistaken to understand and treat words solely like a dress of thoughts, both subsidiary and coextensive with the mental. Wordsworth's famous passage reads:

If words be not (recurring to a metaphor before used) an incarnation of the thought but only a clothing for it, then surely will they prove an ill gift. […] Language, if it do not uphold, and feed, and leave in quiet, like the power of gravitation or the air we breathe, is a counter-spirit, unremittingly and noiselessly at work to derange, to subvert, to lay waste, to vitiate, and to dissolve. (*Prose*, 2. 84–5)

We can see how this passage relates directly to De Quincey's later image of the race between thoughts and words. Both Wordsworth's and De Quincey's accounts imply that thoughts are not only a superficial or coextensive layer supposedly 'covered' by language. The linguistic and its creative powers are not purely a secondary tool. If language were solely ('merely') an additional dress, the division between and extension of the two would be correspondent and well defined (but would turn into the coat of Nessus). However, De Quincey insists that you cannot 'lay the thoughts on the left hand, the language on the right'. Although there is a divide between the mental and the linguistic, the character of this division is more complicated than the analogy with the 'dress' can capture. De Quincey's alternative image of the relation between the two spheres is revealing. According to him, 'poetic thoughts' and language are not divisible like body and garment. They are, rather, all flesh, with no need for a garment at all. The language of these truths is an 'incarnation' of thought, religiously joined together and as inseparable as 'body and soul'. Although it is not necessary to go as far as David Devlin, who claims that 'It is scarcely an exaggeration to say that Wordsworth's image made de Quincey a critic',[26] it is fair to say that the Wordsworthian formulation becomes crucial for De Quincey and his negotiation of language. Importantly for De Quincey, the distinction between thought and language in poetic thought is blurred, if not altogether impossible. 'Every word has a thought corresponding to it' and, presumably, there are still thoughts that lie deeper than words. But once the thoughts are 'incarnated' in the poetic utterance, they are indivisible from their linguistic expression. Words do not sink to the status of garments, and thoughts are transformed into human 'incarnations'. In poetic thought the mental, which corresponds to the soul, is not easily distinguishable from the words, which correspond to the body.

However, the origin of the fundamental fracture, which Wordsworth and De Quincey are intent on covering up, leads both of them to use an image that repeats this division. The 'soul and body' of intellect and language, coming together in a poetic 'incarnation', have ambiguous implications to say the least. As Frances Ferguson reminds us in relation to Wordsworth: 'For the "fallings from us," the "vanishings" within the life of the individual, […] suggest that neither human incarnation nor linguistic incarnation is a fixed form which can be arrived at and sustained.'[27] The traditionally dualistic connotations of the image betray that the supposed unity of 'poetic thought' is more problematic than it seems. It is not clear what kind of life this embodied thought would have. And the insistence on the impossibility of telling the difference between body and soul inversely makes the reader suspicious about attempts to overcome that division. Wordsworth and De Quincey remind us of the impossibility of referring unproblematically to a medium of meaning that could produce and express these 'poetic thoughts'. De Quincey's citation of Wordsworth cannot cover up the fundamental break that lies at the heart of language itself. As much as he attempts to overcome it, his efforts are still bound to a fragmented language which insists on the two-sided nature of the embodied or incarnated thought.

Although the importance of this image of incarnation is often invoked, very little has been written on the specific way in which De Quincey insists on the centrality of poetic thought. It is remarkable how the moments he mentions and cites as examples of such thought often thematise their own double-sided quality. For instance, another of De Quincey's critical comments on Pope reads:

The Essay on Man sins chiefly by want of central principle, and by want therefore of all coherency amongst the separate thoughts. But, taken *as* separate thoughts, viewed in the light of fragments and brilliant aphorisms, the majority of the passages have a mode of truth; not of truth central and coherent, but of truth angular and splintered. (*DQ*, 16. 345)

It is the 'truth angular and splintered' that will be the focus of attention here. The passages by Pope that De Quincey has in mind are 'splinters' that can be cited. Just as De Quincey remembers and reiterates Wordsworth's utterance on the incarnation of thought, he presents Pope's 'passages' as 'brilliant aphorisms'. They turn into truths that can be presented as exemplars of the eminent status of this Augustan poet. As such, they form part of De Quincey's personal memory as well as items in an archive of citations that will become central for his critical project. Both memory and citation here become part of, and begin to stand for, a particular way of recording and archiving texts and literature. In other words, it becomes a question of how the construction of a particular oeuvre (Wordsworth's, Pope's) or of a period (Romanticism) is connected to classifying and preserving writings in a meaningful way. And here the *mode* in which they become truths is relevant. Unless we believe that De Quincey's claim about the truthfulness of Pope's lines is inconsequential, it is reasonable to assume that the form or mode in which they are truthful is also meaningful. The representative citation lies at the heart of an archive that informs our understanding of such collections. Remarkably, though, De Quincey suggests that what makes Pope's lines into representative citations and examples is precisely the kind of splintered, fractured, and broken quality that the Wordsworthian incarnated thought supposedly avoids. The double-movement of the citation is captured in the image of splintered truths. How is a recording of these fragments '*as*' fragments going to be negotiated? De Quincey's use of citation becomes a concentrated enactment of the difficulties this process entails.

In *Suspiria de Profundis*, recording through citation is a matter of the powers of memory and recollection:

Rarely do things perish from my memory that are worth remembering. Rubbish dies instantly. Hence it happens that passages in Latin or English poets which I never could have read but once, (and *that* thirty years ago,) often begin to blossom anew when I am lying awake, unable to sleep. (*DQ*, 15. 153)

De Quincey's selective memory only retains poetical thoughts or truths which are 'worth remembering'. The archival power of his prodigious recalling allows the differentiation (and subsequent representation) to be qualitative rather than quantitative. 'Rubbish' is identified as inferior and 'dies instantly', thus keeping the archive (the texts 'worth remembering') unencumbered. On the other hand, what is remembered is stored and kept successfully; it rarely perishes and thus survives the judgement of both De Quincey's mind and time. Things or texts 'worth remembering', like splinters of truth, become part of an archive of fragments. These poetic passages have an organic and self-regenerating power. Rather than dying instantly, they 'blossom' anew in De Quincey's mind during his nights of insomnia, resembling a Wordsworthian 'renovating virtue'. Their restoring power of renovation is ambivalent, however. De Quincey's boast about his archival memory occurs in a passage of *Suspiria* that is part of the long and famous meditation on the death and funeral of his sister Elizabeth. As John Barrell has brilliantly shown in *The Infection of Thomas De Quincey* (1991), the death of Elizabeth is a scene to which De Quincey returns compulsively. Barrell summarises that 'De Quincey is at once haunted by a hateful memory, and actively colluding with the ghost.'[28] Citation, not part of Barrell's taxonomy of De Quincey's infections, is part of this tension too. In the passage above, the insomnia connected to the death of his sister leads De Quincey to cite blossoming passages that ensure Elizabeth's continued existence via his own autobiography. This revisiting via citation ensures the possibility for De Quincey of revising the scene yet again (as he does in the different versions of the *Confessions*).

That the blossoming citations are connected to death and destruction already foreshadows the fundamental conflict in De Quincey's account. Lying in bed (not quite his coffin), De Quincey continues writing of his memory:

> This being so, it was no great instance of that power – that three separate passages in the funeral service, all of which but one had escaped my notice at the time, and even that one as to the part I am going to mention, but all of which must have struck on my ear, restored themselves perfectly when I was lying awake in bed […]. I will cite all three in an abbreviated form, both for my immediate purpose, and for the indirect purpose of giving to those unacquainted with the English funeral service some specimen of its beauty. (*DQ*, 15. 153–4)

The passages of the funeral service restore themselves in De Quincey's constructing memory. His textual recollection is so acute that he becomes the perfect carrier or embodiment of the 'incarnations of thought' presented in St Paul's first letter to the Corinthians (the text traditionally used at funerals). During his insomnia, De Quincey's memory activates his archive of citations, of 'splintered truths'. They are associated and brought to life by iteration and 'restore themselves' to the mind. That they should stand in relation to the occasion which triggers the insomnia comes as no surprise: as De Quincey reflects on his sister's death, the biblical passages about perishable human nature come to life. This is telling, as the biblical verses are concerned with another kind of incarnation too. The division between corporeal and spiritual body and their respective roles in the resurrection is a central theme of Corinthians 1. The Pauline epistle speaks about the '*glory*' of the afterlife (which later helps to soothe De Quincey's grief about the loss of his sister) and its eternity through the image of the body: 'It is sown a natural body; it is raised a spiritual body. There is a natural body, and there is a spiritual body' (1 Cor. 14.44).[29]

His sister's spiritual body is not the only dimension that De Quincey's open reference to the biblical passage unveils: 'All glories of flesh vanish' (*DQ*, 15. 153). De Quincey is concerned with his own afterlife, too, and the afterlife of his text. To invoke a canonical passage such as Corinthians, which openly thematises different kinds of 'survival', foregrounds the dynamic of self-preservation. In the meditations leading up to the funeral De Quincey writes that

Man is doubtless *one* by some subtle *nexus* that we cannot perceive, extending from the newborn infant to the superannuated dotard: but as, regards many affections and passions incident to his nature at different stages, he is *not* one; the unity of man in this respect is coextensive only with the particular stage to which the passion belongs. Some passions, as that of sexual love, are celestial by one half of their origin, animal and earthly by the other half. (*DQ*, 15. 145)

Although there is hope that, in the end, the spiritual body of his sister will survive, the carnal aspect of sexual love is identified as keeping the subject in the realm of the divisible, making her emphatically '*not*' one. The example De Quincey gives for this anatomy of brokenness is the medical examination of his sister's skull after her death. Conjecturing from having seen 'a similar case' later on in life (his son), he knows that her seat of thought was 'laid in ruins' (*DQ*, 15. 146), broken up and destroyed. De Quincey is reluctant to speak about the 'disfigured images' (*DQ*, 15. 146) that the destruction of his sister's head undoubtedly would have produced. He rather cites the 'similar case', betraying a deep anxiety about the survival of thought and its expression in language.

We can see that De Quincey starts worrying in a number of ways about his own splintered truths *as* separate thoughts, truths worthy of recollection and citation. The resus-citation and eternal life of his corpus and incarnated thoughts are at stake here. Citation performs a central part in this dynamic of preservation. De Quincey suggests that a corpus can be made to grow organically and reach fruition through citation. Often a thought and a line suffice to 'restore' these citations to the status of a memorial by means of recollection. In this way, citation assumes an epitaphic function, a reminder of the possibility of resurrection and eternal life. As a piece of language, it brings to life and ensures both memorial and survival. Thus, the fragmenting power of the citation becomes the means by which to formulate a poetic funeral dirge 'worth' remembering and 'blossom[ing] anew'.

BREAKING THE CURRENT OF THE PASSION

Despite his prodigious memory, the tension between splintered truths and their blossoming, between fragmenting force and organic memory, can become too much even for De Quincey's palimpsest to master. The metaphor of natural unity suggests, against the funereal scene, that his memory reproduces citation flawlessly, without a break or rupture. This fantasy is not sustainable, and De Quincey himself indicates as much elsewhere. In the third essay of 'Dr Samuel Parr and His Contemporaries' (1831), he meditates on the fragmenting power of citation:

> He [Parr] objected, and we think most judiciously, to the employment of direct *quotations* in an epitaph. He did not give his reasons; perhaps he only felt them. On a proper occasion, we fancy that we could develop these reasons at some length. At present it is sufficient to say, that quotations always express a mind not fully possessed by its subject, and abate the tone of earnestness which ought to preside either in very passionate or in very severe composition. (*DQ*, 8. 75)

In this passage the theme of citation becomes a marker for a fracture in language as much as the fracture of the self. De Quincey's comments on Parr are in contrast to his unfailing memory of the funeral service, which could focus the mind on a fitting biblical passage. De Quincey presents the citation as an interrupting figure that is not appropriate in 'very passionate or in very severe composition'. Citation breaks and 'abate[s] the tone of earnestness' that is necessary in the epitaph. Parr's objections are, appropriately, judicious in nature and legal in connotation when bringing citation itself before the judge. The reasons for citation's sentence are not given, but, according to De Quincey, it is enough to feel them. In the essay on Parr, De Quincey points at the criminal trace that citation leaves behind. Full of citations, we become contaminated by others and cannot focus our minds. A citation 'always express[es] a mind not fully possessed by its subject'. The other's language and thought invade and take over. Passionate or severe composition does not allow for this self-abandonment. It cannot permit a rhetorical or conceptual break while developing – which is precisely what citation is and produces. This is no trifle. It is dangerous to expose a fragmented basis to language in matters such as poetry. After these quick assertions, the investigation of the interruption of citation seemingly stops short. Even the ever-digressing De Quincey states that he will not continue his discussion further but will wait until a 'proper occasion' when he can explain Parr more fully.

However, as Hillis Miller reminds us, De Quincey 'can never stop'. [30] And so, we only have to wait until the next sentence for an illustration of De Quincey's argument. He reasserts his agreement with Parr by citing a contemporary source:

A great poet of our own days, in writing an ode, felt that a phrase which he had borrowed ought not to be marked as a quotation; for that this reference to a book had the effect of breaking the current of the passion. (*DQ*, 8. 75)

De Quincey's example remains anonymous, referring only to 'A great poet' and 'an ode'. However, ultimately his investment in this question is sufficient to break his own current of writing. In the 1857 revisions of the essay he inserts an explanatory footnote. He specifies and contextualises his general claim in the following way:

This poet was Wordsworth; the particular case arose in the 'Ode on the Intimations of Immortality;' and I will mention frankly, that it was upon my own suggestion that this secondary and revised view was adopted by the poet. (*DQ*, 8. 470, [n. 75.28])

Omitting the citation saves the 'very passionate' composition. The poet preserves the organic 'current' and flow of his 'ode' and avoids an interruption of its structure. One of the reasons that make Wordsworth 'great' is not only that he writes odes with the same seriousness as epitaphs – a noteworthy suggestion in De Quincey's examples – but also that he follows De Quincey's advice and does not fracture the writing or reading process by citation. De Quincey wants to archive and pass on an unfragmented 'Ode' whose 'current of the passion' is unbroken.

Considering Wordsworth's importance for De Quincey, and in particular the significance of the 'Ode', the concern displayed by this footnote is telling. He convinces Wordsworth that an open display of fracture is detrimental on the grounds that the poem will read (against its own better knowledge and argument) as a more organic whole without it. The citation would reinforce what partly lies at the heart of the 'Ode' – a reminder of the fractures and irretrievable losses within our biographies. Therefore, it is relevant that De Quincey's footnote is actually inaccurate. From the first edition onwards, Wordsworth marks a citation that he takes from the Renaissance poet Samuel Daniel in the main text of the 'Ode'. The seventh stanza highlights this interception by citation marks: 'The little Actor cons another part, / Filling from time to time his "humorous stage"' (line 103).[31] Wordsworth does not write an additional note at the end of the volume as he does in referencing other 'borrowed phrases' in his poems that are not indicated by citation marks. Against De Quincey's judgement, in effect, he does break 'the current of the passion'. Thus De Quincey's interruptive footnote pinpoints the reverse of what it wanted to announce. Citation, and with it fragmentation, find their way into the heart of the 'great poet' as much as into De Quincey's canonisation of Wordsworth as representative for the period. De Quincey's slip allows us a specific insight into how his canonising work as a critic links citation and archivisation. On the one hand, it includes fulfilling a duty to prevent a 'great poet' from using a fragmenting citation. This will ensure the poem's organic growth and natural preserve. On the other hand, De Quincey is deeply aware that it is only through citation that the critical preservation of these poems is possible. The duty of the critic is also to cite. A crucial dynamic of this process is that citation concentrates and repeats this double-movement; in turn, the double movement itself plays an inextricable role in, and becomes a part of, the archivisation of poetical language through criticism.

In view of De Quincey's implicit concern to archive and canonise himself, it comes as no surprise that his anxious fascination with citation's power to reveal a fracture also finds its way into the 1856 version of the *Confessions*. While describing how he is walking from Manchester to Chester, De Quincey notes:

The clouds passed slowly through several arrangements, and in the last of these I read the very scene which six months before I had read in a most exquisite poem of Wordsworth's, extracted entire into a London newspaper (I think the 'St. James's Chronicle'). […] The scene in the poem ('Ruth'), that had been originally mimicked by the poet from the sky, was here re-mimicked and rehearsed to the life, as it seemed, by the sky from the poet. Was I then, in July, 1802, really quoting from Wordsworth? Yes, reader; and I only in all Europe. (*DQ*, 2. 160)

This proud self-advertisement of a prophetic critic is also an anxious examination of the gap that opens in his reading of the representation of nature and its repetition. De Quincey here turns into the Wordsworth of critics, the revolutionary and prophetic figure that he ultimately becomes in contemporary criticism. In his own version, it is he alone who can discover Wordsworth's citation in nature – and quote it. In De Quincey's narrative the poet is followed by the critic who rediscovers the poet's presence in nature. Part of De Quincey's objective is to disentangle the complex web of citation that precedes him. The sky is 're-mimick[ing]' the poet and thereby doubling a citation. Wordsworth's ultimate source lies in the text of nature. He oxymoronically 'orginally mimick[s]' his natural surroundings. Wordsworth's text, in turn, provides the basis for nature's citation from poetry, which is finally recorded by De Quincey. The invocation of a language of nature combines with a concern of how different languages ensure survival. Ultimately, Wordsworth's epitaphic nature lyric relies on the critic, quoting it, to survive. Mary Jacobus in her discussion of De Quincey suggests that he 'vexes the sabbaths of the grave with trepidations that are both echoes and quotations; with language that comes from else-where – from the past.'[32] The language of the past is both the traumatic scene of his sister's death and the language of nature that inspires his fatherly mentor to write the poetry which De Quincey repeats as the wandering prophet. This language of nature, however, is ultimately separated from the human subject that quotes it. De Quincey's construction insists on the fundamental separation between the two spheres, and citation becomes the rhetorical marker of this gap. The fracture also defines the critic's role, part of which is to record precisely this separation. For De Quincey, the Wordsworth of critics (and the critic of Wordsworth), reading and record-ing form part of a more general agenda that makes him the mediator of this Romantic voice, and establishes him as the primary mouthpiece of its inspiration. However, the illustration of this dynamic relies on the image of the fracture and difference between all the separate media (nature, poet, critic). The figure of citation both marks the gap between these spheres and, at the same time, is employed to negotiate between them.

As we saw at the beginning of this chapter, citation mirrors two crucially different aspects in language. The act of citation archives this tension by repeating it. For Benjamin, the two forces at work in citation reflect the fundamentally divided nature of language, even when citation is being recorded. Citation does both: it recalls the destructive moment that lies at the very heart of how our language comes into being. But, by showing us that it is broken out of Language itself, citation also reminds us of its origins in plenitude. To cite Benjamin again:

Before Language, both realms – origin as well as destruction – identify themselves in the citation. And reversely: only where they permeate each other – in the citation – is Language completed. In it [the citation] the language of angels is mirrored, in which all words, disturbed out of the idyllic context [*Zusammenhang*] of sense, have become motti in the book of creation.[33]

This is the mysterious and deepest aspect of citation's double nature. Both spheres, the destructive fracture and the origin, use citation to identify themselves. Citation becomes a concentrated figure of the double nature of language as it repeats language's fracturing predicament. By providing this nexus, citation is also the place where the force of fragmentation ('destruction') and its counterpart ('origin') meet. Here they permeate and interpenetrate each other. Citation records both the loss of Language and also language's coming into being through destruction and fragmentation. But it also records the origin itself, the existence of Language, from which the citation itself is taken. In citation these two lines cross and mirror each other.

It is productive to think about how De Quincey's practice of (and references to) citation relate to Benjamin's terms of loss and creation. The biblical passages that return during De Quincey's insomnia point towards a realm of plenitude. They refer us to spheres that transcend the fallenness of natural languages. Both thought and death are beyond the linguistics of the subject. However, their interrelation, albeit broken, comes to light in the linguistic citation that shows the gap between them to be unbridgeable. Citation breaks and fractures the text, standing as a powerful reminder of the permanent brokenness of language. For all of De Quincey's longing for unity, whether in the funeral service or in the case of the 'Intimations Ode', the citational quality of language accentuates its broken origin. De Quincey's anxious archivisation of himself and the figure of Wordsworth cannot but repeat this double effect. His critical essay 'Wordsworth' (1839), which forms part of the *Lake Reminiscences*, is a case in point.[34]

DE QUINCEY AS ARCHIVING ARAB

De Quincey's practice of citing Wordsworth in his account of Romanticism reaches intricate and complicated levels. Having presented Wordsworth as a poet of the highest order, De Quincey, in a passage that has become canonical, embarks on a discussion of a key moment in the as-yet-unpublished *The Prelude*:

And here I may mention appropriately, and I hope without any breach of confidence, that, in a great philosophic poem of Wordsworth's, which is still in M.S., and will remain in M.S. until after his death, there is, at the opening of one of the books, a dream, which reaches the very *ne plus ultra* of sublimity [...].

I scarcely know whether I am entitled to quote – as my memory (though not refreshed by a sight of the poem for more than twenty years) would well enable me to do – any long extract; but thus much I may allowably say, as it cannot in any way affect Mr. Wordsworth's interests, that the form of the dream is as follows. (*DQ*, 11. 80–1)

De Quincey then gives a detailed description (including citations) of the Arab dream that forms part of what we now know as Book 5 of *The Prelude*. His initial reservations about citing Wordsworth's autobiographical poem are noteworthy on a number of levels. According to De Quincey's argument, 'mention[ing]' a poem is apparently not at all problematic, even if it is still in manuscript form. It is the verbatim reproduction, the citation, which poses the difficulty; especially, as in this case, if the citation is of a poem that has not even reached the public.[35] Also notice that, for De Quincey, the 'breach of confidence' is not a matter of fearing *mis-citation* since his assuredness in his prodigal memory is still intact. For him, it seems, what is contentious is to precede the publication of the literary whole with a fragment displaced to a critical – ultimately receptive – context. Both his and Wordsworth's 'interests' are at stake in this archival sneak preview.

As we know, De Quincey overcomes his doubts and punctuates the essay with fragments from his own memory, citing various scenes from the book 'On Books'. Leaving aside the question of appropriateness (De Quincey's misjudgement and his further estrangement from his former mentor are notorious[36]), it is illuminating to pay attention to precisely how he incorporates and appropriates Wordsworth's poem. De Quincey's passage has provoked a lot of commentary, from philological analysis of source material to retrospective psychoanalytical readings. For a number of years it has been pointed out that in his recounted version De Quincey assigns the dream to Wordsworth himself or to 'the poet', rather than to the narrator of *The Prelude* or, as the 1805 version, to the narrator's 'friend'. The contextualisation of *The Prelude* blurs the intertextual lines indicating who experiences and narrates the Arab dream. Some time ago, Jane W. Smyser pointed out that De Quincey's slip (assuming it was one) comes at the end of a long chain of borrowings, quotations, and appropriations. The dream's ultimate source seems to have been a narration of the last of Descartes's three visionary dreams recounted in Andrien Baillet's *Vie de Descartes* (1692), which were possibly related to Wordsworth by Coleridge or Michel Beaupuy. Smyser remarks on De Quincey's 'curious error' in assigning the dream's source in Wordsworth's narration: 'Remembering with remarkable detail the whole dream passage of Book 5, De Quincey, nevertheless, made one error: he believed that the dreamer was Wordsworth. In the twenty-something years since De Quincey had read *The Prelude* in manuscript, his own artistic sensibility seems to have modified his memory – and in February 1839 he made, in a sense, the change which Wordsworth was to make only a few weeks later.'[37] According to this account, De Quincey's mistake results in a premature Romanticism.

More recent commentators continue to insist on the significance of this slip or 'error'. In some cases Wordsworth's text, and, by proxy, De Quincey's discussion of it, are understood as a citation. Ian Balfour maintains that 'the dream [Wordsworth's] is at least in part a "citation" of one of Descartes's dreams'.[38] While its status as a direct citation is unclear, the intertextual quality of these passages, Wordsworth's and De Quincey's, creates a web of allusions that is impossible to disentangle. This not only affects the difference between 'poet' and 'friend'. Wordsworth's Cartesian vision involves the Arab dream in which a 'semi-Quixote' plays the major role. This is not a straightforward figure either. As Angus Easson has pointed out, albeit in a different context, Wordsworth's poem extends the figure of Don Quixote to the Arab preserving shell and book. The quixotic Arab thereby also becomes 'the equally fictive Cide Hamete Benengeli, the supposed author of Cervantes's story, whose Arabic is feigned to be translated into Castilian for the romance's original readers'.[39] Considering this complex net of influences, allusions, and appropriations, it is significant (but not surprising) that De Quincey's text shifts an aspect of the dream and narration once more. What is remarkable is the *way* he performs it, employing the fracturing device of citation for his version of appropriation and transmission.

Margaret Russett's careful reading of this same passage successfully stresses De Quincey's appropriation of Wordsworth's Arab dream and its sources. She insists how important it is that De Quincey cites this particular part of the poem, including its mnemonic quality. As she shrewdly asks: 'What is the relationship between the apostle of the desert and the apostle who offers these preludic fragments of Wordsworthian shell to many readers of *Tait's*?'[40] Her answer concentrates on questions of influence by suggesting that De Quincey 'resembles a thieving Arab, absconding with someone else's treasure' and that he 'coerces such a recognition by misquoting the *Prelude*'.[41] Russett states that 'Quoting from memory, De Quincey in effect quotes *himself* – the picture of his own mind, receiving its "individual gractification" – rather than the manuscript as a worked artifact.'[42] While this is a very accurate general assessment, it remains to examine in textual detail *how* De Quincey quotes himself or Wordsworth. It transpires that he not only 'coerces' a critical recognition but presents citation *as part of* what is archived and canonised. That is, he makes fracture part of the definition of what is central to Wordsworth's passage. By proxy, it is central to one of Wordsworth's primary concerns in that passage, namely the survival of poetry. Fracture becomes part of the poetry that the thieving Arab De Quincey absconds with and presents to his future readers as the treasure of Romanticism. Importantly, this is not a harmonious process in itself. As several critics have noted in passing, De

Quincey's rich and insomniac memory fails him in 'Wordsworth'. The passages of *The Prelude* in his essay are, with one exception, all mis-citations. This is significant; not for pointing the finger at De Quincey – a rather boring and futile exercise – but because it alerts us to some of the implications of the archival manipulation and distortion involved in citation.

De Quincey places his own role at the very heart of the Wordsworthian passage, not only via canonising the older poet but also by making his own mis-citation part of the archive. He does not heed the citation marks with which *The Prelude* frames the friend's report. As was mentioned above, he transposes the experience to the poet himself: 'He [the poet] had been reading "Don Quixote" by the sea-side […]' (*DQ*, 11. 81) before falling asleep. By citing the wrong person De Quincey creates confusions about which character is the source of the dream. This also blurs which figure, via the citation, stands before the tribunal of the reader. All this is relevant when we consider one of the central subjects of the cited passages – the archivisation and survival of poetry. One way to understand the burial of the shell in the Arab dream is as an image of the preservation of poetry for coming generations. The Arab saves poetry from destruction and stores it for the future, thereby ensuring poetry's status as 'knowledge that endures' and its 'privilege of lasting life, / Exempt from all internal injury […]' (*1805*, 5. 65–7). This is exactly what De Quincey purports to do in his critical essay on Wordsworth. He not only 'resembles' the Arab, but cites himself into this role, in order to fulfil his 'errand' (*1805*, 5. 117) and secure the shell of Wordsworth's poetry for a future generation of readers. Because the method he uses to achieve this goal defines itself by and through fracture, it makes his practice immediately relevant in the larger context of this book.

De Quincey becomes the Arab preserving Wordsworth's text for times to come after the 'deluge now at hand' (*1805*, 5. 99). As we saw in the first chapter, this is no easy task. It is the nature of the shell (or poetry) that poses the most difficult problem. Remember that it is both a shell and a book:

> I plainly saw
> The one to be a Stone, th'other a Shell,
> Nor doubted once but that they both were Books, […].
>
> (*1805*, 5. 111–13)

The Arab carrying the shell also, like his burden, inhabits multiple identities. He is at once Arab and Don Quixote:

> the very Knight
> whose tale Cervantes tells, yet not the Knight,
> But, was an Arab of the Desart too;
> Of these was neither, and was both at once. (*1805*, 5. 123–6)

In paraphrasing, overlapping, and citing these passages De Quincey speaks of the 'other, which is a book and yet not a book, seeming, in fact, a shell as well as a book, sometimes neither, and yet both at once' (*DQ*, 11. 81). The lack of citation marks in De Quincey's reference to the text and the addition of two ambiguous 'seeming[s]' in his paraphrase are revealing. He, not *The Prelude*'s Arab, now carries an object that in his hands becomes 'neither, and yet both at once'. At this point De Quincey collapses Arab and shell into one via his mis-citation.

The problem of the status of what is to be archived, and how it is to be done, produces a pivotal moment. This tension finds its way into De Quincey's text through the practice of citation. His practice illustrates that only through fracturing Wordsworth's poem can it be archived critically. Citation, and hence fracture, is a necessary moment in the survival of poetry. As much as De Quincey's flight into the Arab's role attempts to escape the inherent difficulty, he has to repeat and exemplify the contradictions of his position. By extension, when citing himself into the role of the Arab, De Quincey is archiving not only himself but also the contradiction that his citation makes visible. That is, contradiction and the fracturing power of the citation are archived through De Quincey's practice. Hence it is telling that in his essay he should choose to cite the moment when the Arab carries the shell of poetry – a paradoxical moment that encapsulates the very problem that De Quincey faces. The citation repeats, within itself, the two-sided nature of the object to be archived *and* the form that this process takes. Through his citational and critical practice, De Quincey secures a contradictory mode at the centre of Romanticism. The *ne plus ultra* of sublimity becomes the locus of a double force that lies at the heart of the critical and organising principles of Romanticism.

CHAPTER 7

Philological fractures: Paul de Man's Romantic rhetoric

To connect highest scrupulousness with greatest brutality.[1]

COHERENT FRACTURES

This final chapter wants to take the reader into our Romantic present. It will do so by discussing the purchase fracture and fragmentation have as critical notions in contemporary theorisations of Romanticism. A small selection of texts by Paul de Man will be my main focus. His writings provide an important case for illustrating how fracture and fragmentation function both as critical and as heuristic categories in and for Romantic Studies. In this sense, the chapter is another case study, albeit focusing on texts that are historically situated in the late twentieth century. To argue that this approach is fruitful as well as methodologically sound already reveals part of the assumptions and conclusions that are at stake here. The introduction indicated why there are good reasons to understand de Man and other figures as forming, in significant ways, part of the historical projection termed 'Romanticism'. This not only relates to de Man as one of the most influential figures in the construction and theorisation of this very category. More importantly, it is to understand him as a figure of Romanticism. This is not a matter of simply equating de Man's writings with their Romantic subjects. Rather, it is a question of aligning them in a meaningful trajectory. An insight into certain parallels and affinities (only sometimes elective) between them improves an understanding of how they function as historical and conceptual categories. To shed light on this relation also illustrates how the necessary limitations of this book can form part of its methodological and conceptual force.

There are several reasons why fracture and fragmentation allow for a particularly insightful analysis of de Man's work. The most important of these is quite straightforward. Language stands at the centre of de Man's thought and system. As I will show, de Man himself assumes that the notion of fracture best describes the relation between language and the human. Fracture becomes a fundamental marker which underlies de Man's entire theoretical position. This aspect of his work will form the first point of analysis. Secondly, fragmentation is a term that attains special meaning at important moments of de Man's description of his own oeuvre and its connection to Romanticism in particular. He gives it a specific grammatical connotation, placing it above other notions that emphasise disjunction. Thus fragmentation links and includes the historical object of his study (Romanticism) as well as the surprisingly Romantic character of de Man's own work. That the same texts openly stress the specifically Romantic connotation of fragmentation further supports this choice. However, I should mention one important delimitation of these claims. The discussion does not attempt to represent de Man's position exhaustively: that would require an investigation on a different scale, and ultimately would run counter to the purposes of this book. The present chapter is another combination of minute reading and general claim; and while they are conceived as distinctly directed and powerful, neither of them is understood to be all-encompassing.

De Man's oeuvre has had a complex impact on Romantic Studies. Nearly all the critics mentioned in the introduction, and many more who renegotiate the boundaries between historical and theoretical research, acknowledge de Man as a major formative influence for their work. Figures such as Chandler and Hamilton remain very sceptical of de Man, while Redfield and Keach embrace his writings much more openly. In all of these cases, however, he is acknowledged to play a major role in the critics' thinking about Romanticism. And, while the impact that the discovery of de Man's wartime journalism has had on scholarship is unquestionable, it is also evident that his influence is still pervasive.

In the context of this book it is particularly important to consider how de Man's writings combine strong analytical claims with the constant awareness of their possible overdetermination. This is particularly prevalent in his later work, which continuously re-examines the intersection between history and how linguistic structures shape that history. Despite a strong commitment to clarity in his formal analysis, de Man propagates caution in relation to the terms that are at stake. This is particularly pertinent when he describes the object and medium of that analysis: 'But we seem to assume all too readily that, when we refer to something called "language," we know what it is we are talking about, although there is probably no word to be found in the language that is as overdetermined, self-evasive, disfigured and disfiguring as "language"' (*RT*, 13). This position can be transposed to de

Man's attitude towards period formation and our knowledge claims about such periods. As de Man himself famously suggests, 'The validity of a historical term such as *romantic* can only be evaluated heuristically, by the contribution it can make to the understanding of statements, not the ordering of data.'[2] If we take this invitation seriously, it must affect the object of study as much as the self-understanding of the discipline in which this study takes place: 'By the time a more valid history of romanticism will come to be written, it may well look very different from what we have come to expect literary histories to be.'[3] This means that our idea of history, and therefore literary history, needs examination.

In the process of this examination and construction, de Man seems to imply, the case and role of Romanticism is somehow special. Partly, this is the result of our contemporary position, which is still rooted in Romanticism. The very way the category of the literary is posed today shows our deeply Romantic assumptions. This includes the importance Romantic authors often attribute to the question of their very own history, what Redfield calls 'seeking to explain the history of their own representational possibility'.[4] Moreover, this history, and its Romantic description, is continuously changing. As Rodolphe Gasché, one of de Man's most subtle commentators, points out: 'Already to believe in an eventual and definite separation from Romanticism is indeed illusionary and naive, since it would imply that one already knows what Romanticism is.'[5] Given the lack of sufficient distance, we are unable to describe adequately the way that our Romanticism is altering the conception of history with which this period will subsequently be historicised.

Considering the present focus, the link that de Man establishes between language, history, and Romanticism is particularly important. It is instructive to notice when and where de Man lets his critical guard down in relation to a bind between precisely those central categories. He does so via the notions of fracture and fragmentation, both conceptually and in his vocabulary of analysis. The readings in this chapter will give an example of each case. To use Dickinson's image, quoted at the very beginning of this book: often in his essays de Man finds a 'gap', which he in turn wants to fill with an explanation. He ends up 'insert[ing] the thing that caused it' – and thus reproduces the same gap in his own system. That de Man's own broken origins turn out to be Romantic clarifies a link between contemporary scholarship and eighteenth-century sources. It allows for an insight into de Man's authorship as well as a more general, and positive, assessment of the historical continuity at its basis.

Moments of fracture form an important part of de Man's critical approach and thought. Sometimes he even puts fracture, via rhetoric, at the centre of his oeuvre. Given de Man's general critical method and objective, this is not altogether surprising. Certainly in some of his most important work, an eye for textual fissures combines with a resistance to synthesise too quickly. An emphasis on figures of break and mismatch are typical results. The most eminent and celebrated example is de Man's recuperation of allegory as central for an understanding of Romanticism. In de Man's later work there is a certain correlate about his general assumptions concerning ideology. After all, ideology, in the sense de Man understands it, is the result of a misguided attempt to mend a fracture. As he states: 'What we call ideology is precisely the confusion of linguistic with natural reality, of reference with phenomenalism' (*RT*, 11). By proxy, he emphasises the gap between linguistic and natural reality (albeit in order to insist on its role in ideological constructions).

De Man's texts match the attention given to textual disjunction of conceptual and tropological kind with an emphasis on rigour and systematic procedure that has become nearly proverbial in critical studies. The coherence and methodological precision of de Man's approach and discussion are integral to his critical project. While some readers have found his style alienating or even bureaucratic, there is very little question about its commitment to coherence, rigour, and stability.[6]

A curious tension emerges between de Man's commitment to coherence, on the one hand, and the emphasis on fracture, on the other. This chapter takes its cue from this tension and will use it to illustrate how de Man's work feeds off a broken origin deeply wedded to Romanticism. One of the initial puzzles about his rigorous approach is that he puts fracture at the centre of what amounts to a system. He maintains that both the system and the fracture are stable, or at least that stability is a desirable quality in them. However, as we have learned through de Man himself, a break at the centre of a system always has disruptive qualities. His own method of reading, especially his emphasis on the conceptual import of images and rhetorical figures, forcefully illustrates that. In focusing on the disruptive aspect of fracture and fragmentation, I want to recall my introduction which explained how the dynamics of these notions themselves form part of a figural system.[7] Thus, they cannot be straightforwardly included in a system. By their nature, these notions constantly threaten to disrupt the rhetorical network of which they are a part. They destabilise the system itself; and it is impossible to retain a disruptive force as the stable centre of a system. It is surprising that de Man finds very little to say about the potential disturbance at the heart of his own rhetorics that enables him to perform the sharp and alert discussions of instabilities in the works of

Rousseau, Wordsworth, and others. This translates into a conflict between de Man's style of clinical detachment, consistency, and rigour, and an insistence on fragmentation in a number of meta-theoretical moments in his work.

It becomes clear that to point towards the emphasis of certain rhetorical figures of rupture in his account, such as allegory does not answer how the identification of an unstable centre might affect his analysis of Romanticism. The invitation to read these figures back into de Man's texts is implicit in his work; one need not be a de Manian devotee to read *Allegories of Reading* as itself an allegorical representation of Romanticism. However, de Man's commitment to a broken centre goes deeper than particular figures: it is language itself that he defines through fracture and fragmentation. Albeit rhetorical in its nature, language (rather than rhetoric) is the most fundamental category of the de Manian system. More specifically, the broken relationship between human subject and language forms one of the central and most radical ideas in his writings. It becomes a remarkable example of how a destabilising dynamic of fracture is planted at the centre of de Man's assumptions.

CLEAN BREAKS: THE INHUMAN FRACTURE OF LANGUAGE

A number of openly methodological expositions in de Man's corpus effectively illustrate why the notion of linguistic fracture is a central aspect of his work. The most revealing of these moments is his lecture 'Conclusions: Walter Benjamin's "The Task of the Translator"', held a year before his death. This is an extremely complex text, which is often alluded to, and whose full close analysis remains to be written.[8] In the present context, I will touch on how it presents a number of issues connected to fragmentation and Romanticism.

De Man insists that a thesis about a fundamental break between the human subject and language lies at the heart of Benjamin's essay. He also largely adopts this position as his own, and presents his analysis of Benjamin's exposition accordingly. During the lecture, de Man states with some urgency that 'Benjamin says, from the beginning, that it is not at all certain that language is in any sense human' (*RT*, 87). From the very origin, 'the beginning', according to de Man, Benjamin ponders in absolute terms ('at all [...] any sense') the radical disjunction between human and language. Quizzed in the discussion following the lecture on the radicality of that break, de Man replies to Neil Hertz by again describing the sphere of language as absolutely distinct from the human: 'the inhuman is: linguistic structures, the play of linguistic tensions, linguistic events that occur, possibilities which are inherent in language – independently of any intent or drive or any wish or any desire that we might have' (*RT*, 96). The relentless repetition of 'any' makes it impossible to ignore the absolute character of de Man's claims about the break between language and human. The caesura, separating positive and negative parts of the definition, further underlines the insistence on the disparate nature of the two. The gap between language and the world we inhabit as subjects is at stake when de Man claims that 'Things happen in the world which cannot be accounted for in terms of the human conception of language. And they always happen in linguistic terms [...]' (*RT*, 101). 'Human conception' here denotes an understanding of language as part and parcel of the rational subject's self-definition, much in Schiller's sense, for example. What makes de Man's claim so important is that these 'Things' still happen in linguistic terms. Although the subject is completely severed from language, it is still impossible to conceive of the world in a non-linguistic manner. So it is no wonder that the investigation of the break between language and human is a prime source of intellectual investigation: 'Philosophy originates in this difficulty about the nature of language [...] which is a difficulty about the definition of the human, or a difficulty within the human as such. And I think there is no escape from that' (*RT*, 101). The discipline that de Man pitches against philology – philosophy – has its origin in the gap between the human and language. Insoluble, this problem is both exterior ('the difficulty *about*') and interior ('the difficulty *within*'), both general ('Philosophy originates') and deeply personal ('I think'). De Man is suggesting that the gap itself *and* our conclusion about it are inescapable. Considering the status that de Man assigns language, this complete severance must result in difficulties. Throughout his work, de Man insists that we understand the world around us in linguistic terms. We conceptualise the world and ourselves through language. In an openly Romantic tradition de Man argues that we cannot but understand our surroundings in a specifically linguistic way. Familiar examples include his descriptions of poetry and theory as categories that illustrate the privileged status of language particularly well.

De Man thus suggests that language is the framework through which we understand the world. However, he also argues that there is an inescapable gap between language and the subject. Throughout his oeuvre, de Man negotiates the origins of that fracture and its role in defining the subject. As he does not want to rely on any openly theological argument, this remains a gap in de Man's own theoretical framework.[9] Most importantly, however, this break at the centre of de Man's concerns, between language and subject, remains stable and seemingly well defined. It is not only inescapable, but it also seems to be fixed, or even static. The difficulties that arise from the fracture between language and subject lead de Man to invite us to examine the linguistic traces of what he terms 'initial discrepancies in language' (*RT*, 101). He accomplishes this by a rhetorical analysis which illustrates the consequences of those 'discrepancies' at the origin. Throughout his career he repeats this pattern of masterful historical and analytical readings. These interpretations, then, enforce a sense of the uncontrollable nature of language, ultimately suggesting a disruptive potential. Nevertheless, the origin of these disruptions, the original break of the medium, is curiously unaffected. The break, it seems, is a neat cut; slightly too neat, perhaps.

The cleanliness of the incision is partly the result of de Man's interpretative manoeuvres that present a version of Benjamin that he wants to subscribe to. One of these moves occurs through a famous image of fragmentation. Benjamin likens different languages to the broken pieces of a vessel:

Just as in order to be joined together the broken pieces of a vessel have to correspond to each other in the minutest details without resembling each other, the translation has to lovingly and in detail learn and assimilate the original's way of meaning rather than mimick its sense; this way they both, like a broken piece of a vessel, become recognisable as a broken piece of a bigger Language.[10]

In discussing this passage, de Man only briefly entertains the possibility that this is a 'religious statement about the unity of language' (*RT*, 90). Because he takes it as a given that Benjamin is convinced a 'trope and what it seems to represent do not co-respond' (*RT*, 90), he swiftly discards this possibility. As a result, an uncharacteristically hasty and quick reading leads him to Carol Jacobs's famous analysis of the passage, a variation of which he wants to adopt: 'We have a metonymic, a successive pattern, in which things follow, rather than a metaphorical unifying pattern in which things become one by resemblance. They do not match each other, they follow each other [...]' (RT, 90). Especially in his insistence on the role of metonymy, de Man is drawn into arguing for a very particular way of understanding *any* translation of this passage and disallowing possible ambiguities in either original or translation.

It is widely acknowledged that Harry Zohn's standard translation, which de Man takes as his main critical target in the lecture, is indeed particularly problematic in this passage (I will return to this later); however, the readiness with which de Man follows Jacobs rather than Benjamin in the 'translation' of the passage *and* the image is highly indicative. Benjamin certainly does suggest that the final outcome of translation is a broken part, still fragmentary. However, this does not mean that the history or argument that brings this state into being (and with it the impossibility of achieving totality *in* or *as translation*) is unnecessary or negligible. Nevertheless, Benjamin continuously insists that translation cannot be a matter of achieving perfect equivalence. De Man, however, seems to forget Benjamin's willing renunciation of redemption, and wants him to pronounce on the subject in a more definite manner. De Man (via Jacobs) presents Benjamin as making a point about particular translations and works. However, this interpretation relies on neglecting the wider, and for de Man unpleasantly theological, framework in which the image of the vessel occurs. De Man reads the 'initial fragmentation' as equivalent to the fact that 'any work is totally fragmented in relation to this *reine Sprache*, with which it has nothing in common, and every translation is totally fragmented in relation to the original' (*RT*, 91). The problem occurs because for de Man this apparently untranslatable *reine Sprache* (pure Language) exists, if at all, in relation to a specific natural language. Although he describes it as a language which 'does not exist except as a permanent disjunction which inhabits all languages as such, including the language one calls one's own' (*RT*, 92), he discards the possibility that this disjunction itself could be a link between different natural languages. However, de Man's own formulation of 'languages as such' allows the suggestion that the permanent disjunction might be a binding force for languages, albeit a negative one, on a higher, logically, and mythically prior, plane. The image of the vessel does not present the 'pure language' like an ideal – but structurally similar – version of an actual natural language, like German, French, or Flemish. Benjamin suggests, very much against de Man's will, that the pure Language (*die reine Sprache*) functions as a mythical but real *Ursprache*.

The alternatives, between a unity of language and a fragmented language, are not as stark as de Man suggests when he writes:

What we have here is an initial fragmentation; any work is totally fragmented in relation to this *reine Sprache*, with which it has nothing in common, and every translation is totally fragmented in relation to the original. The translation is the fragment of a fragment, is breaking the fragment – so the vessel keeps breaking, constantly – and never reconstitutes it; there was no vessel in the first place, or we have no knowledge of this vessel, or no awareness, no access to it, so for all intents and purposes there has never been one. (*RT*, 91)

Considering the care and alertness de Man usually displays as a critic, this is a remarkable passage. Its loose argument and structure display an anxiety that is all the more telling because the very centre of his critical system, language, is at stake. The natural language is '*totally* fragmented' (my emphasis), which is no straightforward thing to imagine, considering that this might mean it could lose representational power altogether. This fragmentation keeps occurring and has no redemptive aspect to it; it can never reconstitute even the fragment. The ambiguous continuity implied by the quality of 'breaking constantly' already indicates how de Man's argument attempts to push fragmentation towards stasis.

De Man's drive to stabilise the connotations of Benjamin's image exhibits itself in various ways. For example, notice that, according to de Man, all of these fragments seem similar if not equal in their qualities. When they are considered 'metonymically' they are interchangeable in de Man's system. However, one crucial aspect and insight of Benjamin's image is precisely that these fragments, just as languages, are all different in themselves. Yet they fit together because they derive from the same source. They converged in the mythical past (but may never do so again in the ever-unfulfilled, redemptive future). That does not mean that their sum 'constitutes a totality' in the present, which is what de Man fears. It only means that previously they might have done so. And even then they would have constituted something very different from their present status: precisely by their disjunction, languages retain a reminder of that. De Man invokes the idea of a fallen language throughout his work, and cites that very possibility via Jacobs's article, which specifically links fragmentation and a theological *Ursprache*.[11] However, he does not allow for this model to enter his reading here. Wanting to keep the gap between human and language as neat and untheological as possible ('the more you take the sacred out of this picture the better' [*RT*, 101]) leads him to purge his own readings to a degree that risks a blindness or even a certain dogmatism.

After his highly contentious interpretation of Benjamin's text, de Man makes his final move. He obliterates the image that led him to his reading to begin with. De Man utters in a quasi-biblical pronouncement that 'there was no vessel in the first place'. The repetitive absoluteness of the claims earlier in the paragraph prepares us for the final summary. In one sentence alone de Man claims that it is '*Any* work' at all that is '*totally* fragmented' in relation to a pure language with which it shares '*nothing*', and in turn '*every* translation' is – again – '*totally* fragmented'; ultimately, constant fracture results in '*never*' reconstituting (my emphases). De Man's language shows that the radical terms in which he reads Benjamin do not want to allow for an alternative approach. The system that puts this image in place, and is in turn fed by it, cannot itself afford any gap. Thus it is no surprise that another paratactic string of negatives follows, echoing the anxious radicality of de Man's earlier statements on the abyss between language and human subject ('*any* intent or drive or *any* wish or *any* desire' [my emphases]). Like a mantra, incantation, or funeral dirge, de Man repeats his negations, seemingly associating them with the constant fragmentation he describes ('*no* vessel [...], *no* knowledge [...], *no* awareness, *no* access [...], there has *never* been one' [my emphases]).

A remarkable statement frames de Man's litany: 'there was no vessel in the first place, [...] so for all intents and purposes there has never been one'. He ultimately attempts to smash Benjamin's image of the linguistic container into oblivion. De Man effectively tries to obliterate the source of the very discussion he is pursuing. Because there is neither epistemology ('no knowledge'), nor human consciousness ('no awareness'), through which we can have 'access' to an *Ursprache*, for all 'intents and purposes there has never been one'. 'Intents and purposes' aside – both categories that are at the bedrock of our problematic relation with language – de Man's attempt to erase the material image in Benjamin's text is noteworthy for at least two reasons. First, de Man's argument points towards an uneasy relationship to what supposedly constitutes a central part of his critical outlook, namely fragmentation. Secondly, it exposes the price de Man is willing to pay for keeping the stability of his system. He makes a claim for a stable chain of substitutions whose *telos* is already known by obliterating a specific image of disruptive fragmentation, such as the vessel, that leaves its ultimate outcome open. The desire for stable fracture reaches the point where it has to do away with the material traces of its disruption. Shortly, it will become clear that, rather than its desired outcome, this strategy, in fact, itself creates a further destabilisation of reading.

DE MAN'S TASK: SEEING THINGS CLEARLY

The uncharacteristic insistence on the singularity of a correct interpretation permeates de Man's piece on Benjamin. Even considering its status as a short lecture, it is surprising to encounter so many instances in which de Man fails to mention possible ambiguities of Benjamin's complex text. Strangely enough, the few times when de Man does insist on the inherent multiple meanings of central terms in Benjamin's argument, his points seem strained. Once language itself is at issue, it becomes difficult for de Man to include inevitable misunderstandings as part of his argument. What in other moments in his corpus ranges from humorous inventiveness (Archie Bunker's 'what's the difference?') to attentive sonorous detail (Rousseau's 'Marion') in this essay seems unnecessarily forced and ultimately unconvincing. This contrast appears so starkly precisely because large parts of the lecture stress the importance of one particular way of reading plurality.

For de Man, the prime task of the lecture is a matter of assessing the difference between translations, discarding inadequate ones, and offering substitutions for them. Ultimately, the objective is getting it 'right', and finding out how one might develop a method of discerning between different interpretative options. This all seems straightforward (if not innocent) enough. However, in this case de Man's method goes beyond the theoretical awareness and direction that his interpretative exercises show elsewhere. Throughout his corpus he betrays – much in contrast to misguided accusations of relativism – a legacy to traditional goals of Enlightenment criticism.[12] In this particularly self-reflexive piece, however, his commitment to clarifying the propositional content of what Benjamin is 'really' saying leads him to develop a critical blindness. And, as de Man himself tells us, it often is instructive to understand where exactly those critical blindspots are located.

De Man's Socratic nod towards the rhetorics of humility at the beginning of his lecture is a good case in point. He states that 'We now then ask the simplest, the most naive, the most literal of possible questions [...]: what does Benjamin say?' (*RT*, 79). Just as the string of negative parataxis already quoted, this is a list of absolutes. It ends, half tongue in cheek, with the 'most literal' question about the direct propositional statement of Benjamin's text. This interpretative task is specified further in the next sentence: 'What does he say, in the most immediate sense possible?' (*RT*, 79). Hence, immediacy is the preferred method and access to the propositional content of Benjamin's essay. Considering the notoriety of the text, and de Man's previous statement that 'you are nobody unless you have said something about this text' (*RT*, 73), it is strange that he should consider it apparently 'absurd to ask a question that is so simple, that seems to be so unnecessary [...]' (*RT*, 79). The seemingly simple task is admittedly much harder than previously thought. 'But it seems that, in the case of this text, this is very difficult to establish' (*RT*, 79). While all these statements seem to prepare for a reading that draws out the ambiguities of the text, de Man is maybe slightly too fast in identifying his critical target: 'Even the translators, who certainly are close to the text, [...] don't seem to have the slightest idea of what Benjamin is saying' (*RT*, 79). Not to have 'the slightest idea' is failing to comprehend the propositional content on all levels. It includes not 'see[ing]' 'certain things' (and also things that are certain) which 'Benjamin says […] rather simply in one way' (*RT*, 79) – and one way only, de Man seems to say. The two translators de Man mentions, Harry Zohn and Maurice de Gandillac, fail on all of these accounts. De Man polemically suggests that the philosopher Gandillac must not be capable of telling 'the difference between something *is* and something *is not*' (*RT*, 79), considering that he fails this most basic ontological exercise in his translation. Considering this shortcoming, it is no surprise that he is deemed unsuccessful in transposing Benjamin's meaning correctly from one language into the next. For all the polemics, it is worthwhile attending to de Man's insistence about the assumed simplicity of the task: 'It is not more difficult than that, but somehow he [Gandillac] doesn't get it' (*RT*, 79). This, then, seems to be the mystery: how can somebody get something so simple, so wrong? In other words, de Man is picking up on moments where 'The original is absolutely unambiguous', and 'Benjamin very clearly says' one thing rather than another (*RT*, 81 and 85). In these cases, 'the stress[es]' of the sentences can be determined 'precisely', making the original 'unambiguous' (*RT*, 85). As a de Manian strategy this move seems unusual, especially as it is not always paired with a distancing self-analysis. As a result, the continuous insistence on the clarity and obviousness of Gandillac's and Zohn's mistakes gains a strangely obsessive character.

The image and issue of clarity often permeate de Man's discussion of ambiguity. The lecture is no exception. In a strange move, the translators are repeatedly accused of not seeing an ambiguity clearly enough to make a decision *against* it.[13] De Man's discussion and challenge of Zohn's choice to translate the title of Benjamin's essay as 'The Task of the Translator' (rather than 'The Giving-Up of the Translator' or 'The Defeat of the Translator') are well known. I do not want to dwell too much on the power of de Man's reading,[14] but mention it as an instance where de Man seems to veer away from his trajectory of looking for 'the most immediate sense possible' in both understanding and translation. We begin to see how the disparity between the 'simple' mistake and the 'most immediate sense' begins to diminish substantially. After discussing the multiple meaning of 'Aufgabe', de Man points at yet another moment in Benjamin's text, which he thinks both Zohn and Gandillac crucially misunderstand. Again it is a translation of a noun that de Man takes issue with. He quotes only the last part of the following Benjamin passage (I have italicised the fragment which he chooses to present as 'Benjamin's text'):

Because, like the tone and meaning of great poetry alter completely over the centuries, the mother-tongue of the translator also alters. In fact, while the poetic word in his language remains, even the greatest translation is destined to merge into its own language, and perish in the renewed one. It is so far away from being the deaf equation of two deceased languages *that, in between all forms it is its most characteristic devolvement to call attention to the after-ripening of the foreign word, and to the birth-pangs* [Wehen] *of its own.*[15]

De Man's charge against the translators of this passage is yet again their lack of clear sight, and a misreading of the evident propositional content before their eyes: 'Here too the translators, with considerable unanimity, cannot see this statement' (*RT*, 84–5). De Man's main complaint relates to the last part of Benjamin's passage, and in particular the word *Wehen*. De Man humorously conjectures that an unfortunate mutual agreement across Zohn's English and Gandillac's French has taken place: 'The two translators – I guess they didn't correspond with each other, they did this *d'un commun accord* – translate *Wehen*, pains, as "birth pangs," as being particularly the pains of childbirth' (*RT*, 85). According to de Man, this is yet another quite simple error, and so 'Why they do this is a mystery' (*RT*, 85). However, the translation is neither as clear nor as mysterious as de Man claims (he renders *Wehen* into English as 'sufferings'). In effect, the curious coincidence might have given de Man food for thought. *Wehen*, both in this context and in colloquial use, from the Luther Bible (mentioned as an exemplary translation by de Man) and Grimm's dictionary to Benjamin's era, until today, does indeed have the specific connotation of the pains associated with childbirth. It is not clear whether de Man simply turns a blind eye to this tradition or cannot abide the thought of feminising Benjamin in such a way. Especially, as he himself jokingly points out, because the pangs of childbirth would base the image on experiences of radically limited access: birth pangs are associated with 'producing something – and that is a magnificent moment, you'd be willing to suffer (especially easy for us to say)' (*RT*, 85). Everybody knows who 'us' is here, men, and everybody must know that 'we' cannot have birth pangs. In other words, the experience the image is based on will ultimately be inaccessible, but apparently still something 'we' can know. The 'birth pangs' look quite a lot like translation after all.

However, as the predetermining subclause indicates, de Man wants or needs to read *Wehen* as 'pains' or 'any kind of suffering, without necessarily the connotation of birth and rebirth' (*RT*, 85). There is a specific reason for this, which does not seem too mysterious, but is certainly far away from Benjamin's 'most immediate sense possible'. De Man wants to dissolve the juxtaposition of *Wehen* and *Nachreife* (for which, incidentally, he never gives an English translation, but only a German alternative:

Spätlese). Ultimately, this manoeuvre leads to the rejection of Benjamin's position of balance in favour of a 'stress' that is 'perhaps more on death than on life'. These sufferings, according to de Man, 'are not in any sense human' (*RT*, 85). The reader will recognise how this fits into the larger project on examining and solidifying the rift between human and language. In this particular case, de Man's reading neglects the grammatical and linguistic balance in Benjamin's language in the sentence in question. Benjamin's construction presents an array of carefully chosen concepts and words, which, arranged in pairs, create a striking balance: *zwei* [two]: *Gleichung* [equation]; *alle Formen* [all forms]: *Eigenstes* [the most particular]; *Nachreife* [after-ripening]: *Wehen* [birth pangs]; *fremd* [foreign]: *eigenen* [own]. What is important to pinpoint here is that de Man thinks it is *easy* to see the type of mistake Zohn and Gandillac make, and that it is there for everybody to be inspected. According to de Man it is a 'mystery' how they could translate *Wehen* otherwise, be so insensitive to propositional content and the language of the original. Just as de Man's lists of absolutes, this assumes a type of insight that de Man already had admitted cannot exist without blindness.

At critical moments, then, de Man suggests that the remedy against mistranslation and misunderstanding is quite simple. What is translated is the rupture and fragmentation of language as a whole, but that fracture and the way the transposition is performed remain stable. In the case of the image of the vessel, for example, this seems to be easy enough provided you have the right vision: 'All you have to do, to see that [that translations remain fragmentary], is translate correctly, instead of translating like Zohn […]' (*RT*, 90). This is a peculiar position, the insight sounding dangerously natural to the initiated. In fact, de Man's argument only makes sense if you already know German to begin with, and can transpose correctly. There are two assumptions here that deserve further scrutiny: first, 'seeing' the original is enough to gain its propositional content. Secondly, once this is accomplished, translation will be successful, if you are familiar with both languages. The second might seem obvious, but is in fact far from uncontroversial (as de Man himself points out later); to 'know' German and English might be a necessary but certainly not a sufficient condition to understand and translate Benjamin. The deceptively simple but crucial point about de Man's argument seems to be that, if all this were in place, there would be no need for translation at all. If I understand Benjamin correctly, I can translate him; if I do not understand him, I will mistranslate (like Zohn). However, in relation to both propositional content and the proficiency of language, this can only be part of the story.

It is strange to claim that the only way to 'see' the correct translation is to read the original correctly. This might be a description on de Man's part ('all you have to do'), but it is certainly not an argument for his interpretation of Benjamin's text. The ability to 'see' these mistakes and correct them assumes similar linguistic structures. An extreme consequence of this way of reasoning occurs in de Man's equation of two related but nevertheless different languages. While discussing the question of conceptual and sonorous shifts in connotation through translation (i.e. how is the German *Brot* different from or the same as the French *pain*?) de Man states: 'I was very happy with the word *Brot*, which I hear as a native because my native language is Flemish and you say *brood*, just like in German [...]' (*RT*, 87). De Man's strange claim goes further than arguing for privileged access as a native speaker; it makes Flemish and German 'just' the same, which precisely they are *not*. This is more than another idiosyncratic version of his strategy to claim a special way of accessing conceptual content and its translation into another tongue via a set of connotations.[16] It is precisely because languages are not the same (even if they 'look' it) that one cannot 'just' see things, especially if one does not speak all the respective languages (and even then it is not at all clear that one can). Languages might stand in varying relations to one another, but the Tower of Babel reminds us that they are ultimately separated in kind rather than degree. The simplicity that de Man alludes to is only available for those who do not have a need to translate in the first place (or think they do not have to). In order to present Benjamin as a stable, 'clear' force at the centre of his system, de Man has to minimise the ambiguities his own interpretation relies on.

These slippages in de Man's lecture uncover the importance of fracture for certain central assumptions of his critical framework and imagery. It is not surprising that De Man wants to appropriate Benjamin as a figure who holds very de Manian views. Given the crucial function that Benjamin serves for de Man's critical formation (think of the theory of allegory, for whose articulation Benjamin's seminal *Origin of German Tragic Drama* [1928] is so important), this is not surprising. In this sense, de Man's lecture is *his* 'Task of the Translator' essay. The lecture is de Man's essay on translation, and a supposedly Benjaminian illustration of how to translate 'correctly'. This also makes de Man's essay, like Benjamin's, a 'poetics, a theory of poetic language' (*RT*, 80), and it should be read as such.

De Man points out how a misunderstanding of Benjamin's essay entails a fundamental misrepresentation of language's character per se. His own version of the essay and especially the conclusions his correct translations allow him to draw presumably are of the same stature. As we saw at the beginning of the chapter, one of these conclusions is precisely the localisation of a fracture between human and language. This fracture is nevertheless fixed by de Man 'seeing' the obvious, reading it 'correctly', and presenting its propositional content in a manner that is a variation on a much more general theme in his work. After all, the 'Task' essay is 'just to repeat once more what I [de Man] have been saying since the beginning' (*RT*, 73). It is a repetition of de Man's original utterance, at whose heart lies a linguistic break. Considering its location and function, it is no surprise de Man attempts to preserve the break intact.

THE FRAGMENTARY ASPECT OF THE WHOLE

De Man's lecture exhibits its strong links to the study and practice of Romanticism in various ways. Most openly it occurs through using Benjamin as a backdrop, a figure whose connection to Romanticism, especially in his theory of language, is well known. This choice of material points towards the deep but uneasy relationship of de Man's own Romantic legacy that he negotiates via linguistic fragmentation. In writing his version of the 'Task' as a 'poetics', de Man also subtly places both Benjamin's and his own contribution into the Enlightenment's and Romanticism's traditions of theoretical debates on the origin and nature of language, a topic that recurs throughout de Man's corpus. Just in case anybody overlooked the implicit textual reference of the lecture, he reinforces this trajectory in the discussion following it, mentioning Schiller, Hamann, and other 'funny theories of language in the eighteenth century' (*RT*, 100). It is evident that de Man classifies Benjamin, especially in his statements on language, as a prominent representative of a particular version of Romantic linguistic theory. By placing language at the centre of understanding aesthetics, Benjamin represents a link between the late eighteenth century and de Man. In all of these three cases language is also connected to, or defined through, fragmentation.

De Man, despite some assurances to the contrary, is also firmly embedded in the Romantic line of thinking that is affected by the fragmentary. The link to Romanticism, its construction, and to its description, becomes particularly evident in the short preface to *The Rhetoric of Romanticism* (1984), a text that he wrote in the same year of delivering the 'Task' lecture. While the 'Task' essay is a relatively coded commentary on de Man's relation to earlier sources, the preface makes it much clearer how his linguistic theory of fracture also lies at the centre of his definition of Romanticism.

At the very beginning of the *The Rhetoric of Romanticism*, de Man has to 'confess that I still look back on it [the collection of essays] with some misgivings' (*RR*, viii). The immediate biographical and hermeneutical exercise fills him with Rousseauean apprehension and distrust. One of the sins de Man has to confess is having produced an archetypal enactment and representation of a Romantic ruin: the 'evidence' of de Man's 'failure to make the various readings coalesce is a somewhat melancholy spectacle'. According to de Man, *The Rhetoric of Romanticism* is a Romantic allegory of disjointed parts, a 'melancholy spectacle' of fragmentation for the reader to behold. Here is the passage in full:

Such massive evidence of the failure to make the various individual readings coalesce is a somewhat melancholy spectacle. The fragmentary aspect of the whole is made more obvious still by the hypotactic manner that prevails in each of the essays taken in isolation, by the continued attempt, however ironized, to present a closed and linear argument. (*RR*, viii)

Part of what de Man suggests, tongue very firmly in cheek, by referring to the 'fragmentary aspect of the whole' is an impossibility of claiming to have established a coherent picture of Romanticism in this collection. The inference, that this might not be possible, or desirable, is already embedded in de Man's prose. Correspondingly, the set of critical readings he provides are inextricably linked to his theory of understanding Romanticism, which in turn results from his all-encompassing theory of language. The conviction that there is an irredeemable fracture between language and human, articulated with such force in the 'Task' essay, here finds its way into the assumptions and conclusions underpinning de Man's readings, all of which discover fissures at their subjects' centres.

As we have seen in the lecture on Benjamin's essay, one central tenet of de Man's theory is that the relation between language and subject is irredeemably fractured. In de Manian terms this can be understood as a philological break, in the sense that it precedes the formulation of aesthetic appreciation.[17] The link to philology here is not arbitrary, especially if we consider that Benjamin represents a cornerstone of de Man's philological background. For both figures philology plays a crucial role in understanding the linguistic conditions that result in Romanticism. One of these conditions is the fracture at its linguistic conception. Hence a definition of Romanticism will already contain that break. Thereby de Man's fracture becomes an active element in the description of Romanticism, incorporating it as a defining feature.

However, while de Man is surveying the 'fragmentary aspect' of his work, he is reluctant to admit the intentional placement of such a breaking force.

In fact, he distances his work from approaches that take the 'fragmentary nature' of their object's analysis as a 'stylistic principle of their own critical discourse' (*RR*, ix). After the description of his work as 'fragmentary' this seems strange; particularly if we assume that it is his own system which produces the 'failure to coalesce' that he had just referred to. Instructively, the examples de Man presents to illustrate his statement are Adorno and Erich Auerbach, another two philologists. De Man takes issue with, respectively, Adorno's treatment of parataxis and Auerbach's 'references to the fragmentary style of his own book in the final chapter of *Mimesis*' (*RR*, ix). This is a surprising but telling choice, especially considering de Man's close relation to Benjamin, who very explicitly relies on a highly fragmentary mode in his criticism. We remember that Benjamin's early work on German Romanticism and tragic drama (*Trauerspiel*), alongside his theologically inflected writings on language, links fragmentation and linguistics. And, as always with Benjamin, his insights connect to the 'stylistic principles' with which he presents them. Adorno himself refers to Benjamin's *Arcades Project* along these lines when he writes 'When you yourself describe the work as "unfinished", it would be completely conventional and foolish if I were to contradict you. You know too well how closely the significant is related to the fragmentary here.'[18] Similarly Auerbach's reference to his fragmentary style in *Mimesis* reads more like a description of de Man's comparative method than the aphoristic tendency the latter implies:

It is possible to compare this technique [...] with that of certain modern philologists who hold that the interpretation of a few passages from *Hamlet, Phèdre,* or *Faust* can be made to yield more, and more decisive, information about Shakespeare, Racine, or Goethe and their times than would be a systematic and chronological treatment of their lives and works.[19]

This does not seem so distant a method from de Man's. He wants to convince the reader and himself, however, that his writing does not allow for the fragmentary as 'stylistic principle'. In fact, he can, by contrast, 'of course, make no such claims' of the kind Adorno and Auerbach make. The sub-clause ('of course') attempts to give the examples and his own position an attempted air of self-evidence. However, it masks that this relation is far from straightforward. It relies on de Man's successful description of his own intentions and drives.

Continuing his confession, de Man 'feel[s] [him]self compelled to repeated frustration in a persistent attempt to write as if a dialectical summation were possible beyond the breaks and interruptions that the readings disclose' (*RR*, ix). Against his better knowledge, de Man writes as if he could draw a mathematically balanced conclusion from his approach. 'Beyond the breaks' in this case means both 'after' and 'above' them: in the collection as a whole, and the intellectual coherence the book might present. Despite admitting that his own work discovers and illustrates fractures in the texts that he discusses ('breaks' that the readings 'disclose'), even suggesting their inevitability, de Man here wants to except the intentional manipulation of his writing from this dynamic (this is not always so, as we have seen). Finally, linking fragmentation and Romanticism, de Man continues to comment on Adorno and Auerbach: 'By stating the inevitability of fragmentation in a mode that is itself fragmented, one restores the aesthetic unity of manner and substance that may well be what is in question in the historical study of romanticism' (*RR*, ix). This highly complex statement is a good illustration of how a concern for stability in de Man combines with a rationalisation of the fractured relationship between him and the language he uses for analysis. While he knows that it is a vain belief, he writes in the hope that 'a summation' is possible. However, it is a summation that is different from acknowledging the aesthetic unity of manner and substance. While de Man continuously insists on instabilities, 'breaks and interruptions', he does not want to write in them. The preface, nevertheless, has already intimated that the fractures affect his own textual body too. For all his attempts to escape 'restoring the aesthetic unity of manner and substance', he must still admit that he has composed a Romantic ruin, a 'melancholy spectacle'. In fact, this is the motivation, the urge, and the necessity of the confession.

The tension between the poles around the broken origin of de Man's project dominates the entirety of *The Rhetoric of Romanticism*. De Man gives a telling description of the 'fragmentary whole' which we behold when he singles out the hypotactic manner that prevails in each of the essays taken in isolation. This is motivated 'by the continued attempt, however ironized, to present a closed and linear argument. This apparent coherence *within* each essay is not matched by a corresponding coherence *between* them' (*RR*, viii). De Man's stress on a hypotactic method attempts to present his work in direct opposition to Adorno's stress on parataxis that he has already mentioned. The sentence describing the 'fragmentary whole' itself represents an example of his method, with the interjection of 'however ironized' offering an exemplary hypotactic sub-clause. The problem for de Man, as he himself admits, is that this hypotactic structure still fails to cohere as a whole. *The Rhetoric of Romanticism* is presented as a hypotactic sentence that, for all its attempts to be stable, collapses and fragments because it ultimately fails to sustain grammatical coherence. The words (the essays) of that sentence (the book) might be, at least 'apparent[ly]', cohesive, but they are continuously threatened by severance.

Only through the coherence of the whole can the particles of the sentence correctly and cohesively refer. The crucial aspect of hypotaxis in relation to fragmentation is that 'In hypotaxis the subordinate clause relates either to a constituent of the principal sentence (and thus assumes the function of a sentence-constituent) or to the principal sentence as a whole; this relation is not reversible.'[20]

It is important that the relation between the whole and its fragmentary particles 'is not reversible'. This is one of the ultimate meanings of de Man's 'fragmentary aspect of the whole' and its 'failure to coalesce'. For all of de Man's proverbial rigour, the attempted sentence of *The Rhetoric of Romanticism* as a whole never was, nor will be, nor could be, coherent. However, as Northrop Frye points out in reviewing precisely this passage, 'Perhaps this is true, but [...] the fact need not be a deficiency. What is interesting is that the assumption in *Blindness and Insight* that such books were theoretically very dubious no longer seems to be an assumption.'[21] Ultimately, de Man's essays remain fragments in a wider structure that cannot successfully reproduce that coherence. They are the ruined fragments of the 'melancholy spectacle', and simultaneously give an account of Romanticism that includes that fragmentation in its definition and praxis.

What makes this a forceful, if peculiar, systematic statement on de Man's part is that it is still linked to a vision of fracture at the very basic, philological, level of language. As a linguistic construct, a phrase such as *The Rhetoric of Romanticism* will suffer from the much-cited 'curse' and 'privilege' of language: 'It is the distinctive privilege of language to be able to hide meaning behind a misleading sign, as when we hide rage or hatred behind a smile. But it is the distinctive curse of all language, as soon as any kind of interpersonal relation is involved, that it is forced to act this way.'[22] A rhetorical analysis of a sentence, phrase, or structure, such as *The Rhetoric of Romanticism*, reveals 'that no grammatical decoding, however refined, could claim to reach the determining figural dimensions of a text' (*RT*, 15). As de Man's famous example reminds us, this includes the relation between the text and its severed title. His reading of the multiple meanings of *The Fall of Hyperion* are an invitation to pay similar attention to *Allegories of Reading* or, indeed, *The Rhetoric of Romanticism*. Going further than that, though, we know that de Man conceives of a more radical break that lies at the origin of these linguistic curses, privileges, and irreducible ambiguities, namely, the severance between language and human. By pointing to that fracture de Man's unintentional praxis shows how we might attempt to understand fracture as part of a system whose goal is the description of philology. According to de Man, a break between language and the seemingly intentional production of sentences, be they hypotactical or paratactical, throws its shadow over any further definitions or readings.

It becomes evident that de Man's project of a recovery of philology cannot be solely historical, although it has to take this dimension into account. Fracture haunts de Man's work as a whole, on the most fundamental, theoretical, level. The rigour and systematicity that follow the initial break can only temporarily cover the disruptive force of that origin. While his system might be as coherent as the grammar it analyses – and de Man certainly seems to think about it as a structure akin to language – it also shows the breaks and fissures which the particular readings uncover. Despite his rationalisations to the contrary, it is very much through fracture and fragmentation that de Man defines and writes Romanticism as well as his own critical stance. Not only do they form part of the object and method of inquiry, they also ultimately define the condition and origin of our positions as readers. By emphasising the assumed philological dispute between Auerbach, Adorno, and himself, de Man draws further attention to the fact that his reference to coherence is actually a confession of its necessary disappointment.

For de Man, the original nature of the fracture between human and language must also become a statement about the attempt to define Romanticism. On a macro-critical level, fracture determines language per se, and thus forms a central component in our understanding of the category. On a micro-critical level, the fracture works its rupturing dynamic into the language of Romanticism that he analyses. As de Man himself points out, all the readings of this rhetoric of Romanticism disclose 'breaks and interruptions' at their core. That this also discloses a principle of fracture at the heart of the *Rhetoric* as a whole gives an indication of its rupturing power, just as the strangely confessional volume can be taken to be a fracture at the centre of de Man's oeuvre. However systematic, rigorous, and precise the analysis of the rupture is, it cannot stabilise its disturbing potential.

The impossibility of systematically stabilising the figures (or notions) of fracture or fragmentation evidently has consequences for any definition of Romanticism along their lines. An attempt to focus a period or movement in such a way must remain mobile. The tension inherent in that description is part of its critical potential. However, this must go beyond a mere acknowledgement or affirmation of one's own limits. Part of the argument of this book has seen that fracture and fragmentation illustrate how a specific version of this limitation becomes a Romantic practice that helps us define and understand it as a period, including our position in it. In relation to the rest of the book, the particular case study of de Man introduces us to the idea that his systematic way of describing Romanticism entails a Romantic vision at its centre. It presents yet another way of theorising Romanticism through fracture and putting ourselves at the centre of it. It assumes, as I mentioned before, that it is critically enabling to interpret de Man (and Benjamin, for that matter) as practising a particular form of Romanticism. This does not mean homogenising either de Man's or Benjamin's works, nor the chronologically more removed texts that I discussed earlier. These are all highly particular cases. However, there is a deep relation and affinity between all of them, and this affinity can be described most powerfully through their own language.

As de Man's readings show, admitting this insistence need not be uncritical or an exercise in veneration. It involves recognising the contemporary nature of Romanticism, and the Romantic nature of the present. Our position as contemporary critics improves if we develop a sense for the importance of historical specificity, as well as its relation to analytical statements. De Man's work is a relevant example of how such criticism might be performed and why, even in its problems, it can offer productive insights. It is worth remarking that this is the result, not so much of his specific method of rhetorical reading, but rather of the particular way he performs those readings. In other words: the success of such criticism is not analytically tied or limited to one particular approach – quite the contrary.

It is not new to insist on the desirability of a critical attitude that understands its limits as part of its strength rather than a weakness. However, it does not have to be new in order to be powerful. Knowing and accepting that we are still immersed in Romanticism does not entail that we know what that *exactly means*. Romantic Studies can understand this as an example or an invitation to find out. It depends on the reader, whether our object of inquiry will remind her or him of both. It provides us with a hint for understanding better why we assumed the inquiry was rewarding in the first place, but also why it is advisable not to overestimate our results.

Notes

BROKEN ORIGINS: AN INTRODUCTION

1. Emily Dickinson, *The Poems of Emily Dickinson*, ed. R. W. Franklin (Cambridge, MA: Belknap Press of Harvard University Press, 1999), p. 290.

2. Athenaeum fragment #206, in Friedrich von Schlegel, *Kritische Friedrich-Schlegel-Ausgabe*, ed. Ernst Behler and others, 35 vols. (Paderborn, Munich, and Vienna: Schöningh, 1958–), vol. 2, p. 197. All translations from the German in this book, unless otherwise indicated, are my own.

3. Paul Hamilton, *Metaromanticism: Aesthetics, Literature, Theory* (Chicago: University of Chicago Press, 2003), pp. 2–3.

4. There are many such accounts. For a representative example, see Justus Fletcher, 'Anbrüche: Vorgeschichte und Programm der Fragmentpoetik', in Eckhart Goebel and Martin von Koppenfels, eds., *Die Endlichkeit der Literatur* (Bonn: Akademi, 2002), pp. 62–84.

5. Hamilton, *Metaromanticism*, pp. 2–3.

6. For an overview of the various aspects of this discussion, see Ian Baucom and Jennifer Kennedy, eds., *Afterlives of Romanticism: Special Issue of The South Atlantic Quarterly*, 102 (2003).

7. To name but a few: Peter de Bolla, 'Toward the Materiality of Aesthetic Experience', *Diacritics: A Review of Contemporary Criticism*, 32.1 (2002), 19–37; Clifford Siskin, *The Historicity of Romantic Discourse* (New York: Oxford University Press, 1988); Michel Foucault, *The Order of Things: An Archaeology of the Human Sciences* (London: Tavistock, 1971).

8. For discussions of fragmentation and *Zeitgeist*, see Kathleen M. Wheeler, *Romanticism, Pragmatism, and Deconstruction* (Oxford: Blackwell, 1993). For prolific work in the area of the history of crucial terms and concepts in Romanticism, see Clifford Siskin, *The Work of Writing: Literature and Change in Britain, 1700–1830* (Baltimore and London: Johns Hopkins University Press, 1998). Classic studies of German *Begriffsgeschichte* include Reinhart Koselleck, *Historische Semantik und Begriffsgeschichte* (Stuttgart: Klett-Cotta, 1979); and the ongoing journal and evolving *Archiv für Begriffsgeschichte* now published by Meiner in Hamburg.

9. Peter de Bolla, *The Discourse of the Sublime: Readings in History, Aesthetics, and the Subject* (Oxford and New York: Basil Blackwell, 1989). David Simpson,

Romanticism, Nationalism, and the Revolt against Theory (Chicago: University of Chicago Press, 1993).

10. Ernesto Laclau and Chantal Mouffe, *Hegemony and Socialist Strategy: Towards a Radical Democratic Politics*, 2nd edn (London and New York: Verso, 2001). Friedrich A. Kittler and Horst Turk, eds., *Urszenen: Literaturwissenschaft als Diskursanalyse und Diskurskritik* (Frankfurt am Main: Suhrkamp, 1977).

11. Samuel Beckett, *Worstward Ho* (London: John Calder, 1983), p. 7.

12. Beckett, *Worstward Ho*, p. 7.

13. It is important to acknowledge the heterogeneity within both deconstruction and New Historicism, as well as to be aware of parallels between them. Evidently, my positioning here does not assume that these respective critical approaches are completely static; however, it is reasonable to describe them as being compiled by two distinct groups of scholars each of whom shares a set of similar assumptions. It is their respective common ground that I want to engage with here. Hence, I do not want to present them as a critical stand-off, a common critical move that has begun to look increasingly dated.

14. This goes for the story of literary criticism itself too, and continues to spark debate until today. The acknowledgement of the history of criticism (and all the travail it involves) as a conditioning factor in one's own relation vis-à-vis ideology is important here. Naturally, there are limitations to this (there are many strands of critical and literary work that I cannot discuss here). Despite these difficulties, I believe that this discussion does not suffer from a lack of an appreciation of how the genealogy of Romantic Studies determines its position within it.

15. Jerome J. McGann, *The Romantic Ideology: A Critical Investigation* (Chicago: University of Chicago Press, 1983), p. 1. For a discussion of 'ideology' in the context of Romantic Studies and its contemporary relevance or misconception, see Simon Jarvis, *Wordsworth's Philosophic Song* (Cambridge: Cambridge University Press, 2007), pp. 35–83. For a fierce criticism of Jarvis's project, compare Appendix B of Marjorie Levinson, 'A Motion and a Spirit: Romancing Spinoza', *Studies in Romanticism*, 46.4 (2007), 367–408.

16. Marjorie Levinson, *Wordsworth's Great Period Poems: Four Essays* (Cambridge: Cambridge University Press, 1986), p. 12. Also see Marjorie Levinson, ed., *Rethinking Historicism: Critical Readings in Romantic History* (Oxford: Blackwell, 1989), pp. 1–63.

17. Many important figures of deconstruction, such as Jacques Derrida or Jean-Luc Nancy, in contrast to some of their followers, ponder the differentiation between a deconstruction that 'takes place everywhere' and the specific meaning of the term in its 'current and bookish sense of the word'. See Jacques Derrida, 'Letter to a Japanese Friend', in David Wood and Robert Bernasconi, eds., *Derrida & Différance* (Coventry: Parousia Press, 1985), pp. 1–8 (p. 6).

18. Andrew E. Benjamin, *Philosophy's Literature* (Manchester: Clinamen, 2001), pp. ix and x.

19. John Barrell, *The Spirit of Despotism: Invasions of Privacy in the 1790s* (Oxford: Oxford University Press, 2006), p. 14. Also see John Barrell, *Imagining the*

King's Death: Figurative Treason, Fantasies of Regicide, 1793–1796 (Oxford and New York: Oxford University Press, 2000).

20. Barrell, *The Spirit of Despotism*, p. 14.
21. James K. Chandler, *England in 1819: The Politics of Literary Culture and the Case of Romantic Historicism* (Chicago: University of Chicago Press, 1998). Evidently, many other commentaries that I cannot discuss here fall into this group. The recent work of scholars such as Mary Poovey or Isobel Armstrong immediately comes to mind.
22. Chandler, *England in 1819*, p. 36.
23. Frances Ferguson, 'Romantic Memory', in Helen Regueiro Elam and Frances Ferguson, eds., *The Wordsworthian Enlightenment: Romantic Poetry and the Ecology of Reading* (Baltimore: Johns Hopkins University Press, 2005), pp. 71–93 (p. 87).
24. Ian Balfour, *The Rhetoric of Romantic Prophecy* (Stanford: Stanford University Press, 2002).
25. Marc Redfield, *Phantom Formations: Aesthetic Ideology and the Bildungsroman* (Ithaca: Cornell University Press, 1996), p. 11.
26. William Keach, *Arbitrary Power: Romanticism, Language, Politics* (Princeton: Princeton University Press, 2004), p. ix.
27. Leon Chai, *Romantic Theory: Forms of Reflexivity in the Revolutionary Era* (Baltimore: Johns Hopkins University Press, 2006), p. ix.
28. Thomas McFarland, *Romanticism and the Forms of Ruin: Wordsworth, Coleridge and the Modalities of Fragmentation* (Princeton: Princeton University Press, 1981), p. 5.
29. McFarland, *Romanticism and the Forms of Ruin*, p. 55.
30. Marjorie Levinson, *The Romantic Fragment Poem: A Critique of Form* (Chapel Hill: University of North Carolina Press, 1986), p. 11. As I point out above, I believe Levinson's more recent work, albeit not directly related to fragmentation, modulates this impulse more convincingly. Nevertheless, this early book remains one of the most widely read accounts in relation to the fragment and therefore serves well as a contrast to McFarland's study.
31. Levinson, *The Romantic Fragment Poem*, p. 6.
32. For these studies, see Anne Janowitz, 'Coleridge's 1816 Volume: Fragment as Rubric', *Studies in Romanticism*, 24.1 (1985), 21–39; Anne Janowitz, *England's Ruins: Poetic Purpose and the National Landscape* (Oxford: Blackwell, 1990); Elizabeth Harries, *The Unfinished Manner: Essays on the Fragment in the Later Eighteenth Century* (Charlottesville: University Press of Virginia, 1994); Sophie Thomas, *Romanticism and Visuality: Fragments, History, Spectacle* (New York and London: Routledge, 2008). In several ways these substantial accounts hark back to a much older divide between readings. One can think here, on the one hand, of Edward Bostetter's classification of fragmentation as a paradigmatic sign of Romanticism's decline, as well as of D. F. Rauber's discussion of the fragment and infinity. On the other hand, there is Ilse Gugler, who ultimately doubts the importance of the fragment for English studies. For these accounts, see Edward E. Bostetter, *The Romantic Ventriloquists: Wordsworth, Coleridge,*

Keats, Shelley, Byron (Seattle: University of Washington Press, 1963); D. F. Rauber, 'The Fragment as Romantic Form', *Modern Language Quarterly*, 30 (1969), 212–21; Ilse Gugler, *Das Problem der fragmentarischen Dichtung in der englischen Romantik* (Berne: A. Francke, 1944). For a more recent discussion, also see Fletcher, 'Anbrüche: Vorgeschichte und Programm der Fragmentpoetik'.

33. In John Keats, *A Critical Edition of the Major Works*, ed. Elizabeth Cook, (Oxford and New York: Oxford University Press, 1990), p. 592. However, if we survey the titles published under the heading of 'fragment' between 1790 and 1830, it becomes evident that although 'fragment' is a term with relatively wide circulation it is by no means clearly defined as genre. 'Fragments' take such different forms as long grammatical treatises, political essays, instructions in landscape architecture, theological argument, travelogues, or sentimental war narratives. The category of 'the fragment' during that time in Britain seems, in fact, too heterogeneous to qualify as an established literary category as Cook understands it.

34. Philippe Lacoue-Labarthe and Jean-Luc Nancy, *The Literary Absolute: The Theory of Literature in German Romanticism* (Albany: State University of New York Press, 1988).

35. Maurice Blanchot, *The Infinite Conversation* (Minneapolis: University of Minnesota Press, 1993), pp. 351–9. Maurice Blanchot, *The Writing of the Disaster* (Lincoln: University of Nebraska Press, 1986).

36. Jean-Luc Nancy, *The Birth to Presence* (Stanford: Stanford University Press, 1993), pp. 266–78. For a representative starting point, containing a variety of examples of how contemporary critical responses on the fragment are articulated, see Lucien Dällenbach and Christian L. Hart Nibbrig, eds., *Fragment und Totalität* (Frankfurt am Main: Suhrkamp, 1984).

I A BROTHERHOOD IS BROKEN

1. All biblical citations are to the King James version, and will be given in the main text.

2. For a recent overview on this aspect of Benjamin's work, see Andrew E. Benjamin and Beatrice Hanssen, eds., *Walter Benjamin and Romanticism* (New York: Continuum, 2002). My final chapter will deal with how this aspect of Benjamin's legacy weaves itself into the current reception of his thought (and how it is linked to the suggestion that his thinking on language remains fundamentally theological). Benjamin's latent and idiosyncratic Romanticism has been written about extensively. This includes the extremely complicated question how Benjamin's theory of language influences the redemptive-messianic, or revolutionary, quality of Benjamin's thought. It is still open whether Benjamin's peculiar version of historical materialism leads him to change his linguistics. Out of the vast literature on Benjamin, language, and Romanticism, the following contributions helpfully discuss this point: Winfried Menninghaus, *Walter Benjamins Theorie der Sprachmagie* (Frankfurt

am Main: Suhrkamp, 1980); Benjamin, *Philosophy's Literature*; Carol Jacobs, 'The Monstrosity of Translation', *MLN*, 90.6 (1975), 755–66; Howard Caygill, *Walter Benjamin: The Colour of Experience* (London: Routledge, 1998); Alexander García-Düttman, *The Gift of Language: Memory and Promise in Adorno, Benjamin, Heidegger, and Rosenzweig*, trans. Arline Lyons (London: Athlone, 2000); Peter Fenves, 'The Genesis of Judgment: Spatiality, Analogy, and Metaphor in Benjamin's "On Language as Such and on Human Language"', in David Ferris, ed., *Walter Benjamin: Theoretical Questions* (Stanford: Stanford University Press, 1996), pp. 75–93.

3. Walter Benjamin, *Gesammelte Schriften*, ed. Rolf Tiedemann, 7 vols. (Frankfurt am Main: Suhrkamp, 1991), vol. 2.1, p. 147. Further references to Benjamin's texts are to this edition (*GS*).

4. The most accessible account of a variety of these projects is found in Umberto Eco, *The Search for the Perfect Language*, trans. James Fentress (Oxford: Blackwell, 1995). Also see Umberto Eco, *Serendipities: Language and Lunacy*, Italian Academy Lectures (New York: Columbia University Press, 1998).

5. *GS* 4.1, pp. 13–14; p. 19.

6. *GS* 2.1, p. 155.

7. Geoffrey Hartman, *The Unremarkable Wordsworth* (London: Methuen, 1987), p. 171. Notice Hartman's direct reference to Benjamin (p. 238, n. 4).

8. William Wordsworth, *'The Ruined Cottage' and 'The Pedlar'*, ed. James Butler (Ithaca: Cornell University Press, 1979), line 73. Further references to *The Ruined Cottage* are to this edition (*RC*) and are indicated by line numbers in the main text. Unless stated otherwise, I am quoting from MS. D.

9. *GS* 2.1, p. 155.

10. William A. Ulmer, 'Wordsworth, the One Life, and *The Ruined Cottage*', *Studies in Philology*, 93.3 (1996), 304–31 (p. 305).

11. For a reading that explores the rift between the metaphysical sphere and the human in a similar way, see J. Hillis Miller, *The Disappearance of God: Five Nineteenth-Century Writers* (Cambridge, MA: Belknap Press of Harvard University Press, 1963), p. 5.

12. On this aspect of the myth, see Jacques Derrida, 'Des Tours de Babel', in Joseph F. Graham, ed., *Difference in Translation* (Ithaca and London: Cornell University Press, 1985), pp. 165–207 (esp. pp. 166–8).

13. The image of language as a fragmented container or vessel is common in imaginative and theoretical writing. Benjamin's essay 'The Task of the Translator' is a well-known case in point. There Benjamin argues that, 'Just as in order to be joined together the broken pieces of a vessel have to correspond to each other in the minutest details without resembling each other, the translation has to lovingly and in detail learn and assimilate the original's way of meaning rather than mimick its sense; this way they both, like a broken piece of a vessel, become recognisable as a broken piece of a bigger Language' (*GS* 4.1, p. 18). Gershom Scholem famously insists on the importance of the vessel as a biblical image in Gershom Scholem, *Zur Aktualität Walter Benjamins* (Frankfurt am Main: Suhrkamp, 1972), pp. 132–3. Also see Paul de Man's

discussion of Benjamin's essay (and Harry Zohn's standard translation of it) highlighting the importance of fragmentation in Paul de Man, *The Resistance to Theory* (Manchester: Manchester University Press, 1986), pp. 73–105. This last text will be discussed in Chapter 7 below; further references are to this edition (*RT*) and will be given in the main text.

14. Also see Jonathan Wordsworth, *The Music of Humanity: A Critical Study of Wordsworth's 'Ruined Cottage', Incorporating Texts from a Manuscript of 1799–1800* (London: Nelson, 1969), p. 125. For an analysis of the temporal aspect of fragmentation and mourning in this text, see Kurt Fosso, 'Community and Mourning in William Wordsworth's *The Ruined Cottage*, 1797–1798', *Studies in Philology*, 92.3 (1995), 329–45 (p. 335).

15. For a discussion of the corresponding passage in *The Excursion*, see Frances Ferguson, *Wordsworth: Language as Counter-Spirit* (New Haven and London: Yale University Press, 1977), pp. 214–16.

16. A comparison with *The Five-Book Prelude* and the 1805 version also reveals a fragmentation of the whole Wordsworthian corpus on this matter. In both of these later versions the old man has become the (poetical) narrator himself. In all these texts we can detect a fundamental destabilisation of the autobiographical mode. The identification with any 'I' is therefore made even harder than before, especially as we are aware that this 'eye' becomes the shorthand for certain 'powers'. See in this context Cynthia Chase's criticism of de Man's discussion of the 1805 passage in Cynthia Chase, *Decomposing Figures: Rhetorical Readings in the Romantic Tradition* (Baltimore and London: Johns Hopkins University Press, 1986), pp. 82–112. Also see Ferguson, *Wordsworth*, p. 200.

17. Fosso, 'Community and Mourning', pp. 344–5.

18. Unless otherwise indicated, *The Prelude* refers to the 1805 version (thirteen-book *Prelude*). I quote from volume 1 of Reed's edition. See William Wordsworth, *The Thirteen-Book 'Prelude'*, ed. Mark L. Reed, 2 vols. (Ithaca: Cornell University Press, 1991). Further references to *The Prelude* are to this edition (*1805*) and are indicated by volume and line numbers in the main text.

19. On the 'language of the dream', also see Mary Jacobus, *Romanticism, Writing and Sexual Difference: Essays on 'The Prelude'* (Oxford: Clarendon Press, 1989), pp. 97–125.

20. Also see Balfour, *The Rhetoric of Romantic Prophecy*, pp. 24–6.

21. It is worth observing that the Pentecostal image of the shell reappears, albeit with more directly Christian connotations, in *The Excursion*. There the Wanderer sees 'A curious Child, who dwelt upon a tract / Of inland ground, applying to his ear / The convolutions of a smooth-lipped Shell; / To which, in silence hushed, his very soul / Listened intensely; and his countenance soon / Brightened with joy; for murmurings from within / Were heard, – sonourous cadences! whereby, / To his belief, the Monitor expressed / Mysterious union with its native Sea. / Even such a Shell the Universe itself / Is to the ear of Faith […]'. William Wordsworth, *The Excursion*, ed. Sally Bushell, James A. Butler, and Michael C. Jaye, with the assistance of David García (Ithaca:

Cornell University Press, 2007), 4. 1126–36. Further references to *The Excursion* are to this edition (*Excursion*) and indicated by volume and line numbers. This self-referencing by Wordsworth is also a self-editing. The ideal of the earlier powers has become a mode that is specific ('the') and capitalised in its religious direction ('Faith'). Nothing actually occurs and changes ('pass'd') anymore in this framework; it is a more rigid 'universe itself', in danger of being heard only with the ear of a very particular Christian 'Faith'.

22. On this point, also see Balfour, *The Rhetoric of Romantic Prophecy*, pp. 19–81.
23. William Wordsworth, *The Prose Works of William Wordsworth*, ed. W. J. B. Owen and Jane Worthington Smyser, 3 vols. (Oxford: Clarendon, 1974), vol. 2, p. 66. Further references to Wordsworth's prose writings are to this edition (*Prose*) and cited by page number in the main text.
24. For the two views, see, respectively, D. D. Devlin, *De Quincey, Wordsworth and the Art of Prose* (London and Basingstoke: Macmillan, 1983); and Angus Easson, *The Lapidary Wordsworth: Epitaphs and Inscriptions* (Winchester: King Alfred's College, 1981).
25. Hartman, *The Unremarkable Wordsworth*, p. 39.
26. For all of these examples, see William Wordsworth, *'Lyrical Ballads', and Other Poems, 1797–1800*, ed. James Butler and Karen Green (Ithaca: Cornell University Press, 1992).
27. Also see *Excursion* 7. 494–8. Also see Wordsworth's description in the *Guide through the District of the North*: 'A not unpleasing sadness is induced by this perplexity and those images of decay; while the prospect of a body of pure water unattended with groves and other cheerful rural images by which fresh water is usually accompanied, and unable to give furtherance to the meagre vegetation around it – excites a sense of some repulsive power strongly put forth, and thus deepens the melancholy natural to such scenes' (*Prose* 2. 187).
28. For 'Hart-leap Well' and, later, 'Nutting' as well as ''Tis said that some have died for love' see Wordsworth, *'Lyrical Ballads', and Other Poems*. In my discussion of 'The Solitary Reaper' line references are to the text given in William Wordsworth, *'Poems, in Two Volumes', and Other Poems, 1800–1807*, ed. Jared Curtis (Ithaca: Cornell University Press, 1983).
29. Lord (Henry Home) Kames, *Elements of Criticism*, 3rd edn, 2 vols. (London and Edinburgh: 1765), vol. 1, p. 494. Also see Herbert Rauter, *Die Sprachauffassung der englischen Frühromantik in ihrer Bedeutung für die Literaturkritik und Dichtungstheorie der Zeit* (Bad Homburg, Berlin, and Zurich: Gehlen, 1970), pp. 117–25.
30. James Beattie, *Dissertations Moral and Critical* (London, 1783), p. 633. For a contemporary theorisation of how silence and aesthetic experience relate see Peter de Bolla, *Art Matters* (Cambridge, MA: Harvard University Press, 2001).
31. Peter Larkin, 'Relations of Scarcity: Ecology and Eschatology in *The Ruined Cottage*', *Studies in Romanticism*, 39.3 (2000), 347–64 (p. 351).
32. Wordsworth, *'Poems, in Two Volumes', and Other Poems*. This is a constant theme in Wordsworth's oeuvre. The early *Epitaphs from Chiabrera* record how Titus is called 'to the perpetual silence of the grave' (line 18). See William

Wordsworth, *Shorter Poems 1807–1820*, ed. Carl H. Ketcham (Ithaca: Cornell University Press, 1989), Epitaph 'Perhaps some needful service of the State'. The 'Elegiac Stanzas' in *Memorials of a Tour on the Continent, 1820* remind us that 'Calm is the grave and calmer none' (line 22). See William Wordsworth, *Sonnet Series and Itinerary Poems, 1820–1845*, ed. Geoffrey Jackson (Ithaca: Cornell University Press, 2004). In the 1850 version of *The Prelude*, Edmund Burke is reported to be 'Now mute, for ever mute in the cold grave'. William Wordsworth, *The Fourteen-Book 'Prelude'*, ed. W. J. B. Owen (Ithaca: Cornell University Press, 1985), 7. 518.

33. Also the passage in *Excursion* 7. 412–98.
34. In this context, also see Mary Jacobus, 'Composing Sound: The Deaf Dalesman, "The Brothers", and Epitaphic Signs', in Alexander Regier and Stefan H. Uhlig, eds., *Wordsworth's Poetic Theory* (Basingstoke: Palgrave Macmillan, 2010), pp. 176–94.
35. Arno Borst, *Der Turmbau von Babel*, 4 vols. (Stuttgart: Hiersemann, 1957), vol. 4, p. 2002.

2 FIGURING IT OUT

1. Jean-Jacques Rousseau, 'Essay on the Origin of Languages', trans. John T. Scott, in *The Collected Writings of Rousseau*, ed. Roger Masters and Christopher Kelly, 13 vols. (Hanover, NH, and London: University Press of New England, 1990–), vol. 7 (1998), pp. 289–332 (p. 293).
2. See Rauter, *Die Sprachauffassung der englischen Frühromantik*; James H. Stam, *Inquiries into the Origin of Language: The Fate of a Question* (New York: Harper and Row, 1976); Hans Aarsleff, *The Study of Language in England 1780–1860* (London: Athlone, 1983); Sabrina Hausdörfer, 'Die Sprache ist Delphi: Sprachursprungstheorie, Geschichtsphilosophie und Sprach-Utopie bei Novalis, Friedrich Schlegel und Hölderlin', in Joachim Gessinger and Wolfert von Rahden, eds., *Theorien vom Ursprung der Sprache*, 2 vols. (Berlin and New York: De Gruyter, 1989), vol. 1, pp. 468–97; Robert E. Norton, *Herder's Aesthetic and the European Enlightenment* (Ithaca: Cornell University Press, 1991); Richard Marggraf Turley, *The Politics of Language in Romantic Literature* (Basingstoke and New York: Palgrave Macmillan, 2002).
3. Johann Georg Hamann, *Sämtliche Werke*, 6 vols. (Vienna: Thomas Morus Presse in Verlag Herder, 1949–57), vol. 2, p. 197. A. W. Schlegel, *Vorlesungen über schöne Litteratur und Kunst* (Heilbronn: Henninger, 1884), p. 263.
4. While not itself particulary original, Blair's work has rightly been called a 'summarising moment of eighteenth-century linguistic theory', in Rauter, *Die Sprachauffassung der englischen Frühromantik*, p. 219. For the mentioned sources, see Thomas Blackwell, *An Enquiry into the Life and Writings of Homer* (London, 1735); Hugh Blair, *Lectures on Rhetoric and Belles Lettres*, 2 vols. (London, 1783); John Brown, *The History of the Rise and Progress of Poetry, through it's several Species* (Newcastle, 1764); Lord (James Burnet) Monboddo, *Of the Origin and Progress of Language*, 6 vols. (Edinburgh, 1773–92); Johann Gottfried Herder,

Abhandlung über den Ursprung der Sprache (Munich and Vienna: Hanser, 1978); William Warburton, *The Divine Legation of Moses* (London, 1738).

5. Blair, *Lectures*, vol. i, p. 101.
6. Blair, *Lectures*, vol. i, p. 101.
7. Blair, *Lectures*, vol. i, p. 102.
8. Blair, *Lectures*, vol. i, p. 112.
9. Blair, *Lectures*, vol. i, p. 115.
10. Blair, *Lectures*, vol. i, p. 116.
11. This last point is particularly important because, despite having lost its mainstream status, the idea of a conjunction of poetical and linguistic origin (and its subsequent change in the development of language) remains important from the eighteenth century until today. Structurally, William Wordsworth, for instance, reiterates large parts of the above arguments in the 'Appendix to Preface to *Lyrical Ballads*' (1802) and the 'Essay, Supplementary to the Preface' (1815). While he retains the basic structure of its historical speculation, he reverses the assessment. For him linguistic development is a history of decline from passionate towards mechanical language rather than a narrative of laudable progress of increasing rationality. It is instructive to invoke Wordsworth here because it seems there is a larger argument to be made about the continuity of questions concerning the origin of language from at least the eighteenth century onwards. As Frances Ferguson eloquently reminds us, 'Wordsworth's and Coleridge's explicit discussions of language and the origins of language thus take their place with the numerous conjectural histories of language as versions of the Romantic tendency to disclose the limitations of their own discoveries and creations [...]'. Ferguson, *Wordsworth*, p. 6. Also see Robert Crawford, *The Modern Poet: Poetry, Academia and Knowledge since the 1750's* (Oxford: Oxford University Press, 2001), pp. 54–5.
12. Blackwell, *An Enquiry*, p. 40.
13. Blackwell, *An Enquiry*, p. 41.
14. Blackwell, *An Enquiry*, p. 163.
15. Blackwell, *An Enquiry*, pp. 100–1.
16. Rousseau, *Essay*, p. 294.
17. In his notes John Scott points out that 'Rousseau draws on Bernard Lamy's discussion of tropes and figurative language in his *La rhétorique, ou l'art de parler* (4th edn, 1701), II, 3: "Tropes are names that are transferred from the thing of which they are the proper name, to apply them to things which they signify only indirectly: thus all tropes are metaphors, for the word, which in Greek, means translation".'
18. One of the few exceptions is Paul de Man's essay 'Anthropomorphism and the Trope in the Lyric'. See Paul de Man, *The Rhetoric of Romanticism* (New York: Columbia University Press, 1984), pp. 239–62. Other aspects of de Man's book will be discussed in Chapter 7 below; further references to *The Rhetoric of Romanticism* are to this edition (*RR*), and will be given in the main text. In the wake of de Man's essay on anthropomorphism, see the following: Rodolphe Gasché, *The Wild Card of Reading: On Paul de Man* (Cambridge,

MA, and London: Harvard University Press, 1998), pp. 187 and 233. Barbara Johnson, 'Anthropomorphism in Lyric and Law', in Tom Cohen and others, eds., *Material Events* (Minneapolis and London: University of Minnesota Press, 2001), pp. 205–28; Cynthia Chase, 'Double-Take: Reading Paul de Man and Derrida Writing on Tropes', in Marc Redfield, ed., *Legacies of Paul de Man* (New York: Fordham University Press, 2007), pp. 17–28.

19. One of the few literary handbooks to have an entry on the term is Martin Gray, *A Dictionary of Literary Terms*, 2nd revised edn (Harlow: Longman, 1992), p. 26. It reads: '**Anthropomorphism.** (Gk. "human-form-ism") The attribution of a human form to God, to abstractions or even to animals and inanimate objects.'

20. David Hume, *Dialogues concerning Natural Religion* (Oxford and New York: Oxford University Press, 1993), p. 88.

21. Also see Hans Graubner, 'Zum Problem des Anthropomorphismus in der Theologie (Hume, Kant, Hamann)', in Bernhard Gajek, ed., *Johan Georg Hamann und England, Hamann und die englischsprachige Aufklärung: Acta des siebten internationalen Hamann-Kolloquium zu Marburg/Lahn 1996* (Frankfurt am Main: Lang, 1999), pp. 381–95.

22. Graubner, 'Zum Problem des Anthropomorphismus in der Theologie', p. 399.

23. De Man raises a similar point when discussing Kant's notion of the sublime (which will concern me later), in Paul de Man, *Aesthetic Ideology* (Minneapolis: University of Minnesota Press, 1996), p. 86.

24. Herder, *Abhandlung über den Ursprung der Sprache*, p. 109. The English translations available omit this (second) part of the *Essay*.

25. De Man here insists on yet another problem that the figure of anthropomorphism throws up, which is its reliance on what he calls the constructed and pretended 'identification of substance' in relation to a temporal framework. It is not meaningless to ask whether 'anthropomorphism' or the human concept of 'nature' came first. In fact, this rephrasing of de Man's comment indicates the kind of impasse any answer to this question will face.

26. Herder, *Abhandlung über den Ursprung der Sprache*, p. 109.

27. Hamann, *Sämtliche Werke*, vol. 3, p. 18. Also see Elfriede Büchsel, *Johann Georg Hamanns Hauptschriften erklärt*, ed. Fritz Blanke and Lothar Schreiner, 7 vols. (Gütersloh: Mohn, 1963), vol. 4 (*Über den Ursprung der Sprache*), p. 139. For another commentary, compare Stam, *Inquiries into the Origin of Language*, pp. 110–77. Until some years ago English-speaking scholarship rarely discussed Hamann in detail. Gwen Dickson's and Kenneth Haynes's relatively recent introductions and translations promise that this might change. See Gwen Griffith Dickson, *Johann Georg Hamann's Relational Metacriticism* (Berlin and New York: de Gruyter, 1995). Also see Johann Georg Hamann, *Writings on Philosophy and Language*, trans. Kenneth Haynes (Cambridge: Cambridge University Press, 2007). A good recent commentary on *Aesthetica in Nuce* can be found in Carol Jacobs, *Skirting the Ethical* (Stanford: Stanford University Press, 2008), pp. 111–30. The literature on Hamann in German is extensive; in relation to conjectural histories of language, his writings on biblical

hermeneutics are particularly relevant. For first guidance in this wide field, see Fritz Blanke, Karlfried Günder, and Lothar Schreiner, *Johann Georg Hamanns Hauptschriften erklärt*, 7 vols. (Gütersloh: Bertelsmann, 1956–), vol. 1 (*Die Hamann Forschung*); Oswald Bayer, Benjamin Gleede, and Ulrich Moustakas, *Vernunft ist Sprache: Hamanns Metakritik Kants* (Stuttgart-Bad Cannstatt: Frommann-Holzboog, 2002). For the historical dimension of 'galimathias', see Gert Ueding and others, *Historisches Wörterbuch der Rhetorik* (Tübingen: Max Niemeyer, 1992), vol. 3, pp. 524–8. Hamann's review of Herder is an instance of what de Man, invoking Hamann in his own theory of allegory, calls 'the polemical utterances of Hamann against Herder on the problem of the origin of language', which in his view 'are closely related to Hamann's considerations on the allegorical nature of all language, as well as with his literary praxis that mingles allegory with irony'. Paul de Man, *Blindness and Insight: Essays in the Rhetoric of Contemporary Criticism*, 2nd rev. edn (London: Methuen, 1983), p. 189. There is a book yet to be written about Hamann's influence on de Man himself and how, especially via various Romantic sources and Walter Benjamin (an admirer of Hamann), he determines de Man's thinking about figuration.

28. Stam, *Inquiries into the Origin of Language*, p. 152.
29. The important qualification is that this implies a shortcoming on man's part and thus is nothing but an admission that the fundamental rift between deity and human, as well as between the human and the natural, is irreversible. Graubner points out how one might extend Hamann's pulling together of the epistemological and theological arguments to the actual meaning of the term 'anthropomorphism' itself. See Graubner, 'Zum Problem des Anthropomorphismus in der Theologie', p. 393.
30. Kames, *Elements*, p. 233.
31. James Harris, *Hermes: or, a Philosophical Inquiry Concerning Language and Universal Grammar* (London, 1751), pp. 41–2.
32. Harris, *Hermes*, p. 43.
33. John Horne Tooke, *Diversions of Purley*, reprint of 1829 edn, 2 vols. (London and Tokyo: Thoemmes Press/Routledge, 1993), vol. 1, p. 54.
34. Blair, *Lectures*, vol. 1, p. 145.
35. Blair, *Lectures*, vol. 1, p. 146.
36. Blair, *Lectures*, vol. 1, p. 146.
37. Blair, *Lectures*, vol. 1, p. 146.
38. Blair, *Lectures*, vol. 1, p. 147.
39. Hugh Blair, *Critical Dissertation on the Poems of Ossian the Son of Fingal* (London, 1763), p. 65.
40. Beattie, *Dissertations Moral and Critical*, p. 630.
41. Kames, *Elements*, vol. 2, p. 226.
42. Kames, *Elements*, vol. 2, p. 226.
43. Kames, *Elements*, vol. 2, p. 233.
44. Beattie, *Dissertations Moral and Critical*, p. 630.
45. Harris, *Hermes*, p. 43.

46. Note that Harris speaks about the distinctions that entail gendered nouns, rather than identifying a problem that such a distinction (which implies anthropomorphism) is drawn in the first place.
47. Harris, *Hermes*, p. 43.
48. Harris's reference is to *Paradise Lost*, 8. 151. Milton's 'natural distinction' is between male and female light, rather than between the human sexes. This is an *already* anthropomorphic projection of the human qualities onto what is then interpreted as the life-giving force (the light). It comes as no surprise that this section of the Miltonic epic is very much about the problem of anthropomorphism. Raphael is conversing with Adam and reminds him that 'God, to remove his ways from human sense, / Placed heav'n from earth so far, that earthly sight, / If it presume, might err in things too high […]' (*Paradise Lost*, 8. 119–21). John Milton, *Poetical Works* (Oxford and New York: Oxford University Press, 1992).
49. Harris, *Hermes*, p. 44.
50. Harris, *Hermes*, p. 45.
51. Harris produces a number of examples, including planets that are anthropomorphised in Classical literature. However, interestingly enough for this discussion, he ignores Germanic languages, where the assignation of gender to the sun and moon – which he does list as an illustrative example in other languages – is the reverse. John Horne Tooke picks up on this, shortly after referring to the quoted passage from Harris in scathing manner: 'with the rest of it [that part of the book], he had much better have let it alone. And as for his poetical authorities; the Muses (as I have heard Mrs. Peachum say of her own sex in cases of murder) are bitter bad judges in matter of philosophy.' Tooke, *Diversions of Purley*, vol. 1, pp. 52–3.
52. Harris, *Hermes*, p. 48.
53. Harris, *Hermes*, p. 51.
54. Harris, *Hermes*, p. 54.
55. Harris, *Hermes*, pp. 49–50.
56. Kames, *Elements*, vol. 2, p. 248.
57. Blair, *Lectures*, vol. 1, p. 145.
58. Blair, *Lectures*, vol. 1, pp. 147–8.
59. Blair, *Lectures*, vol. 1, p. 324.
60. Blair, *Lectures*, vol. 1, p. 324.
61. Blair, *Lectures*, vol. 1, p. 325.
62. Blair, *Lectures*, vol. 1, p. 324.
63. Blair, *Lectures*, vol. 1, p. 331.

3 FORCES TREMBLING UNDERNEATH

1. Thomas Mann, *Der Zauberberg*, in *Gesammelte Werke* (Frankfurt am Main: Fischer, 1960), vol. 3, p. 349.
2. Johann Wolfgang von Goethe, *From My Life: Poetry and Truth*, trans. Eithne Wilkins and Ernst Kaiser (Princeton: Princeton University Press, 1994), p. 34.

Also see Hans Blumenberg, *Begriffe in Geschichten* (Frankfurt am Main: Suhrkamp, 1998), pp. 230–5. Here Blumenberg writes about Goethe's changing reception and conceptualisation of the disaster. For Lisbon's significance for German literature as a whole see Karl-Heinz Bohrer, *Nach der Natur: Über Politik und Ästhetik* (Munich and Vienna: Hanser, 1988), pp. 133–61.

3. The standard accounts of the earthquake's chronology can be found in T. D. Kendrick, *The Lisbon Earthquake* (London: Methuen, 1956); and Ulrich Löffler, *Lissabons Fall–Europas Schrecken: Die Deutung des Erdbebens von Lissabon im deutschsprachigen Protestantismus des 18. Jahrhunderts* (Berlin and New York: Walter de Gruyter, 1999).

4. One of the most extraordinary examples is the building of a cyclorama in London during 1848, a purpose-built structure where members of the public, including a certain Thackeray, experienced a show that re-created the devastating earthquake. See Richard D. Altick, *The Shows of London* (Cambridge, MA and London: Belknap Press of Harvard University Press, 1978), pp. 158–60.

5. The description of this particular link has to remain quite general here. The discussion between Hans Blumenberg and Karl Löwith shows how hard it is to describe adequately the connection between secularisation and modernity. The difficulties (or impossibilities) of defining the latter, especially 'against' Romanticism, are notorious. In this context it is worth remarking that Blumenberg, while insisting on the 'legitimacy' of modernity, describes the Lisbon earthquake as 'putting an end to the optimism of the first half of the [eighteenth] century' and therefore helping Kant in formulating the basis for a subsequent secular outlook. See Hans Blumenberg, *Die Legitimität der Neuzeit* (Frankfurt am Main: Suhrkamp, 1966), p. 244.

6. Especially the year 2005 saw a variety of events and publications that, openly or not, invoke the anniversary of the events of 1755. This includes a number of conferences in the sciences and the humanities as well as publications in different countries, such as Theodore E. D. Braun and John B. Radner, eds., *The Lisbon Earthquake of 1755: Representations and Reactions* (Oxford: Voltaire Foundation, 2005); Horst Günther, *Das Erdbeben von Lissabon und die Erschütterung des aufgeklärten Europa* (Frankfurt am Main: Fischer, 2005); Grégory Quenet, *Les tremblements de terre aux XVIIe et XVIIIe siècles: La naissance d'un risque* (Seyssel: Champ Vallon, 2005); *Lisbonne 1755: Un tremblement de terre et de ciel*, ed. Jean Mondot (Bordeaux: Presses Universitaires de Bordeaux, 2005); Jan T. Kozák, Victor S. Moreira, and David R. Oldroyd, *Iconography of the 1755 Lisbon Earthquake* (Prague: Geophysical Institute of the Academy of Sciences of the Czech Republic, 2005).

7. See Susan Neiman, *Evil in Modern Thought: An Alternative History of Philosophy* (Princeton: Princeton University Press, 2002), pp. 4 and 267. Neiman provides a new and refreshing look at the history of philosophy. However, for all its interest, Neiman's study is deeply problematic when it comes to her use of the historical event of the earthquake as part of her argument. Her information about the event and its reception seems to rely on quite a selective list of

secondary sources, as she herself indicates (p. 333, n. 2). This actually affects
the argument of her book. The introduction opens with the claim that 'The
eighteenth century used the word *Lisbon* much as we use the word *Auschwitz*
today' (p. 1). Given Neiman's wider argument about theodicy as an alternative
lens to understand the history of philosophy, it is not surprising that Adorno is
a constant presence in this text. It therefore makes a difference *not* to point
out that Adorno himself writes about the event in Portugal in a manner that
directly relates to and challenges Neiman's core argument: 'The earthquake of
Lisbon sufficed to cure Voltaire of the theodicy of Leibniz, and the visible
disaster of the first nature was insignificant in comparison with the second,
social one, which defies human imagination as it distills a real hell from human
evil.' Theodor W. Adorno, *Negative Dialectics*, trans. E. B. Ashton (London:
Routledge, 1990), p. 361. Another relevant and thought-provoking study in
this context is Gene Ray's recent intervention which links, in quite different
terms from Neiman's, contemporary philosophy with the Lisbon catastrophe
and Immanuel Kant's writings on the earthquake. See Gene Ray, 'Reading the
Lisbon Earthquake: Adorno, Lyotard, and the Contemporary Sublime', *Yale
Journal of Criticism*, 17.1 (2004), 1–18. Also see Richard Hamblyn, 'Notes
from the Underground: Lisbon after the Earthquake', *Romanticism*, 14.2
(2008), 108–18.

 8. See William Blake, *The Complete Poetry and Prose of William Blake*, ed., David
Erdman, new rev. edn (Berkeley: University of California Press, 1982), p. 614;
Heinrich von Kleist, *Das Erdbeben in Chili*, in *Sämtliche Werke*, Brandenburger
Ausgabe (Basel and Frankfurt am Main: Stroemfeld Verlag, 1993), vol. 2.3;
Bertrand Russell, *A History of Western Philosophy* (New York: Simon and
Schuster, 1945), pp. 689–90. For a discussion of Wollstonecraft's and
Benjamin's writings on Lisbon, see the end of the chapter.

 9. See Voltaire, 'Poem on the Destruction of Lisbon', in *The Works of M. de
Voltaire*, 24 vols. (Dublin: Moncrieffe, 1772), vol. 20, pp. 219–30. The Lisbon
episode in chapter 5 of *Candide* (1759) is the poem's variant in prose; see
Voltaire, *Candide and Other Stories*, trans. Joan Spencer (London: Oxford
University Press, 1966).

10. Examples of the more general literary historical accounts include Wolfgang
Breidert, ed., *Die Erschütterung der vollkommenen Welt: Die Wirkung des
Erdbebens von Lissabon im Spiegel europäischer Zeitgenossen* (Darmstadt:
Wissenschaftliche Buchgesellschaft, 1994); Olaf Briese, *Die Macht
der Metaphern: Blitz, Erdbeben, Kometen im Gefüge der Aufklärung*
(Stuttgart: Metzler, 1998); Franz Eybl, H. Heppner, and F. Kernbauer, eds.,
*Elementare Gewalt, Kulturelle Bewältigung: Aspekte der Naturkatastrophe im 18.
Jahrhundert* (Vienna: WUV Universitätsverlag, 2000); Horst Günther, *Das
Erdbeben von Lissabon erschüttert die Meinungen und setzt das Denken in
Bewegung* (Berlin: Wagenbach, 1994); Andreas Schmidt, *'Wolken krachen,
Berge zittern, und die ganze Erde weint': zur kulturellen Vermittlung von
Naturkatastrophen in Deutschland 1755 bis 1855* (Münster: Waxmann, 1999).
Harald Weinrich, 'Literaturgeschichte eines Weltereignisses: Das Erdbeben

von Lissabon', in *Literatur für Leser: Essays und Aufsätze zur Literaturwissenschaft* (Stuttgart: Kohlhammer, 1971), pp. 64–76.

11. David Simpson, *Irony and Authority in Romantic Poetry* (London and Basingstoke: Macmillan, 1979), p. 118.

12. *Philosophical Transactions being an Appendix to those for the year 1750: Consisting of several Papers laid before the Royal Society, concerning several Earthquakes felt in England and some neighbouring countries in the year 1750* (London: Royal Society, 1750). The numerous other contemporary commentaries on this event include *A Chronological and Historical Account of the most memorable Earthquakes that have happened in the World, from the Beginning of the Christian Period to the present year 1750* (Cambridge, 1750); and Samuel Chandler, *The Scripture Account of the Cause and Intention of Earthquakes, in a Sermon Preached at the old-jury March 11, 1749–50, on Occasion of the two Shocks of an earthquake, the first on February 8, the other March 8* (London, 1750).

13. There is a vast number of sources on this event. Even a very limited selection from outside the 'scientific' environment of the Society gives the reader an idea how widespread and common the engagement with the catastrophe was. Apart from the many entries in the *Philosophical Transactions* and other sources discussed later, see especially the anonymous *Reflections physical and moral, upon the various and numerous uncommon phenomena in the air, water, or earth, which have happened from the earthquake at Lima, to the present time: In a series of familiar letters from a Member of Parliament in town to his friend in the country* (London, 1756). Also see John D. D. Milner, *Ruin prevented by repentance, applied to civil societies. In two discourses delivered at Peckham in Surrey. On the general fast, February 6, 1756. Occasioned by the late dreadful earthquake at Lisbon, and the apprehension of nearer threatning calamities. – – With two hymns.* (London, 1756).

14. *The Lisbon Earthquake of 1755: British Accounts*, ed. Judite Nozes (Lisbon: British Historical Society of Portugal and Lisóptima, 1990), p. 36.

15. *The Lisbon Earthquake of 1755*, p. 54.

16. John Biddulph, *A Poem on the Earthquake of Lisbon* (London: 1755), p. 7.

17. Perry, 'An Account of the Earthquake felt in the Island of Sumatra, in the East-Indies, in November and December 1756. In a Letter from Mr. Perry to the Rev. Dr. Stukeley, dated at Fort Malborough, in the Island of Sumatra, Feb 20. 1757. Communicated by the Rev. Wm. Stukeley, M.D. F.R.S.', *Philosophical Transactions of the Royal Society of London*, 50 (1758), 491–2 (p. 491).

18. *The Lisbon Earthquake of 1755*, pp. 42–3.

19. *The Lisbon Earthquake of 1755*, pp. 42 and 44.

20. See J. Latham, 'Letter from Mr. J. Latham, dated at Zsusqueira, Dec. 11, 1755, to his Uncle in London. Communicated by Peter Daval, Esq; Secret. R.S.', *Philosophical Transactions of the Royal Society of London*, 49 (1755), 411–13 (p. 412).

21. Anthony Pereira, *A Narrative of the Earthquake and Fire of Lisbon of the Congregation of the Oratory, an Eyewitness thereof. Translated from the Latin* (London, 1756), pp. 5–6.

22. John Mendes Saccheti, 'A Copy of Part of Two Letters, written by John Mendes Saccheti, M.D. F.R.S. to Dr. DeCastro, F.R.S. dated from the Fields of Lisbon, on the 7th of November, and the 1st of December, 1755', *Philosophical Transactions of the Royal Society of London*, 49 (1755), 409–11 (p. 409).

23. *The Lisbon Earthquake of 1755*, p. 184.

24. *The Lisbon Earthquake of 1755*, pp. 42 and 44.

25. *The Lisbon Earthquake of 1755*, p. 52.

26. *The Lisbon Earthquake of 1755*, p. 52.

27. *The Lisbon Earthquake of 1755*, p. 52.

28. *The Lisbon Earthquake of 1755*, p. 42. Not only in Lisbon do material and mental confusion correspond. In Madrid, for example, 'Every body at first thought, that they were seized with a swimming in their heads; and, afterwards, that the houses, in which they were, were falling.' John Ellicot, 'Letter from Madrid, to the Spanish Consul, residing in London. Translated from the Spanish. Communicated by Mr. John Ellicot, F.R.S.', *Philosophical Transactions of the Royal Society of London*, 49 (1755), 423–4 (p. 423).

29. *The Lisbon Earthquake of 1755*, p. 52.

30. *The Lisbon Earthquake of 1755*, p. 116.

31. *The Lisbon Earthquake of 1755*, pp. 150 and 140.

32. *The Lisbon Earthquake of 1755*, pp. 238 and 178.

33. *The Lisbon Earthquake of 1755*, p. 196.

34. *The Lisbon Earthquake of 1755*, p. 76.

35. *The Lisbon Earthquake of 1755*, pp. 188 and 132.

36. Here I especially have in mind work by Cathy Caruth, Geoffrey Hartman, or Dominic LaCapra in the area of trauma studies. In contrast, I want to move the discussion in a direction that is more concerned with the philosophical underpinnings and representations of the sublime as part of, and articulated within, a larger frame of the aesthetic. For guidance in the extensive field of trauma studies, see Cathy Caruth, ed., *Trauma: Explorations in Memory* (Baltimore and London: Johns Hopkins University Press, 1995); Dominick LaCapra, *Representing the Holocaust: History, Theory, Trauma* (Ithaca and London: Cornell University Press, 1994); Geoffrey Hartman, *Scars of the Spirit: The Struggle against Inauthenticity* (New York and Basingstoke: Palgrave Macmillan, 2002); Jonathan Elmer and others, eds., *Trauma and Psychoanalysis: Special Issue of Diacritics*, 28.4 (1998).

37. Edmund Burke, *A Philosophical Enquiry into the Origin of our Ideas of the Sublime and Beautiful*, ed. J. T. Boulton (London: Routledge and Kegan Paul, 1958), pp. 47–8.

38. In his editorial notes, Boulton links this passage to the 1750 earthquake in London; see Burke, *A Philosophical Enquiry*, ed. Boulton, p. 47. David Womersley also mentions the link to Lisbon. See Edmund Burke, *A Philosophical Enquiry into the Origin of our Idea of the Sublime and Beautiful and other Pre-Revolutionary Writings*, ed. David Womersley (Harmondsworth: Penguin, 1998), p. 448 (n. 424).

39. James Hallifax, *A sermon preach'd in St. John's chapel in the parish of St. Andrew, Holborn, on Sunday February 8, 1756. being the Sunday after the day appointed by proclamation for a general fast and humiliation, on account of the dreadful earthquake at Lisbon* (London, 1756), p. 17.

40. *An Address to the Inhabitants of Great Britain; occasioned by the late Earthquake at Lisbon. To which is added, A Postscript, particularly addressed to the Merchants and others, who are Sufferers in that awful Calamity. The Second Edition* (London, 1755), p. 4.

41. The question whether the Burkean sublime can be understood as a 'reaction' to the Lisbon earthquake, and how far its historical influences are reflected in (or necessary to) his specific account, belongs to the much larger question of anachronism. The present chapter alludes to this wider discussion in terms of the interdependent presuppositions (about this precise issue) that govern the supposed tension between an empirical (Burkean) and a formalist (Kantian) argument. I can only gesture towards this dynamic in the following pages, by reminding the reader of the strong interdependence of Burke's and Kant's accounts, whose ideas are often presented as opposed. Kant openly adopts crucial categorisations from Burke (the division between the beautiful and the sublime, for instance). Furthermore, the empirical experience of the sublime *as a certain type of experience* (which *has* to be empirical) is a necessary stepping stone for Kant's formal argument to take off the ground. Inversely, the characterisation of Burke's account as one of purely empirical or descriptive psychology falls short of the analytical (and ultimately formal) claims he makes about the universality and structure of human experience and mental make-up. This highly complex discussion relates to epistemological, ethical, and aesthetic judgements, their formal structure, and the empirical experiences that fill them with meaning. Speaking of aesthetic judgements, Marc Redfield helpfully comments on the 'circular predicament of taste. The example is only an example thanks to the formalizing power of judgment, yet common sense depends on examples for its appearance and development […]. The a priori act of formalization that is exemplarity is thus always marked by the "prior" formalization: the exemplary is always belated with respect to itself. This paradox may be inverted: the exemplary is always ahead of itself, moving toward an ideal, precisely because of the lag or lapse inherent within the example.' Redfield, *Phantom Formations*, p. 19. One crucial point of reference for Redfield here is de Man, *Aesthetic Ideology*, pp. 70–90.

42. This is not to make reference to the continuous debate about the aestheticisation of disasters or catastrophic events. The present focus lies somewhere slightly different, namely, on the structural presuppositions that the sublime requires philosophically.

43. *The Lisbon Earthquake of 1755*, p. 224.

44. The particular issue of how the concept of distance is connected with the position (or indeed creation) of the self or subject has been a common point of interest for a number of very different studies over the past decades. For the

most important accounts on this, see the following: Thomas Weiskel, *The Romantic Sublime: Studies in the Structure and Psychology of Transcendence* (Baltimore: Johns Hopkins University Press, 1976); Neil Hertz, *The End of the Line: Essays on Psychoanalysis and the Sublime* (New York: Columbia University Press, 1985); De Bolla, *The Discourse of the Sublime*; Frances Ferguson, *Solitude and the Sublime: Romanticism and the Aesthetics of Individuation* (New York and London: Routledge, 1992).

45. Burghart Schmidt, *Postmoderne–Strategien des Vergessens: Ein kritischer Bericht*, 4th edn (Frankfurt am Main: Suhrkamp, 1994), pp. 143–61.

46. Mary Wollstonecraft, *The Works of Mary Wollstonecraft*, ed. Janet Todd and Marilyn Butler (London: William Pickering, 1989), vol. 1, p. 26. Wollstonecraft's own visit to Lisbon is recorded in Janet Todd, *Mary Wollstonecraft: A Revolutionary Life* (London: Weidenfeld and Nicolson, 2000), pp. 70–2.

47. Wollstonecraft, *The Works*, p. 34.

48. Wollstonecraft, *The Works*, p. 91.

49. Wollstonecraft, *The Works*, p. 91.

50. Wollstonecraft, *The Works*, p. 92.

51. Wollstonecraft, *The Works*, p. 92.

52. Immanuel Kant, *Critique of Judgment*, trans. Werner S. Pluhar (Indianapolis: Hackett, 1987). Further references are to this translation, and given in the main text (*CJ*). When alluding to the original German, I refer to the 1793 text of the *Critique* in Immanuel Kant, 'Kritik der Urteilskraft', ed. Otto Buek, vol. 5 of *Immanuel Kants Werke* (Hildesheim: Gerstenberg, 1973), pp. 177–568. Sometimes, I will also make reference to Guyer's and Matthews's translation; for these see Immanuel Kant, *Critique of the Power of Judgment*, trans. Paul Guyer and Eric Matthews (Cambridge: Cambridge University Press, 2000). All translations of Kant's pre-critical writings are my own.

53. Recent commentaries on this aspect include Jean-François Lyotard, *Lessons on the Analytic of the Sublime*, trans. Elizabeth Rottenberg (Stanford: Stanford University Press, 1994); Henry E. Allison, *Kant's Theory of Taste: A Reading of the Critique of Aesthetic Judgment* (Cambridge: Cambridge University Press, 2001), pp. 302–44; Howard Caygill, *Art of Judgement* (Oxford: Blackwell, 1989). To prevent a misunderstanding: this 'rationalisation' is not equivalent to 'rationality'. My discussion is not interested in (wrongly) claiming that Kant conceives of *reason* (or even rationality) per se as a domesticating and distancing category; after all, he thinks reason itself needs to be controlled through one's critical faculty.

54. This is not to confuse epistemological and aesthetic judgements as understood by Kant. It only links the two areas by the common notion of a subject that makes judgements of *any* kind and plays a vital role in the Kantian investigation of uncovering how these judgements are made and how to describe their conditions of possibility.

55. One could argue that one such moment is that the Kantian *sensus communis* (and thereby the entire question of judgement per se) might depend on the success of the argument on the sublime as a *formal* one, which ensures the identical *type* of self-construction for human beings.

56. A recent exception is Iain Hamilton Grant, 'Kant after Geophilosophy: The Physics of Analogy and the Metaphysics of Nature', in Andrea Rehberg and Rachel Jones, eds., *The Matter of Critique: Readings in Kant's Philosophy* (Manchester: Clinamen, 2000), pp. 37–60.

57. Immanuel Kant, 'Geschichte und Naturbeschreibung der merkwürdigsten Vorfälle des Erdbebens welches an dem Ende des 1755sten Jahres einen großen Teil der Erde erschüttert hat', ed. Artur Buchenau, vol. 1 of *Immanuel Kants Werke* (Hildesheim: Gerstenberg, 1973), pp. 439–73 (p. 471).

58. Immanuel Kant, 'Immanuel Kants fortgesetzte Betrachtung der seit einiger Zeit wahrgenommenen Erderschütterungen', ed. Artur Buchenau, vol. 1 of *Immanuel Kants Werke* (Hildesheim: Gerstenberg, 1973), pp. 475–84; Immanuel Kant, 'Von den Ursachen der Erderschütterungen bei Gelegenheit des Unglücks, welches die westlichen Länder von Europa gegen Ende des vorigen Jahres betroffen hat', ed. Artur Buchenau, vol. 1 of *Immanuel Kants Werke* (Hildesheim: Gerstenberg, 1973), pp. 427–37.

59. Kant, 'Geschichte und Naturbeschreibung', p. 467. Intriguingly, Kant's vocabulary of a 'punishing rod' unwittingly blurs the very point he is trying to make, giving the disaster a castigatory quality that could only be traced back to an anthropomorphised deity.

60. Rousseau writes: 'Without departing from your subject of Lisbon, admit, for example, that nature did not construct twenty thousand houses of six to seven stories there, and that if the inhabitants of this great city had been more equally spread out and more lightly lodged, the damage would have been much less, and perhaps of no account. [...] [T]hey [earthquakes] even cause little harm to the animals and Savages who dwell scattered in isolated places, and who fear neither the fall of housetops, nor the conflagration of houses.' Jean-Jacques Rousseau, 'Letter from Rousseau to Voltaire', trans. Roger Masters, Judith Bush, Christopher Kelly, and Terence Marshall, in *The Collected Writings of Rousseau*, ed, Roger Masters and Christopher Kelly, 13 vols. (Hanover, NH, and London: University Press of New England, 1990–), vol. 3 (1992), pp. 108–21 (p. 110). On the 'theology of earthquakes' in relation to these two figures see again Russell, *A History of Western Philosophy*, pp. 689–90. For the link between Kant and Rousseau, see Günther, *Das Erdbeben von Lissabon erschüttert die Meinungen und setzt das Denken in Bewegung*, p. 42.

61. Kant, 'Geschichte und Naturbeschreibung', p. 472.

62. Kant, 'Geschichte und Naturbeschreibung', p. 468.

63. *GS*, 7.1, p. 221. Tellingly, a paperback collection of Benjamin's writings for radio broadcast containing the essay on Lisbon is entitled *Aufklärung für Kinder [Enlightenment for Children]*. Walter Benjamin, *Aufklärung für Kinder* (Frankfurt am Main: Suhrkamp, 1985). For a more recent exponent of a similar position to Benjamin's, see Erhard Oeser, 'Das Erdbeben von Lissabon im Spiegel der zeitgenössischen Philosophie', in F. Eybl, H. Heppner, and A. Kernbauer, eds., *Elementare Gewalt. Kulturelle Bewältigung: Aspekte der Naturkatastrophe im 18. Jahrhundert* (Vienna: WUV Universitätsverlag, 2000), pp. 185–95. Considering Kant's influence on the early Benjamin, see Caygill, *Walter Benjamin*, pp. 27–9.

64. *GS*, 7.1, p. 221.
65. *GS*, 7.1, p. 222.
66. *GS*, 7.1, p. 223.
67. A variant of this position occurs in *The Magic Mountain* (1924). The humanist Settembrini understands his question to Castorp ('Have you heard of the earthquake of Lisbon?'), cited in the epigraph, as a shorthand for a 'modern' and enlightened outlook. Castorp's confused answer (he thinks Settembrini is referring to a contemporary event) gives Settembrini the chance to begin one of his arguments for the superiority of rational and secular ways of inquiry and thought.
68. To my knowledge, Gene Ray's article in *Yale Journal of Criticism* cited earlier is the only other place that links this passage of the *Critique* to the Lisbon earthquake. Also see Ray's monograph (which includes a version of the article as a chapter): Gene Ray, *Terror and the Sublime in Art and Critical Theory: From Auschwitz to Hiroshima to September 11* (New York: Palgrave Macmillan, 2005). Without discussing it further, Weiskel glosses Kant's passage as a moment when 'Fascination and dread coincide' rather than follow from one another or stand in a continuous tension. See Thomas Weiskel, *The Romantic Sublime: Studies in the Structure and Psychology of Transcendence* (Baltimore: Johns Hopkins University Press, 1976), p. 104. A more extensive study of this material would have to include how far the *Gemüt* – already identified as a term central to Kant – is a category through which the larger ramifications of the subverting and shattering force of fragmentation can be theorised via notions of the self. This can complement a historically motivated claim such as de Bolla's, who suggests that 'Kant's critical philosophy has become sublimated within our perception of the sublime.' In fact, de Bolla's historically specific examination as to how 'they [Edmund Burke and Archibald Alison] set out to [...] investigate the theoretical and discursive production of th[e] subject' gains unsuspected force when reassessing the more unstable side of the subject in the Kantian texts. De Bolla, *The Discourse of the Sublime*, p. 293.

4 A BLUE CHASM

1. John Keats, *The Letters of John Keats*, ed. Hyder Edward Rollins, 2 vols. (Cambridge: Cambridge University Press, 1958), vol. 1, p. 319. Further references to the *Letters* are to this edition (*L*) and indicated by volume and page numbers in the main text.
2. Revd Joseph A. M. Robertson, *An Essay on Punctuation* (London: 1785), p. 115.
3. F. Francillon, *An Essay on Punctuation, with Incidental Remarks on Composition* (London, 1842), p. 33. Also see George Smallfield, *The Principles of English Punctuation, Preceded by Brief Explanations of the Parts of Speech* (London, 1838); John Best Davidson, *The Difficulties of English Grammar and Punctuation Removed* (London, 1839); Robert Morehead, *Explanations of Some Passages in the Epistles of St. Paul, Chiefly by Means of an Amended Punctuation* (Edinburgh,

1843); James Burrow, *De Ratione et Usu Interpungendi: An Essay on Punctuation* (London, 1872); Justin Brenan, *Composition and Punctuation* (n.p.: Crosby Lockwood, 1889).

4. Heinrich Lausberg, *Handbuch der literarischen Rhetorik: Eine Grundlegung der Literaturwissenschaft* (Munich: Max Hueber, 1960), §860. Also note the similarity to the related figure of anacoluthon ('the want of grammatical sequence; the passing from one construction to the another before the former is completed' [*OED*]). The importance of the anacoluthon for contemporary German writers interested in fragmentation is explained in Winfried Menninghaus, *Unendliche Verdopplung: Die frühromantische Grundlegung der Kunsttheorie im Begriff absoluter Selbstreflexion* (Frankfurt am Main: Suhrkamp, 1987), pp. 142–8. For other entries on these rhetorical terms, see Alex Preminger and T. V. F. Brogan, eds., *The New Princeton Encyclopedia of Poetry and Poetics* (Princeton: Princeton University Press, 1993). Ueding and others, *Historisches Wörterbuch der Rhetorik*.

5. Thomas O. Sloane, ed., *Encyclopedia of Rhetoric* (Oxford: Oxford University Press, 2001), p. 553.

6. Derrida indicates these dimensions only in passing. See Jacques Derrida, *Limited Inc* (Evanston, IL: Northwestern University Press, 1988), pp. 131–7. Other commentaries concentrate on quite particular angles and mostly restrict their analysis to the parenthesis as a grammatical phenomenon. See Sylwia Gibs, 'Les fonctions de la parenthèse dans *Nadja* d'André Breton', in Yves Gohin and Robert Ricatte, eds., *Recherches en sciences des textes* (Grenoble: Presses Universitaires de Grenoble, 1977), pp. 181–8; Gabrielle Parker, 'Michèle Perrein: The Parenthesis as Metaphor for the Female Condition', in Margaret Atack and Phil Powrie, eds., *Contemporary French Fiction by Women: Feminist Perspectives* (Manchester and New York: Manchester University Press, 1990), pp. 116–25; Jean-Jacques Thomas, 'Dada ne signifie rien, fermez la parenthèse', *L'Ésprit Créateur*, 20.2 (1980), 5–11; Garin W. Dowd, '"Connect-I-Cut": George Oppen's *Discrete Series* and a Parenthesis by Jacques Derrida', *Angelaki*, 5.1 (2000), 123–8.

7. The wider definition of parenthesis also refers to rules (hyphen and dash) and so-called 'special sorts' (asterisk, paragraph).

8. In Wordsworth's case, as with many of his contemporaries, punctuation can be editorial (the lunulae at the beginning of 'Nutting' are one example). In a letter written on 29 July 1800 to Humphrey Davy, Wordsworth suggests that he is 'no adept' at punctuation. See William Wordsworth and Dorothy Wordsworth, *The Letters of William and Dorothy Wordsworth*, ed. Ernest De Selincourt and others, 2nd edn, 8 vols. (Oxford: Clarendon Press, 1967–93), vol. 1, p. 289. Considering this, I have only used passages of *The Prelude* in which the lunulae appear in the manuscripts. I am aware that these are not always in Wordsworth's own hand. However, if this were to prevent us from taking their precise form and position seriously, much textual scholarship relating to Wordsworth would be impossible. The more abstract methodological question in how far Wordsworth's own interest regarding

punctuation impinges on my argument I want to answer through my readings. However, I want to take this opportunity to thank Duncan Wu for making me aware of this difficulty and generously helping – while ultimately disagreeing with me – on precisely this point.

9. John Lennard, *But I Digress: The Exploitation of Parentheses in English Printed Verse* (Oxford: Clarendon Press, 1991), pp. 114–38. Also see Robert Grant Williams, 'Reading the Parenthesis', *Substance*, 22.1 (1993), 53–66. These are the only two recent studies to deal with parenthesis in English literature. Of the very few longer publications on the subject that appear earlier, most restrict themselves to genealogical investigations and strictly technical rhetorical studies. Eduard Schwyzer, *Die Parenthese im engeren und weiteren Sinne* (Berlin: Verlag der Akademie der Wissenschaften, 1939); Michael von Albrecht, *Die Parenthese in Ovids Metamorphosen und ihre dichterische Funktion* (Hildesheim: Olms, 1964). In relation to linguistics, see Sabine Pétillon-Boucheron, *Les détours de la langue: Etude sur la parenthèse et le tiret double* (Louvain and Dudley, MA: Éditions Peeters, 2002). For a broad historical survey, see M. B. Parkes, *Pause and Effect: An Introduction to the History of Punctuation in the West* (Berkeley: University of California Press, 1993). For a commentary on citation and cultural studies, refer to Marjorie Garber, *Quotation Marks* (New York; London: Routledge, 2003), pp. 7–32. Bearing Lennard's study in mind, I want to assume that the parenthesis maintains its disruptive quality in terms of narratorial and grammatical structure even when it is seemingly inclusive, such as in a digressive list.

10. Lennard, *But I Digress*, p. 136.

11. As in other cases that I discuss, the non-verbal variants between the different versions also affect the parenthetical punctuation.

12. Jacobus, *Romanticism, Writing and Sexual Difference*, p. 276.

13. William Wordsworth, *The Five-Book Prelude*, ed. Duncan Wu (Oxford and Malden, MA: Blackwell, 1997), App 1, lines 1–11.

14. This is an apt moment to mention the related discussion on the hermeneutic gap and the figure of allegory, specifically as understood through de Man (via Gadamer and Benjamin). As will become increasingly clear, de Man's writings are present in the background of this chapter. For a selection of sources on the link between hermeneutic gap and allegory, see Hans-Georg Gadamer, *Wahrheit und Methode: Grundzüge einer philosophischen Hermeneutik*, 4th edn (Tübingen: Mohr, 1975), pp. 66–77. De Man, *Blindness and Insight*, pp. 187–228. Paul de Man, *Allegories of Reading: Figural Language in Rousseau, Nietzsche, Rilke and Proust* (New Haven and London: Yale University Press, 1979), pp. 188–220. In direct relation to allegory and Romanticism, also see Geoffrey Hartman, *Beyond Formalism: Literary Essays, 1958–1970* (New Haven and London: Yale University Press, 1970), pp. 303–4. Nancy, *The Birth to Presence*, pp. 48–81.

15. William Wordsworth, *The Prelude, 1798–1799*, ed. Stephen Parrish (Ithaca: Cornell University Press, 1977), vol. 1, lines 247–8. Further references to the

1799 *Prelude* are to this edition (*1799*) and indicated by volume and line numbers in the main text.

16. Astonishingly, this is a phrase that both Wordsworth and Friedrich Nietzsche use in relation to particular mental states. See the *Prelude*'s 'Strange rendezvous my mind was at that time' (*1805*, 4. 346), and Nietzsche's description of the hysteric: 'He [the hysteric] is not a person anymore, at most a rendezvous of persons […]'. See Friedrich Nietzsche, *Kritische Gesamtausgabe*, ed. Giorgio Colli and Mazzino Montenari, vol. 8.3 (Berlin and New York: de Gruyter, 1972), p. 314.

17. Judith Butler, 'Giving an Account of Oneself', *Diacritics: A Review of Contemporary Criticism*, 31.4 (2001), pp. 22–40 (p. 34). Also see Ferguson, 'Romantic Memory'.

18. Susan J. Wolfson, 'The Illusion of Mastery: Wordsworth's Revisions of "The Drowned Man of Esthwaite," 1799, 1805, 1850', *PMLA*, 99.5 (1984), 917–35 (p. 922). Also see Peter J. Manning, 'Reading Wordsworth's Revisions: Othello and the Drowned Man', *Studies in Romanticism*, 22.1 (1983), 3–28; William A. Ulmer, 'Rousseau's *Émile* and Wordsworth's Drowned Man of Esthwaite', *English Language Notes*, 33.1 (1995), 15–19.

19. On the spots of time as memorials, see Harold Bloom, *The Visionary Company: A Reading of English Romantic Poetry*, revised and enlarged edn (Ithaca and London: Cornell University Press, 1971), p. 161. The reading advanced here is compatible with recent psychoanalytic interpretations such as Eugene Stelzig's which see the haunting corpse as a 'symbolic correlative and covert signifier […] of the death of the [poet's] father'. Eugene Stelzig, 'Wordsworth's Bleeding Spots: Traumatic Memories of the Absent Father in "The Prelude"', *European Romantic Review*, 15.4 (2004), 533–45 (p. 540). Hartman comments on the importance of the figure of the garment in a similar context, cross-referencing this passage to other parts of *The Prelude*. See Hartman, *Beyond Formalism*, p. 308.

20. Chase, *Decomposing Figures*, p. 24.

21. For how 'the Romantic mind' rebuilds (and mythologises) Romance, see Hartman, *Beyond Formalism*, p. 307. The textualisation of the world brings with it a necessary suppression of its non-textual sources.

22. For the other intertextual reference to the *Arabian Nights* and its importance in relation to Wordsworth's text, see Peter L. Caraciolo, 'Introduction', in Peter L. Caraciolo, ed., *The Arabian Nights in English Literature: Studies in the Reception of The Thousand and One Nights into British Culture* (Basingstoke and London: Macmillan, 1988), pp. 1–80 (esp. pp. 6–10).

23. For a related discussion around the topic of spectres, see Jacques Derrida, *Specters of Marx: The State of the Debt, the Work of Mourning, and the New International*, trans. Peggy Kamuf (New York and London: Routledge, 1994), pp. 1–48. In relation to Wordsworth and ghosts, see Geoffrey Hartman, *Wordsworth's Poetry: 1787–1814* (New Haven and London: Yale University Press, 1964), p. 78. Deeane Westbrook, *Wordsworth's Biblical Ghosts* (New York and Basingstoke: Palgrave, 2001).

24. See A. C. Bradley, *Oxford Lectures on Poetry* (London: Macmillan, 1909). More contemporary classics are Hartman, *The Unremarkable Wordsworth*, pp. 75–89. Neil Hertz, *The End of the Line: Essays on Psychoanalysis and the Sublime* (New York: Columbia University Press, 1985), pp. 136–64. Weiskel, *The Romantic Sublime*, pp. 167–204. Departing from these psychoanalytic approaches into Kleinean themes is John Turner, 'Wordsworth and the Psychogenesis of the Sublime', *Romanticism*, 6.1 (2000), 20–34. For an overview and close readings of the early Wordsworth, see Klaus P. Mortensen, *The Time of Unrememberable Being: Wordsworth and the Sublime, 1787–1805* (Copenhagen: Museum Tusculanum Press, 1998). In relation to the sublime and economy, see Charles J. Rzepka, 'Wordsworth between God and Mammon: The Early "Spots of Time" and the Sublime as Sacramental Commodity', in J. Robert Barth, ed., *The Fountain Light: Studies in Romanticism and Religion in Honor of John L. Mahoney* (New York: Fordham University Press, 2002), pp. 73–89.

25. Wordsworth, *'Lyrical Ballads', and Other Poems, 1797–1800*. For an instructive textual comparison with 'A Night Piece' and *Descriptive Sketches* (492–511), where the Snowdon episode first enters Wordsworth's corpus, see Jonathan Wordsworth, 'The Climbing of Snowdon', in Jonathan Wordsworth, ed., *Bicentenary Wordsworth Studies: In Memory of John Alban Finch* (Ithaca and London: Cornell University Press, 1970), pp. 449–74.

26. Alan Liu, *Wordsworth: The Sense of History* (Stanford: Stanford University Press, 1989), p. 466.

27. Liu, *Wordsworth*, p. 447.

28. Hartman, *Wordsworth's Poetry: 1787–1814*, p. 187.

29. There has been a tendency, especially in some commentary that wants to provide a more definite textual account of the episode, to ignore the continuous power of this second aspect of Wordsworth's text. For example, W. J. B Owen's classic reading argues that 'The meaningless data take on form and meaning by passing through the channel of the Imagination.' W. J. B. Owen, 'The Perfect Image of a Mighty Mind', *The Wordsworth Circle*, 10.1 (1979), 3–16 (p. 8). Owen, similarly to Liu, seems to belittle the genuinely creative effect of the confusion Wordsworth describes.

30. Simpson, *Irony and Authority in Romantic Poetry*, p. 117.

5 LETTERS FROM THE GRAVE

1. Athenaeum fragment #77, in Schlegel, *Kritische Friedrich-Schlegel-Ausgabe*, vol. 2, p. 176.

2. T. S. Eliot is an interesting exception, stating that Keats's letters will prove to be his ultimate legacy to the literary canon. T. S. Eliot, 'Shelley and Keats', in *The Use of Poetry and the Use of Criticism*, 2nd edn (London: Faber and Faber, 1949), pp. 87–102.

3. Robin Mayhead, 'The Letters', in *John Keats* (Cambridge: Cambridge University Press, 1967), pp. 112–26 (p. 112).

4. See Susan J. Wolfson, 'Keats the Letter-Writer: Epistolary Poetics', *Romanticism Past and Present*, 6.2 (1982), 43–61. Timothy Webb, '"Cutting Figures": Rhetorical Strategies in Keats's *Letters*', in Michael O'Neill, ed., *Keats: Bicentenary Readings* (Edinburgh: Edinburgh University Press, 1997), pp. 144–69.

5. John Barnard, 'Keats's Letters: "Remembrancing and enchaining"', in Susan J. Wolfson, ed., *The Cambridge Companion to Keats* (Cambridge: Cambridge University Press, 2001), pp. 120–34 (pp. 120–1).

6. It includes critics such as Andrew Bennett, who insists that the 'pragmatic nature of epistolary discourse' is classified as paradigmatic for 'private' writing. Andrew Bennett, *Romantic Poets and the Culture of Posterity* (Cambridge: Cambridge University Press, 1999), p. 36. Also see Jürgen Habermas, *Strukturwandel der Öffentlichkeit: Untersuchungen zu einer Kategorie der bürgerlichen Gesellschaft* (Frankfurt am Main: Suhrkamp, 1962), pp. 107–21. In his important study, Karl-Heinz Bohrer makes the letter a 'period' genre, arguing, however, for its fundamental change into a fully auto-poetic mode in the Romantic era; see Karl Heinz Bohrer, *Der romantische Brief: Die Enstehung ästhetischer Subjektivität* (Munich and Vienna: Suhrkamp, 1989).

7. Hyder Rollins's editorial notes inform us that in this letter Keats is referring to *Correspondence originale et inédite de J. J. Rousseau avec Mme. Latour de Franqueville et M. du Peyrou* (*L*, 2. 266, n. 4).

8. Such is Benjamin Bailey's project when he remarks to Richard Milnes, who had compiled *The Life, Letters and Literary Remains of John Keats*: 'Would you allow me to suggest that, in a future edition, this & the other Sonnets included in letters, be restored to their several & appropriate places? [...] All the other poems, sent in letters *are* so printed. They would obviously have lost their peculiar zest, had they been divorced from their original destination; & so do the sonnets.' Hyder Edward Rollins, ed., *The Keats Circle*, 2 vols. (Cambridge, MA: Harvard University Press, 1965), vol. 2, p. 281. Further references are to this edition (*KC*) and are indicated by volume and page number in the main text.

9. Gilles Deleuze and Félix Guattari, *Kafka: Toward a Minor Literature* (Minneapolis: University of Minnesota Press, 1986), p. 30.

10. Frances Ferguson, 'The Unfamiliarity of Familiar Letters', in Christopher Ricks, ed., *The State of the Language* (Berkeley, Los Angeles, and London: University of California Press, 1990), pp. 78–88 (p. 88). Also see Frances Ferguson, 'Interpreting the Self through Letters', *Centrum*, 1.2 (1981), 107–12. These passages also echo Humboldt's insight that all exchanges of speech reinforce the difference between interlocutors (rather than their commonality). See Wilhelm von Humboldt, 'Über den Dualis', in *Werke in Fünf Bänden*, ed. Andreas Flitner and Klaus Giel, vol. 3 (Stuttgart: Cotta, 1963), pp. 113–43.

11. To classify letters as dialogue or a specifically feminine form is a commonplace in letter-writing and its theory from the Classical age onwards. For a selection of sources, see Angelika Ebrecht, Regina Nörtemann, and Herta Schwarz, eds.,

Brieftheorie des 18. Jahrhunderts: Texte, Kommentare, Essays (Stuttgart: Metzler, 1990). William Henry Irving, *The Providence of Wit in English Letter Writers* (Durham, NC: Duke University Press, 1955); Felix Pryor, ed., *The Faber Book of Letters* (London: Faber and Faber, 1988); Anita Runge and Lieselotte Steinbrügge, eds., *Die Frau im Dialog: Studien zur Theorie des Briefes* (Stuttgart: Metzler, 1991); Bernhard Siegert, *Relais: Geschichte der Literatur als Epoche der Post 1751–1913* (Berlin: Brinkmann and Bose, 1993). I do not understand my use of the terms 'dialogue' and 'dialogism' in a Bakhtinian sense. Bakhtin's specific generic restrictions do not allow this and here would lead into a critical cul-de-sac.

12. The complexity of this position gains a further layer when it is considered that only through past experiences, through 'remember[ing] Ways and Manners and actions', is writing made possible in the first place.

13. Curiously, Schlegel combines the imagery of the two Keats brothers when writing to Novalis: 'I think that you [Novalis] will express your ideas more piquantly and boldly in letters to me than in a dissertation.' Schlegel, *Kritische Friedrich-Schlegel-Ausgabe*, vol. 24, p. 56.

14. Nevertheless, Seneca's *De Beneficiis* is usually cited as the major influence. See Linda Levy Peck, *Court Patronage and Corruption in Early Stuart England* (London: Unwin Hyman, 1990), pp. 12–14; Natalie Zemon Davis, *The Gift in Sixteenth-Century France* (Oxford: Oxford University Press, 2000), pp. 17–21. For Mauss's foundational text, see Marcel Mauss, *The Gift: The Form of Reason for Exchange in Archaic Societies*, trans. W. D. Halls (London: Routledge, 1990). In relation to the epistolary mode and reciprocity, also see Jacques Derrida, 'Envois', trans. Alan Bass, in *The Postcard: From Socrates to Freud and Beyond* (Chicago and London: University of Chicago Press, 1987), pp. 1–256.

15. Jonathan Parry, '*The Gift*, the Indian Gift and the "Indian Gift"', *Man*, 21.3 (1985), 453–73 (p. 458). Also see Simon Jarvis who argues that 'Economy is *essentially* characterized not only by the ubiquity of exchange, but also by a reduction to purity of the gift. [...] *The reduction of the gift to the purity of non-being is a condition of the possibility of economism.*' Simon Jarvis, 'Problems in the Phenomenology of the Gift', *Angelaki*, 6.2 (2001), 67–78 (p. 75).

16. Michael Wetzel, 'Liebesgaben: Streifzüge des literarischen Eros', in Michael Wetzel and Jean-Michel Rabaté, eds., *Ethik der Gabe: Denken nach Jacques Derrida* (Berlin: Akademie, 1993), pp. 223–47 (p. 240).

17. Simon Jarvis, 'Wordsworth's Gift of Feeling', *Romanticism*, 4.1 (1998), 90–103 (p. 100).

18. John Keats, *The Poems of John Keats*, ed. Jack Stillinger (London: Heinemann, 1978).

19. Hamann, *Sämtliche Werke*, vol. 2, p. 129.

20. Jochen Hörisch, *Kopf oder Zahl: Die Poesie des Geldes* (Frankfurt am Main: Suhrkamp, 1996), p. 307.

21. Jarvis, 'Wordsworth's Gift of Feeling', pp. 93–4. Unfortunately, Hörisch ignores the anthropological aspects of this question (e.g. Mauss's avoidance of the question of purely monetary exchange in his *Essai*), from which Jarvis

takes his cue. For the deep-seated nexus of linguistics and exchange also see Florian Coulmas, *Die Wirtschaft mit der Sprache: Eine sprachsoziologische Studie* (Frankfurt am Main: Suhrkamp, 1992). There is a book yet to be written about metaphor *as* currency, including the image of the coin as both figure and material of exchange; the variations of this idea can be traced through Hobbes, Locke, Leibniz, Hume, Hamann, Kant, Herder, and Nietzsche.

22. Nicholas Roe, *John Keats and the Culture of Dissent* (Oxford: Clarendon Press, 1997), p. vii.

23. Nicholas Roe, *Keats and History* (Cambridge and New York: Cambridge University Press, 1995). See especially Wolfson's contribution 'Keats Enters History: Autopsy, *Adonais*, and the Fame of Keats', pp. 17–45.

24. Hamilton, *Metaromanticism*, p. 107. This is part of a larger discussion on Keats and monetary theories (see pp. 102–14).

25. Bennett, *Romantic Poets and the Culture of Posterity*, p. 151.

26. Bennett would disagree with this move; see Andrew Bennett, *Keats, Narrative and Audience: The Posthumous Life of Writing* (Cambridge: Cambridge University Press, 1994), pp. 36–47. Also see Benjamin (*GS* 5.1, p. 95) in this context who speaks of the letter as a 'testimony' (*Zeugnis*).

27. Concerning the temporal aspects of the construction of an archive, see Jacques Derrida, *Archive Fever: A Freudian Impression*, trans. Eric Prenowitz (Chicago and London: University of Chicago Press, 1996), pp. 29 and 36.

28. See Robert Gittings, *John Keats* (London: Heinemann, 1968), p. 405.

29. Richard Monckton Milnes, ed., *Life, Letters and Literary Remains of John Keats* 2 vols. (London: Edward Moxon, 1848), vol. 2, p. 91. Further references to the *Life* are in the main text (*Life*) and are indicated by volume and page numbers.

30. As Hyder Rollins points out, it is used by Catullus, Bacon, Chapman, Beaumont and Fletcher, and Donne (see *KC*, 2. 91, n. 72). For contemporary examples, see David Rothenberg and Marta Ulvaeus, eds., *Writing on Water* (Cambridge, MA: MIT Press, 2001).

31. Jackson Bate, for example, fantasises that 'As he [Keats] lay in his corner room next to the Spanish Steps, listening night after night to the constant play of water in the fountain outside, the words kept coming back to him from a play of Beaumont and Fletcher (*Philaster*): "all your better deeds / Shall be in water writ".' Walter Jackson Bate, *John Keats* (London: Chatto and Windus, 1979), p. 694. For other relevant sources concerning the history of Keats's tombstone, see Joseph Severn, *Joseph Severn: Letters and Memoirs*, ed. Grant F. Scott (Aldershot: Ashgate, 2005), especially p. 174 (n. 179); and *KC*, 2. 91, n. 72. In relation to the epitaph, see Oonagh Lahr, 'Greek Sources of "Writ in Water"', *Keats–Shelley Journal*, 21–2 (1972), 17–18.

32. Jonathan Barnes, *The Presocratic Philosophers*, rev. edn (London and Boston: Routledge, 1982), p. 66 (45: B 91 = 40 (C^3) M).

33. See Severn, *Joseph Severn*, p. 174.

34. For Marx's famous letter mentioning Heraclitus (written on 25 February 1859), see Karl Marx and Friedrich Engels, *Karl Marx–Friedrich Engels Gesamtausgabe*

(MEGA) (Amsterdam: Akademie, 2003), vol. 3.9, pp. 325–30. Also see Karl Marx and Friedrich Engels, *Collected Works* (London: Lawrence and Wishart, 1975–), vol. 40 (*Marx and Engels: 1856–59*), p. 394. For a recent intervention on the link between money and Heraclitus, see Richard Seaford, *Money and the Early Greek Mind: Homer, Philosophy, Tragedy* (Cambridge: Cambridge University Press, 2004), pp. 231–42.

35. Marc Shell, *The Economy of Literature* (Baltimore: Johns Hopkins University Press, 1978), p. 50. Similarly to Jarvis, Shell is interested in the role of exchange in the genesis of the division between the figural and the literal.

36. Marc Shell, *Money, Language and Thought: Literary and Philosophical Economies from the Medieval to the Modern Era* (Berkeley and London: University of California Press, 1982), p. 2.

37. Barnes, *The Presocratic Philosophers*, p. 66 (44: B 49a = 40 (c²) M).

38. Shell, *The Economy of Literature*, p. 50.

39. Shell, *The Economy of Literature*, pp. 50–1.

40. Johann Wilhelm Ritter, *Fragmente aus dem Nachlasse eines jungen Physikers: Ein Taschenbuch für Freunde der Natur* (Leipzig and Weimar: Kiepenheuer, 1984), p. 181.

6 THE DOUBLING FORCE OF CITATION

1. Ritter, *Fragmente aus dem Nachlasse eines jungen Physikers*, p. 181.

2. Ralph Waldo Emerson, 'Quotation and Originality', in *Emerson's Complete Works*, 12 vols. (Boston and New York: Houghton Mifflin, 1892–4), vol. 8, pp. 169–94 (pp. 170–2). See Stanley Cavell's exceptional contribution on Emerson and citation in relation to the construction of the Romantic canon. Strangely, Cavell does not mention Emerson's overt intervention on the subject. Stanley Cavell, *In Quest of the Ordinary: Lines of Skepticism and Romanticism* (Chicago: University of Chicago Press, 1988), pp. 30–6 and 105–20.

3. Emerson, 'Quotation and Originality', p. 183.

4. Jacques Ehrmann, 'The Death of Literature', *New Literary History*, 3.1 (1971), 31–47 (p. 37).

5. M. M. Bakhtin, *Speech Genres and Other Late Essays*, trans. Vern W. McGee (Austin: University of Texas Press, 1986), p. 339.

6. Bakhtin, *Speech Genres and Other Late Essays*, p. 374. Bakhtin makes a suspiciously sharp distinction between fictional and non-fictional quotation. He therefore does not seem willing to read his insights back into his own theoretical prose. That is, he seems reluctant to look for 'another's discourse' that might have shaped his own theory; or turn into his own 'given author'. In relation to Bakhtin, literary analysis, and quotation, see S. Stevenson, 'Poetry Deleted, Parody Added, Watergate, Spark Style, and Bakhtin Stylistics', *Ariel*, 24.4 (1993), 71–85. V. Creelman, 'Quotation and Self-fashioning in Margaret Paston's Household Letters', *English Studies in Canada*, 30.3 (2004), 111–28; Nina Perlina, *Varieties of Poetic Utterance: Quotation in The Brothers Karamazov* (Lanham, MD: University Press of America, 1985).

7. Nigel Leask, *British Romantic Writers and the East: Anxieties of Empire* (Cambridge and New York: Cambridge University Press, 1992), p. 187.

8. Leask, *British Romantic Writers and the East*, p. 188.

9. Grevel Lindop, 'De Quincey's Wordsworthian Quotations', *The Wordsworth Circle*, 26.2 (1995), 58–65 (p. 58).

10. Antoine Compagnon, *La seconde main: ou Le travail de la citation* (Paris: Éditions du Seuil, 1979).

11. Balfour, *The Rhetoric of Romantic Prophecy*, p. 5.

12. Thomas Drewitt [attributed], *The Force of Contrast: or Quotations, Accompanied by Remarks* (Bath: Hazard, 1801).

13. Thomas Toke Lynch, *The Ethics of Quotation, with a Preliminary Letter to the Secretaries of the Congregational Union* (London: William Freeman, 1856), p. i.

14. Blanchot, *The Writing of the Disaster*, p. 37.

15. *GS*, 2.1, pp. 362–3. In relation to Benjamin and citation, see Josef Fürnkäs, 'Zitat und Zerstörung: Karl Kraus und Walter Benjamin', in Jacques Le Rider and Gérard Raulet, eds., *Verabschiedung der (Post-)Moderne? Eine interdisziplinäre Debatte* (Tübingen: Gunther Narr, 1987), pp. 209–26; James L. Rolleston, 'The Politics of Quotation: Walter Benjamin's Arcades Project', *PMLA*, 104.1 (1984), 13–27; Ian Balfour, 'Reversal, Quotation (Benjamin's History)', *Modern Language Notes*, 106.3 (1991), 622–47.

16. *GS*, 2.1, p. 363.

17. See Manfred Voigts, '"Die Mater der Gerechtigkeit": Zur Kritik des Zitat-Begriffes bei Walter Benjamin', in Norbert W. Bolz and Richard Faber, eds., *Antike und Moderne: Zu Walter Benjamins 'Passagen'* (Würzburg: Königshausen and Neumann, 1986), pp. 97–115 (p. 100). For Voigts's more recent work on Benjamin and citation, see Manfred Voigts, 'Zitat', in *Benjamins Begriffe*, ed. Michael Opitz and Erdmut Wizisla, 2 vols. (Frankfurt am Main: Suhrkamp, 2000), vol. 2, pp. 826–50.

18. In his *Trauerspiel* book, Benjamin dedicates a section to a discussion of Ritter's conception of language, relating it to the (post-Babelian) musical and allegorical sign (*GS*, 1.1, pp. 387–9). An edition of Ritter's *Fragmente* is Benjamin's object of desire in the famous 'Unpacking my Library' (*GS*, 4.1, pp. 388–96). According to Voigts, Benjamin's second major influence in thinking about this topic is Goethe's report in *Dichtung und Wahrheit* about reading Georg Hamann. Benjamin adapts Goethe's idea, exemplified in the latter's reading of Hamann's citations in manuscript, that citation is a writerly strategy for the multiplication of meaning. Through endless referencing and referring, it allows for the possibility of the perpetual creation of meaning in an infinite variety of contexts. For Goethe's passage see Johann Wolfgang von Goethe, *Werke, Hamburger Ausgabe*, ed. Lieselotte Blumenthal, 9th rev. edn, 14 vols. (Munich: Beck, 1981), vol. 9, pp. 512–17.

19. Ritter, *Fragmente aus dem Nachlasse eines jungen Physikers*, pp. 208–9.

20. Thomas De Quincey, *The Works of Thomas De Quincey*, ed. Grevel Lindop, and others, Pickering Masters, 21 vols. (London and Brookfield, VT: Pickering and Chatto, 2000–3), vol. 16, p. 354. Further references to De

Quincey's *Works* are to this edition (*DQ*) and are indicated by volume and page numbers in the main text.

21. Frederick Burwick, *Thomas De Quincey: Knowledge and Power* (Basingstoke: Palgrave, 2001), p. 160.

22. Alina Clej, *A Genealogy of the Modern Self: Thomas De Quincey and the Intoxication of Writing* (Stanford: Stanford University Press, 1995), pp. v and 8.

23. Joel Faflak, 'De Quincey Collects Himself', in Joel Faflak and Julia M. Wright, eds., *Victorian Recollections of Romanticism*, (Albany, NY: State University of New York Press, 2004), pp. 23–46 (p. 25). Also see Josephine McDonagh, *De Quincey's Disciplines* (Oxford: Clarendon, 1994).

24. Margaret Russett, *De Quincey's Romanticism: Canonical Minority and the Forms of Transmission* (Cambridge: Cambridge University Press, 1997), p. 189.

25. Russett, *De Quincey's Romanticism*, p. 190.

26. Devlin, *De Quincey, Wordsworth and the Art of Prose*, p. 46.

27. Ferguson, *Wordsworth*, p. xvi.

28. John Barrell, *The Infection of Thomas De Quincey: A Psychopathology of Imperialism* (New Haven and London: Yale University Press, 1991), p. 24.

29. For a different reading of the episode recording Elizabeth's death that is receptive to the biblical allusions and implications, see Charles Rzepka, *Sacramental Commodities: Gift, Text, and the Sublime in De Quincey* (Amherst: University of Massachusetts Press, 1995), pp. 111–22.

30. Miller, *The Disappearance of God*, p. 55.

31. Wordsworth, *'Poems, in Two Volumes', and Other Poems, 1800–1807*, p. 274. Also see William Wordsworth, *The Manuscript of William Wordsworth's 'Poems, in Two Volumes'*, ed. W. H. Kelliher (London: British Library, 1984), p. 109. William Wordsworth, *Poems in Two Volumes* (London, 1807), p. 153. In his editorial notes Robert Morrison mentions this strange footnote and its mis-directed reference; his suggestion is that De Quincey might in fact be alluding to a passage in *Hamlet*. See *DQ*, 8, p. 395 (n. 108).

32. Mary Jacobus, 'The Art of Managing Books: Romantic Prose and the Writing of the Past', in Arden Reed, ed., *Romanticism and Language* (London: Methuen, 1984), pp. 215–46 (p. 224).

33. *GS*, 2.1, p. 363.

34. The publishing history of this essay is well documented. Originally, it appeared in instalments in *Tait's Edinburgh Magazine*, 1839. A revised version finds its way into *Selections Grave and Gay* ed. James Hogg (1854). In the Masson edition it is collected under the heading 'Literary and Lake Reminiscences', whereas now it is best known as part of *Recollections of the Lakes and the Lake Poets*. See Julian North's remarks in *DQ*, 11, pp. 40–3. Also cf. Thomas De Quincey, *Recollections of the Lakes and the Lake Poets*, ed. David Wright (Harmondsworth: Penguin, 1970), pp. 28–9.

35. De Quincey's hesitation also relates to what kind of sublime he is trying to establish via Wordsworth here. Charles Rzepka shows how De Quincey figures the experience of the sublime in a particular way that is linked to the categories of gift exchange and sacrifice. See Rzepka, *Sacramental Commodities*. For an

account of the ambiguity of the supposedly stereotypically 'male' sublime in De Quincey, see Tim Fulford, 'De Quincey's Literature of Power', *The Wordsworth Circle*, 31.3 (2000), 158–64.

36. See John E. Jordan, *De Quincey to Wordsworth: A Biography of a Relationship* (Berkeley and Los Angeles: University of California Press, 1962), p. 349.

37. Jane Worthington Smyser, 'Wordsworth's Dream of Poetry and Science: "The Prelude", v', *PMLA*, 71.1 (1956), 269–75 (p. 274). For an earlier discussion of how the 'Wordsworth' essay discusses more than just Book 5, also see John E. Wells, 'De Quincey and "The Prelude" in 1839', *Philological Quarterly*, 20 (1941), 1–24. For the dream itself, Georges Poulet, *Études sur le temps humain*, 4 vols. (Edinburgh: Edinburgh University Press, 1949–68), vol. 1, pp. 63–92.

38. Ian Balfour, 'The Future of Citation: Blake, Wordsworth, and the Rhetoric of Romantic Prophecy', in David Wood, ed., *Writing the Future* (London and New York: Routledge, 1990), pp. 115–28 (p. 119).

39. Easson, *The Lapidary Wordsworth*, p. 7.

40. Russett, *De Quincey's Romanticism*, p. 196.

41. Russett, *De Quincey's Romanticism*, pp. 203 and 204.

42. Russett, *De Quincey's Romanticism*, p. 202.

7 PHILOLOGICAL FRACTURES

1. Walter Benjamin describing the act of translation (see *GS*, 6, p. 159).

2. Paul de Man, *Romanticism and Contemporary Criticism: The Gauss Seminar and Other Papers*, ed. E. S. Burt, Kevin Newmark, and Andrzej Warminski (Baltimore: Johns Hopkins University Press, 1993), p. 95. Further references are to this edition (*Gauss*), and will be given in the main text.

3. De Man, *Romanticism and Contemporary Criticism*, p. 97.

4. Redfield, *Phantom Formations*, p. 11.

5. Gasché, *The Wild Card of Reading*, p. 46.

6. Famously, John Guillory likens de Manian rigour to scholarly bureaucracy. See John Guillory, *Cultural Capital: The Problem of Literary Canon Formation* (Chicago and London: University of Chicago Press, 1993), pp. 176–268. Also note Simpson on the 'abjection' of de Man owing to his style, in Simpson, *Romanticism, Nationalism, and the Revolt against Theory*, p. 181.

7. Both de Man's own work and subsequent de Manian analyses of it, such as in Lindsay Waters's seminal collection, invite further considerations along these lines. See Lindsay Waters and Wlad Godzich, eds., *Reading de Man Reading* (Minneapolis: University of Minnesota Press, 1989).

8. Some of the more substantial discussions of the piece can be found in Derrida, 'Des Tours de Babel'. Also see Karl-Heinz Bohrer, ed., *Ästhetik und Rhetorik: Lektüren zu Paul de Man* (Frankfurt am Main: Suhrkamp, 1993); Andrew E. Benjamin and Peter Osborne, eds., *Walter Benjamin's Philosophy: Destruction and Experience,* 2nd edn (Manchester: Clinamen, 2000).

9. In its widest sense the issue of language in de Man is part of a much larger discussion about the theological nature of many post-structuralist projects.

The question remains whether the manner in which de Man insists on the secular nature of the gap indicates that his argument must ultimately remain theological. This extremely complicated but rewarding discussion must be displaced here. Suffice it to say that Benjamin was very aware of the theological dimension, even of his later work (which is characterised by a notoriously idiosyncratic version of historical materialism). As he subtly puts it in *The Arcades Project*: 'My thinking relates to theology like blotting paper to ink. It is wholly sucked full of it. If the blotting paper had its way, however, nothing that is written would remain' (*GS*, 5.1, p. 588 [N7, 7]). Benjamin repeats the intriguing image of the blotting paper in his short *Eidos und Begriff* (*GS*, 5.1, pp. 29 and 31). For further discussion see Hent De Vries, *Philosophy and the Turn to Religion* (Baltimore: Johns Hopkins University Press, 1999).

10. *GS*, 4.1, p. 18.

11. Jacobs, 'The Monstrosity of Translation', p. 763. Jacobs maintains that Benjamin rejects a link between an organic *Ursprache* and the 'broken part' which is what translations reveal languages to be. However, it still seems that admitting that the fragments will never be united does not entail that they need not have been so in order for them to become fragments. That unity may not have been organic, but it presumably preceded the fragments. I want to take this opportunity to thank Carol Jacobs and Andrew Benjamin for a number of long and detailed discussions on this topic.

12. See Ortwin de Graef, *Serenity in Crisis: A Preface to Paul de Man, 1939–1960* (Lincoln, NE, and London: University of Nebraska Press, 1993), pp. 21–6.

13. In an extremely insightful article, Rei Terada comments on the importance of the metaphors of light and vision in de Man. See Rei Terada, 'Seeing Is Reading', in Marc Redfield, ed., *Legacies of Paul de Man* (New York: Fordham University Press, 2007), pp. 162–77. However, her focus is de Man's notion of reading, and she does not mention translation. Terada's longer *Feeling in Theory* (2001) also provides a subtle reading of de Man. Rei Terada, *Feeling in Theory: Emotion after the 'Death of the Subject'* (Cambridge, MA: Harvard University Press, 2001).

14. For all its apparent originality, Carol Jacobs already makes this point in the piece later cited by de Man. Jacobs, 'The Monstrosity of Translation', p. 765. The qualities and shortcomings of de Man are helpfully discussed (albeit in a reactionary tone) in Jeffrey Grossman, 'The Reception of Walter Benjamin in the Anglo-American Literary Institution', *German Quarterly*, 65.3–4 (1992), 414–28 (p. 422). Also see Dieter Freundlieb, 'Dekonstruktivismus als interpretatorische Zwangsjacke. Paul de Mans (Fehl)Lektüre von Walter Benjamin', *Orbis Litterarum*, 54.2 (1999), 100–33. Stanley Corngold perceptively comments on de Man's use of the term *Wehen* in the context of his 'second birth' in US criticism, a 'second birth' after his darker past in Europe. Stanley Corngold, 'Paul de Man on the Contingency of Intention', in Luc Herman, Kris Humbeeck, and Lernout Geert, eds., *(Dis)continuities: Essays on Paul de Man* (Amsterdam: Rodopi, 1989), pp. 27–42 (p. 40, n. 43). I still think that Corngold's separate mention of '*Wähen* (which are quiches of sorts)' when writing on Benjamin and about attending de Man's lectures is more than an

odd coincidence; it represents a truly funny insight. See Stanley Corngold, 'Genuine Obscurity Shadows the Semblance Whose Obliteration Promises Redemption: Reflections on Benjamin's "Goethe's Elective Affinities"', in Gerhard Richter, ed., *Benjamin's Ghosts: Interventions in Contemporary Literary and Cultural Theory* (Stanford: Stanford University Press, 2002), pp. 154–68 (p. 154).

15. *GS*, 4.1, p. 13.
16. Maybe this is why de Man makes the initial move about *Wehen*, which are much more medical and circumscribed in their connotation than the Flemish *ween* seem to be. Incidentally, de Man is exhibiting a surprising optimism about the ability to 'see', 'hear', and consequently understand as well as translate 'correctly'.
17. See *RT*, 24.
18. Quoted in *GS*, 5.2, p. 1110.
19. Erich Auerbach, *Mimesis: The Representation of Reality in Western Literature* (Princeton: Princeton University Press, 1953), p. 484.
20. Ueding and others, *Historisches Wörterbuch der Rhetorik*, vol. 6.
21. Northrop Frye, *Collected Works of Northrop Frye*, ed. Robert D. Denham (Toronto and Buffalo: University of Toronto Press, 1996), vol. 17, p. 219.
22. De Man, *Blindness and Insight*, p. 11. This distinction, even into its exact phraseology, remains a constant in de Man's critical career (cf. *Gauss*, 12).

Bibliography

Aarsleff, Hans, *The Study of Language in England, 1780–1860* (London: Athlone, 1983)

An Address to the Inhabitants of Great Britain; occasioned by the late Earthquake at Lisbon. To which is added, A Postscript, particularly addressed to the Merchants and others, who are Sufferers in that awful Calamity. The Second Edition (London, 1755)

Adorno, Theodor W., *Negative Dialectics*, trans. E. B. Ashton (London: Routledge, 1990)

Albrecht, Michael von, *Die Parenthese in Ovids Metamorphosen und ihre dichterische Funktion* (Hildesheim: Olms, 1964)

Allison, Henry E., *Kant's Theory of Taste: A Reading of the Critique of Aesthetic Judgment* (Cambridge: Cambridge University Press, 2001)

Altick, Richard D., *The Shows of London* (Cambridge, MA, and London: Belknap Press of Harvard University Press, 1978)

Auerbach, Erich, *Mimesis: The Representation of Reality in Western Literature* (Princeton: Princeton University Press, 1953)

Bakhtin, M. M., *Speech Genres and Other Late Essays*, trans. Vern W. McGee (Austin: University of Texas Press, 1986)

Balfour, Ian, 'The Future of Citation: Blake, Wordsworth, and the Rhetoric of Romantic Prophecy', in David Wood, ed., *Writing the Future* (London and New York: Routledge, 1990), pp. 115–28

'Reversal, Quotation (Benjamin's History)', *Modern Language Notes*, 106.3 (1991), 622–47

The Rhetoric of Romantic Prophecy (Stanford: Stanford University Press, 2002)

Barnard, John, 'Keats's Letters: "Remembrancing and enchaining"', in Susan J. Wolfson, ed., *The Cambridge Companion to Keats* (Cambridge: Cambridge University Press, 2001), pp. 120–34

Barnes, Jonathan, *The Presocratic Philosophers*, rev. edn (London and Boston: Routledge, 1982)

Barrell, John, *The Infection of Thomas De Quincey: A Psychopathology of Imperialism* (New Haven and London: Yale University Press, 1991)

Imagining the King's Death: Figurative Treason, Fantasies of Regicide, 1793–1796 (Oxford and New York: Oxford University Press, 2000)

The Spirit of Despotism: Invasions of Privacy in the 1790s (Oxford: Oxford University Press, 2006)

Bate, Walter Jackson, *John Keats* (London: Chatto and Windus, 1979)

Baucom, Ian, and Jennifer Kennedy, eds., *Afterlives of Romanticism: Special Issue of The South Atlantic Quarterly*, 102 (2003)

Bayer, Oswald, Benjamin Gleede, and Ulrich Moustakas, *Vernunft ist Sprache: Hamanns Metakritik Kants* (Stuttgart-Bad Cannstatt: Frommann-Holzboog, 2002)

Beattie, James, *Dissertations Moral and Critical* (London, 1783)

Beckett, Samuel, *Worstward Ho* (London: John Calder, 1983)

Benjamin, Andrew E., *Philosophy's Literature* (Manchester: Clinamen, 2001)

Benjamin, Andrew E., and Beatrice Hanssen, eds., *Walter Benjamin and Romanticism* (New York: Continuum, 2002)

Benjamin, Andrew E., and Peter Osborne, eds., *Walter Benjamin's Philosophy: Destruction and Experience*, 2nd edn (Manchester: Clinamen, 2000)

Benjamin, Walter, *Aufklärung für Kinder* (Frankfurt am Main: Suhrkamp, 1985)
  Gesammelte Schriften, 7 vols. (Frankfurt am Main: Suhrkamp, 1991)

Bennett, Andrew, *Keats, Narrative and Audience: The Posthumous Life of Writing* (Cambridge: Cambridge University Press, 1994)
  Romantic Poets and the Culture of Posterity (Cambridge: Cambridge University Press, 1999)

Biddulph, John, *A Poem on the Earthquake of Lisbon* (London, 1755)

Blackwell, Thomas, *An Enquiry into the Life and Writings of Homer* (London, 1735)

Blair, Hugh, *Critical Dissertation on the Poems of Ossian the Son of Fingal* (London, 1763)
  Lectures on Rhetoric and Belles Lettres, 2 vols. (London, 1783)

Blake, William, *The Complete Poetry and Prose of William Blake*, ed. David Erdman, new rev. edn (Berkeley: University of California Press, 1982)

Blanchot, Maurice, *The Writing of the Disaster* (Lincoln: University of Nebraska Press, 1986)
  The Infinite Conversation (Minneapolis: University of Minnesota Press, 1993)

Blanke, Fritz, Karlfried Gründer, and Lothar Schreiner, *Johann Georg Hamanns Hauptschriften erklärt*, vol. 1 (*Die Hamann Forschung*), 7 vols. (Gütersloh: Bertelsmann, 1956)

Bloom, Harold, *The Visionary Company: A Reading of English Romantic Poetry*, revised and enlarged edn (Ithaca and London: Cornell University Press, 1971)

Blumenberg, Hans, *Die Legitimität der Neuzeit* (Frankfurt am Main: Suhrkamp, 1966)
  Begriffe in Geschichten (Frankfurt am Main: Suhrkamp, 1998)

Bohrer, Karl-Heinz, *Nach der Natur: Über Politik und Ästhetik* (Munich and Vienna: Hanser, 1988)
  Der romantische Brief: Die Enstehung ästhetischer Subjektivität (Munich and Vienna: Suhrkamp, 1989)
  ed., *Ästhetik und Rhetorik: Lektüren zu Paul de Man* (Frankfurt am Main: Suhrkamp, 1993)

Borst, Arno, *Der Turmbau von Babel*, 4 vols. (Stuttgart: Hiersemann, 1957)

Bostetter, Edward E., *The Romantic Ventriloquists: Wordsworth, Coleridge, Keats, Shelley, Byron* (Seattle: University of Washington Press, 1963)

Bradley, A. C., *Oxford Lectures on Poetry* (London: Macmillan, 1909)

Braun, Theodore E. D., and John B. Radner, eds., *The Lisbon Earthquake of 1755: Representations and Reactions*, Studies on Voltaire and the Eighteenth Century (Oxford: Voltaire Foundation, 2005)

Breidert, Wolfgang, ed., *Die Erschütterung der vollkommenen Welt: Die Wirkung des Erdbebens von Lissabon im Spiegel europäischer Zeitgenossen* (Darmstadt: Wissenschaftliche Buchgesellschaft, 1994)

Brenan, Justin, *Composition and Punctuation* (n.p.: Crosby Lockwood, 1889)

Briese, Olaf, *Die Macht der Metaphern: Blitz, Erdbeben, Kometen im Gefüge der Aufklärung* (Stuttgart: Metzler, 1998)

Brown, John, *The History of the Rise and Progress of Poetry, through it's several Species* (Newcastle, 1764)

Büchsel, Elfriede, *Johann Georg Hamanns Hauptschriften erklärt*, vol. 4 (*Über den Ursprung der Sprache*), 7 vols. (Gütersloh: Mohn, 1963)

Burke, Edmund, *A Philosophical Enquiry into the Origin of our Ideas of the Sublime and Beautiful*, ed. J. T. Boulton (London: Routledge and Kegan Paul, 1958)

   A Philosophical Enquiry into the Origin of our Ideas of the Sublime and Beautiful and other Pre-Revolutionary Writings, ed. David Womersley (Harmondsworth: Penguin, 1998)

Burrow, James, *De Ratione et Usu Interpungendi: An Essay on Punctuation* (London, 1872)

Burwick, Frederick, *Thomas De Quincey: Knowledge and Power* (Basingstoke: Palgrave, 2001)

Butler, Judith, 'Giving an Account of Oneself', *Diacritics: A Review of Contemporary Criticism*, 31.4 (2001), 22–40

Caraciolo, Peter L., 'Introduction', in *The Arabian Nights in English Literature: Studies in the Reception of The Thousand and One Nights into British Culture*, ed. Peter L. Caraciolo (Basingstoke and London: Macmillan, 1988), pp. 1–80

Caruth, Cathy, ed., *Trauma: Explorations in Memory* (Baltimore and London: Johns Hopkins University Press, 1995)

Cavell, Stanley, *In Quest of the Ordinary: Lines of Skepticism and Romanticism* (Chicago: University of Chicago Press, 1988)

Caygill, Howard, *Art of Judgement* (Oxford: Blackwell, 1989)

   Walter Benjamin: The Colour of Experience (London: Routledge, 1998)

Chai, Leon, *Romantic Theory: Forms of Reflexivity in the Revolutionary Era* (Baltimore: Johns Hopkins University Press, 2006)

Chandler, James K., *England in 1819: The Politics of Literary Culture and the Case of Romantic Historicism* (Chicago: University of Chicago Press, 1998)

Chandler, Samuel, *The Scripture Account of the Cause and Intention of Earthquakes, in a Sermon Preached at the old-jury March 11, 1749–50, on Occasion of the two Shocks of an earthquake, the first on February 8, the other March 8* (London, 1750)

Chase, Cynthia, *Decomposing Figures: Rhetorical Readings in the Romantic Tradition* (Baltimore and London: Johns Hopkins University Press, 1986)

    'Double-Take: Reading Paul de Man and Derrida Writing on Tropes', in Marc Redfield, ed., *Legacies of Paul de Man* (New York: Fordham University Press, 2007), pp. 17–28

A Chronological and Historical Account of the most memorable Earthquakes that have happened in the World, from the Beginning of the Christian Period to the present year 1750 (Cambridge, 1750)

Clej, Alina, *A Genealogy of the Modern Self: Thomas De Quincey and the Intoxication of Writing* (Stanford: Stanford University Press, 1995)

Compagnon, Antoine, *La seconde main: ou le travail de la citation* (Paris: Éditions du Seuil, 1979)

Corngold, Stanley, 'Paul de Man on the Contingency of Intention', in Luc Herman, Kris Humbeeck, and Lernout Geert, eds., *(Dis)continuities: Essays on Paul de Man* (Amsterdam: Rodopi, 1989), pp. 27–42

    'Genuine Obscurity Shadows the Semblance Whose Obliteration Promises Redemption: Reflections on Benjamin's "Goethe's Elective Affinities"', in Gerhard Richter, ed., *Benjamin's Ghosts: Interventions in Contemporary Literary and Cultural Theory* (Stanford: Stanford University Press, 2002), pp. 154–68

Coulmas, Florian, *Die Wirtschaft mit der Sprache: Eine sprachsoziologische Studie* (Frankfurt am Main: Suhrkamp, 1992)

Crawford, Robert, *The Modern Poet: Poetry, Academia and Knowledge since the 1750's* (Oxford: Oxford University Press, 2001)

Creelman, V., 'Quotation and Self-fashioning in Margaret Paston's Household Letters', *English Studies in Canada*, 30.3 (2004), 111–28

Dällenbach, Lucien, and Christian L. Hart Nibbrig, eds., *Fragment und Totalität* (Frankfurt am Main: Suhrkamp, 1984)

Davidson, John Best, *The Difficulties of English Grammar and Punctuation Removed* (London, 1839)

Davis, Natalie Zemon, *The Gift in Sixteenth-Century France* (Oxford: Oxford University Press, 2000)

de Bolla, Peter, *The Discourse of the Sublime: Readings in History, Aesthetics, and the Subject* (Oxford and New York: Basil Blackwell, 1989)

    Art Matters (Cambridge, MA: Harvard University Press, 2001)

    'Toward the Materiality of Aesthetic Experience', *Diacritics: A Review of Contemporary Criticism*, 32.1 (2002), 19–37

de Man, Paul, *Allegories of Reading: Figural Language in Rousseau, Nietzsche, Rilke and Proust* (New Haven and London: Yale University Press, 1979)

    Blindness and Insight: Essays in the Rhetoric of Contemporary Criticism, 2nd rev. edn (London: Methuen, 1983)

    The Rhetoric of Romanticism (New York: Columbia University Press, 1984)

    The Resistance to Theory (Manchester: Manchester University Press, 1986)

    Romanticism and Contemporary Criticism: The Gauss Seminar and Other Papers (Baltimore: Johns Hopkins University Press, 1993)

    Aesthetic Ideology (Minneapolis: University of Minnesota Press, 1996)

De Quincey, Thomas, *Recollections of the Lakes and the Lake Poets* (Harmondsworth: Penguin, 1970)

The Works of Thomas De Quincey, Pickering Masters, 21 vols. (London and Brookfield, VT: Pickering and Chatto, 2000–3)

De Vries, Hent, *Philosophy and the Turn to Religion* (Baltimore: Johns Hopkins University Press, 1999)

Deleuze, Gilles, and Félix Guattari, *Kafka: Toward a Minor Literature* (Minneapolis: University of Minnesota Press, 1986)

Derrida, Jacques, 'Des Tours de Babel', in Joseph F. Graham, ed., *Difference in Translation* (Ithaca and London: Cornell University Press, 1985), pp. 165–207

'Letter to a Japanese Friend', in David Wood and Robert Bernasconi, eds., *Derrida & Differance* (Coventry: Parousia Press, 1985), pp. 1–8

'Envois', trans. Alan Bass, in *The Postcard: From Socrates to Freud and Beyond* (Chicago and London: University of Chicago Press, 1987), pp. 1–256

Limited Inc (Evanston, IL: Northwestern University Press, 1988)

Specters of Marx: The State of the Debt, the Work of Mourning, and the New International, trans. Peggy Kamuf (New York and London: Routledge, 1994)

Archive Fever: A Freudian Impression, trans. Eric Prenowitz (Chicago and London: University of Chicago Press, 1996)

Devlin, D. D., *De Quincey, Wordsworth and the Art of Prose* (London and Basingstoke: Macmillan, 1983)

Dickinson, Emily, *The Poems of Emily Dickinson*, ed. R. W. Franklin (Cambridge, MA: Belknap Press of Harvard University Press, 1999)

Dickson, Gwen Griffith, *Johann Georg Hamann's Relational Metacriticism* (Berlin and New York: de Gruyter, 1995)

Dowd, Garin W., '"Connect-I-Cut": George Oppen's *Discrete Series* and a Parenthesis by Jacques Derrida', *Angelaki*, 5.1 (2000), 123–8

Drewitt, Thomas [attributed], *The Force of Contrast: or Quotations, Accompanied by Remarks* (Bath: Hazard, 1801)

Easson, Angus, *The Lapidary Wordsworth: Epitaphs and Inscriptions* (Winchester: King Alfred's College, 1981)

Ebrecht, Angelika, Regina Nörtemann, and Herta Schwarz, eds., *Brieftheorie des 18. Jahrhunderts: Texte, Kommentare, Essays* (Stuttgart: Metzler, 1990)

Eco, Umberto, *The Search for the Perfect Language*, trans. James Fentress (Oxford: Blackwell, 1995)

Serendipities: Language and Lunacy, Italian Academy Lectures (New York: Columbia University Press, 1998)

Ehrmann, Jacques, 'The Death of Literature', *New Literary History*, 3.1 (1971), 31–47

Eliot, T. S., 'Shelley and Keats', in *The Use of Poetry and the Use of Criticism*, 2nd edn (London: Faber and Faber, 1949), pp. 87–102

Ellicot, John, 'Letter from Madrid, to the Spanish Consul, residing in London. Translated from the Spanish. Communicated by Mr. John Ellicot, F.R.S.', *Philosophical Transactions of the Royal Society of London*, 49 (1755), 423–4

Elmer, Jonathan, and others, eds., *Trauma and Psychoanalysis: Special Issue of Diacritics*, 28.4 (1998)

Emerson, Ralph Waldo, 'Quotation and Originality', in *Emerson's Complete Works*, 12 vols. (Boston and New York: Houghton Mifflin, 1892–4), vol. 8, pp. 169–94

Eybl, Franz, H. Heppner, and F. Kernbauer, eds., *Elementare Gewalt, Kulturelle Bewältigung: Aspekte der Naturkatastrophe im 18. Jahrhundert* (Vienna: WUV Universitätsverlag, 2000)

Faflak, Joel, 'De Quincey Collects Himself', in Joel Faflak and Julia M. Wright, eds., *Victorian Recollections of Romanticism*, (Albany: State University of New York Press, 2004), pp. 23–46

Fenves, Peter, 'The Genesis of Judgment: Spatiality, Analogy, and Metaphor in Benjamin's "On Language as Such and on Human Language"', in David Ferris, ed., *Walter Benjamin: Theoretical Questions* (Stanford: Stanford University Press, 1996), pp. 75–93

Ferguson, Frances, *Wordsworth: Language as Counter-Spirit* (New Haven and London: Yale University Press, 1977)

'Interpreting the Self through Letters', *Centrum*, 1.2 (1981), 107–12

'The Unfamiliarity of Familiar Letters', in Christopher Ricks, ed., *The State of the Language* (Berkeley, Los Angeles, and London: University of California Press, 1990), pp. 78–88

Solitude and the Sublime: Romanticism and the Aesthetics of Individuation (New York and London: Routledge, 1992)

'Romantic Memory', in Helen Regueiro Elam and Frances Ferguson, eds., *The Wordsworthian Enlightenment: Romantic Poetry and the Ecology of Reading* (Baltimore: Johns Hopkins University Press, 2005), pp. 71–93

Fletcher, Justus, 'Anbrüche: Vorgeschichte und Programm der Fragmentpoetik', in Eckhart Goebel and Martin von Koppenfels, eds., *Die Endlichkeit der Literatur* (Bonn: Akademi, 2002), pp. 62–84

Fosso, Kurt, 'Community and Mourning in William Wordsworth's *The Ruined Cottage*, 1797–1798', *Studies in Philology*, 92.3 (1995), 329–45

Foucault, Michel, *The Order of Things: An Archeology of the Human Sciences* (London: Tavistock, 1971)

Francillon, F., *An Essay on Punctuation, with Incidental Remarks on Composition* (London, 1842)

Freundlieb, Dieter, 'Dekonstruktivismus als interpretatorische Zwangsjacke. Paul de Mans (Fehl)Lektüre von Walter Benjamin', *Orbis Litterarum*, 54.2 (1999), 100–33

Frye, Northrop, *Collected Works of Northrop Frye*, ed. Robert D. Denham (Toronto and Buffalo: University of Toronto Press, 1996)

Fulford, Tim, 'De Quincey's Literature of Power', *The Wordsworth Circle*, 31.3 (2000), 158–64

Fürnkäs, Josef, 'Zitat und Zerstörung: Karl Kraus und Walter Benjamin', in Jacques Le Rider and Gérard Raulet, eds., *Verabschiedung der (Post-) Moderne? Eine interdisziplinäre Debatte* (Tübingen: Gunther Narr, 1987), pp. 209–26

Gadamer, Hans-Georg, *Wahrheit und Methode: Grundzüge einer philosophischen Hermeneutik*, 4th edn (Tübingen: Mohr, 1975)

Garber, Marjorie, *Quotation Marks* (New York and London: Routledge, 2003)

García-Düttman, Alexander, *The Gift of Language: Memory and Promise in Adorno, Benjamin, Heidegger, and Rosenzweig*, trans. Arline Lyons (London: Athlone, 2000)

Gasché, Rodolphe, *The Wild Card of Reading: On Paul de Man* (Cambridge, MA, and London: Harvard University Press, 1998)

Gibs, Sylwia, 'Les fonctions de la parenthèse dans *Nadja* d'André Breton', in Yves Gohin and Robert Ricatte, eds., *Recherches en sciences des textes* (Grenoble: Presses Universitaires de Grenoble, 1977), pp. 181–8

Gittings, Robert, *John Keats* (London: Heinemann, 1968)

Goethe, Johann Wolfgang von, *Werke, Hamburger Ausgabe*, 9th rev. edn, 14 vols. (Munich: Beck, 1981)

   From My Life: Poetry and Truth, trans. Eithne Wilkins and Ernst Kaiser (Princeton: Princeton University Press, 1994)

Graef, Ortwin de, *Serenity in Crisis: A Preface to Paul de Man, 1939–1960* (Lincoln, NE, and London: University of Nebraska Press, 1993)

Grant, Iain Hamilton, 'Kant after Geophilosophy: The Physics of Analogy and the Metaphysics of Nature', in Andrea Rehberg and Rachel Jones, eds., *The Matter of Critique: Readings in Kant's Philosophy* (Manchester: Clinamen, 2000), pp. 37–60

Graubner, Hans, 'Zum Problem des Anthropomorphismus in der Theologie (Hume, Kant, Hamann)', in Bernhard Gajek, ed., *Johan Georg Hamann und England, Hamann und die englischsprachige Aufklärung: Acta des siebten internationalen Hamann-Kolloquium zu Marburg/Lahn 1996* (Frankfurt am Main: Lang, 1999), pp. 381–95

Gray, Martin, *A Dictionary of Literary Terms*, 2nd rev. edn (Harlow: Longman, 1992)

Grossman, Jeffrey, 'The Reception of Walter Benjamin in the Anglo-American Literary Institution', *German Quarterly*, 65.3–4 (1992), 414–28

Gugler, Ilse, *Das Problem der fragmentarischen Dichtung in der englischen Romantik* (Berne: A. Francke, 1944)

Guillory, John, *Cultural Capital: The Problem of Literary Canon Formation* (Chicago and London: University of Chicago Press, 1993)

Günther, Horst, *Das Erdbeben von Lissabon erschüttert die Meinungen und setzt das Denken in Bewegung* (Berlin: Wagenbach, 1994)

   Das Erdbeben von Lissabon und die Erschütterung des aufgeklärten Europa (Frankfurt am Main: Fischer, 2005)

Habermas, Jürgen, *Strukturwandel der Öffentlichkeit: Untersuchungen zu einer Kategorie der bürgerlichen Gesellschaft* (Frankfurt am Main: Suhrkamp, 1962)

Hallifax, James, *A sermon preach'd in St. John's chapel in the parish of St. Andrew, Holborn, on Sunday February 8, 1756. being the Sunday after the day appointed by proclamation for a general fast and humiliation, on account of the dreadful earthquake at Lisbon* (London, 1756)

Hamann, Johann Georg, *Sämtliche Werke*, 6 vols. (Vienna: Thomas Morus Presse im Verlag Herder, 1949–57)

    Writings on Philosophy and Language, trans. Kenneth Haynes (Cambridge: Cambridge University Press, 2007)

Hamblyn, Richard, 'Notes from the Underground: Lisbon after the Earthquake', *Romanticism*, 14.2 (2008), 108–18

Hamilton, Paul, *Metaromanticism: Aesthetics, Literature, Theory* (Chicago: University of Chicago Press, 2003)

Harries, Elizabeth, *The Unfinished Manner: Essays on the Fragment in the Later Eighteenth Century* (Charlottesville: University Press of Virginia, 1994)

Harris, James, *Hermes: or, a Philosophical Inquiry Concerning Language and Universal Grammar* (London, 1751)

Hartman, Geoffrey, *Wordsworth's Poetry, 1787–1814* (New Haven and London: Yale University Press, 1964)

    Beyond Formalism: Literary Essays 1958–1970 (New Haven and London: Yale University Press, 1970)

    The Unremarkable Wordsworth (London: Methuen, 1987)

    Scars of the Spirit: The Struggle against Inauthenticity (New York and Basingstoke: Palgrave, 2002)

Hausdörfer, Sabrina, 'Die Sprache ist Delphi: Sprachursprungstheorie, Geschichtsphilosophie und Sprach-Utopie bei Novalis, Friedrich Schlegel und Hölderlin', in Joachim Gessinger and Wolfert von Rahden, eds., *Theorien vom Ursprung der Sprache*, vol. 1 (Berlin and New York: De Gruyter, 1989), pp. 468–97

Herder, Johann Gottfried, *Abhandlung über den Ursprung der Sprache*, ed. Wolfgang Pross (Munich and Vienna: Hanser, 1978)

Hertz, Neil, *The End of the Line: Essays on Psychoanalysis and the Sublime* (New York: Columbia University Press, 1985)

Hörisch, Jochen, *Kopf oder Zahl: Die Poesie des Geldes* (Frankfurt am Main: Suhrkamp, 1996)

Humboldt, Wilhelm von, *Werke in fünf Bänden*, ed. Andreas Flitner, Klaus Giel, Ulrich Herrmann, Philip Mattson, Rose Unterberger, et al., 5 vols. (Stuttgart: Cotta, 1963)

Hume, David, *Dialogues concerning Natural Religion* (Oxford and New York: Oxford University Press, 1993)

Irving, William Henry, *The Providence of Wit in English Letter Writers* (Durham, NC: Duke University Press, 1955)

Jacobs, Carol, 'The Monstrosity of Translation', *Modern Language Notes*, 90.6 (1975), 755–66

    Skirting the Ethical (Stanford: Stanford University Press, 2008)

Jacobus, Mary, 'The Art of Managing Books: Romantic Prose and the Writing of the Past', in Arden Reed, ed., *Romanticism and Language* (London: Methuen, 1984), pp. 215–46

    Romanticism, Writing and Sexual Difference: Essays on 'The Prelude' (Oxford: Clarendon Press, 1989)

'Composing Sound: The Deaf Dalesman, "The Brothers", and Epitaphic Signs', in Alexander Regier and Stefan H. Uhlig, eds., *Wordsworth's Poetic Theory* (Basingstoke: Palgrave Macmillan, 2010)

Janowitz, Anne, 'Coleridge's 1816 Volume: Fragment as Rubric', *Studies in Romanticism*, 24.1 (1985), 21–39

England's Ruins: Poetic Purpose and the National Landscape (Oxford: Blackwell, 1990)

Jarvis, Simon, 'Wordsworth's Gift of Feeling', *Romanticism*, 4.1 (1998), 90–103

'Problems in the Phenomenology of the Gift', *Angelaki*, 6.2 (2001), 67–78

Wordsworth's Philosophic Song (Cambridge: Cambridge University Press, 2007)

Johnson, Barbara, 'Anthropomorphism in Lyric and Law', in Tom Cohen and others, eds., *Material Events* (Minneapolis and London: University of Minnesota Press, 2001), pp. 205–28

Jordan, John E., *De Quincey to Wordsworth: A Biography of a Relationship* (Berkeley and Los Angeles: University of California Press, 1962)

Kames, Lord (Henry Home), *Elements of Criticism*, 3rd edn, 2 vols. (London and Edinburgh, 1765)

Kant, Immanuel, *Immanuel Kants Werke*, ed. Ernst Cassirer, Hermann Cohen, Artur Buchenau, Otto Buek, et al., 11 vols. (Hildesheim: Gerstenberg, 1973)

Critique of Judgment, trans. Werner S. Pluhar (Indianapolis: Hackett, 1987)

Critique of the Power of Judgment, trans. Paul Guyer and Eric Matthews (Cambridge: Cambridge University Press, 2000)

Keach, William, *Arbitrary Power: Romanticism, Language, Politics* (Princeton: Princeton University Press, 2004)

Keats, John, *The Letters of John Keats*, ed. Hyder Edward Rollins, 2 vols. (Cambridge: Cambridge University Press, 1958)

The Poems of John Keats, ed. Jack Stillinger (London: Heinemann, 1978)

A Critical Edition of the Major Works, ed. Elizabeth Cook (Oxford and New York: Oxford University Press, 1990)

Kendrick, T. D., *The Lisbon Earthquake* (London: Methuen, 1956)

Kittler, Friedrich A., and Horst Turk, eds., *Urszenen: Literaturwissenschaft als Diskursanalyse und Diskurskritik* (Frankfurt am Main: Suhrkamp, 1977)

Kleist, Heinrich von, *Das Erdbeben in Chili*, in *Sämtliche Werke,* Brandenburger Ausgabe, vol. 2.3 (Basel and Frankfurt am Main: Stroemfeld Verlag, 1993)

Koselleck, Reinhart, *Historische Semantik und Begriffsgeschichte* (Stuttgart: Klett-Cotta, 1979), in F. Eybl, H. Heppner, and A. Kernbauer, eds., *Elementare Gewalt Kulturelle Bewältigung: Aspekte der Naturkatastrophe im 18. Jahrhundert*, (Vienna: WUV Universitätsverlag, 2000), pp. 185–95

Kozák, Jan T., Victor S. Moreira, and David R. Oldroyd, *Iconography of the 1755 Lisbon Earthquake* (Prague: Geophysical Institute of the Academy of Sciences of the Czech Republic, 2005)

LaCapra, Dominick, *Representing the Holocaust: History, Theory, Trauma* (Ithaca and London: Cornell University Press, 1994)

Laclau, Ernesto, and Chantal Mouffe, *Hegemony and Socialist Strategy: Towards a Radical Democratic Politics*, 2nd edn (London and New York: Verso, 2001)

Lacoue-Labarthe, Philippe, and Jean-Luc Nancy, *The Literary Absolute: The Theory of Literature in German Romanticism* (Albany: State University of New York Press, 1988)

Lahr, Oonagh, 'Greek Sources of "Writ in Water"', *Keats–Shelley Journal*, 21–2 (1972), 17–18

Larkin, Peter, 'Relations of Scarcity: Ecology and Eschatology in *The Ruined Cottage*', *Studies in Romanticism*, 39.3 (2000), 347–64

Latham, J., 'Letter from Mr. J. Latham, dated at Zsusqueira, Dec. 11, 1755, to his Uncle in London. Communicated by Peter Daval, Esq; Secret. R.S.', *Philosophical Transactions of the Royal Society of London*, 49 (1755), 411–13

Lausberg, Heinrich, *Handbuch der literarischen Rhetorik: Eine Grundlegung der Literaturwissenschaft* (Munich: Max Hueber, 1960)

Leask, Nigel, *British Romantic Writers and the East: Anxieties of Empire* (Cambridge and New York: Cambridge University Press, 1992)

Lennard, John, *But I Digress: The Exploitation of Parentheses in English Printed Verse* (Oxford: Clarendon Press, 1991)

Levinson, Marjorie, *The Romantic Fragment Poem: A Critique of Form* (Chapel Hill: University of North Carolina Press, 1986)

    Wordsworth's Great Period Poems: Four Essays (Cambridge: Cambridge University Press, 1986)

    ed., *Rethinking Historicism: Critical Readings in Romantic History* (Oxford: Blackwell, 1989)

    'A Motion and a Spirit: Romancing Spinoza', *Studies in Romanticism*, 46.4 (2007), 367–408

Lindop, Grevel, 'De Quincey's Wordsworthian Quotations', *The Wordsworth Circle*, 26.2 (1995), 58–65

Liu, Alan, *Wordsworth: The Sense of History* (Stanford: Stanford University Press, 1989)

Löffler, Ulrich, *Lissabons Fall–Europas Schrecken: Die Deutung des Erdbebens von Lissabon im deutschsprachigen Protestantismus des 18. Jahrhunderts* (Berlin and New York: De Gruyter, 1999)

Lynch, Thomas Toke, *The Ethics of Quotation, with a Preliminary Letter to the Secretaries of the Congregational Union* (London: William Freeman, 1856)

Lyotard, Jean-François, *Lessons on the Analytic of the Sublime*, trans. Elizabeth Rottenberg (Stanford: Stanford University Press, 1994)

Mann, Thomas, *Der Zauberberg*, in *Gesammelte Werke*, vol. 3 (Frankfurt am Main: Fischer, 1960)

Manning, Peter J., 'Reading Wordsworth's Revisions: Othello and the Drowned Man', *Studies in Romanticism*, 22.1 (1983), 3–28

Marx, Karl, and Friedrich Engels, *Collected Works*, vol. 40 (*Marx and Engels: 1856–59*) (London: Lawrence and Wishart, 1983)

    Karl Marx–Friedrich Engels Gesamtausgabe (MEGA), vol. 3.9 (Amsterdam: Akademie, 2003)

Mauss, Marcel, *The Gift: The Form of Reason for Exchange in Archaic Societies*, trans. W. D. Halls (London: Routledge, 1990)

Mayhead, Robin, 'The Letters', in *John Keats* (Cambridge: Cambridge University Press, 1967), pp. 112–26

McDonagh, Josephine, *De Quincey's Disciplines* (Oxford: Clarendon, 1994)

McFarland, Thomas, *Romanticism and the Forms of Ruin: Wordsworth, Coleridge and the Modalities of Fragmentation* (Princeton: Princeton University Press, 1981)

McGann, Jerome J., *The Romantic Ideology: A Critical Investigation* (Chicago: University of Chicago Press, 1983)

Menninghaus, Winfried, *Walter Benjamins Theorie der Sprachmagie* (Frankfurt am Main: Suhrkamp, 1980)

    Unendliche Verdopplung: Die frühromantische Grundlegung der Kunsttheorie im Begriff absoluter Selbstreflexion (Frankfurt am Main: Suhrkamp, 1987)

Miller, J. Hillis, *The Disappearance of God: Five Nineteenth-Century Writers* (Cambridge, MA: Belknap Press of Harvard University Press, 1963)

Milner, John D. D., *Ruin prevented by repentance, applied to civil societies. In two discourses delivered at Peckham in Surrey. On the general fast, February 6, 1756. Occasioned by the late dreadful earthquake at Lisbon, and the apprehension of nearer threatning calamities. – – With two hymns* (London, 1756)

Milnes, Richard Monckton, ed., *Life, Letters and Literary Remains of John Keats*, 2 vols. (London: Edward Moxon, 1848)

Milton, John, *Poetical Works* (Oxford and New York: Oxford University Press, 1992)

Monboddo, Lord (James Burnet), *Of the Origin and Progress of Language*, 6 vols. (Edinburgh, 1773–92)

Mondot, Jean, ed., *Lisbonne 1755: Un tremblement de terre et de ciel* (Bordeaux: Presses Universitaires de Bordeaux, 2005)

Morehead, Robert, *Explanations of Some Passages in the Epistles of St. Paul, Chiefly by Means of an Amended Punctuation* (Edinburgh, 1843)

Mortensen, Klaus P., *The Time of Unrememberable Being: Wordsworth and the Sublime, 1787–1805* (Copenhagen: Museum Tusculanum Press, 1998)

Nancy, Jean-Luc, *The Birth to Presence* (Stanford: Stanford University Press, 1993)

Neiman, Susan, *Evil in Modern Thought: An Alternative History of Philosophy* (Princeton: Princeton University Press, 2002)

Nietzsche, Friedrich, *Kritische Gesamtausgabe*, vol. 8.3 (Berlin and New York: de Gruyter, 1972)

Norton, Robert E., *Herder's Aesthetic and the European Enlightenment* (Ithaca: Cornell University Press, 1991)

Nozes, Judite, ed., *The Lisbon Earthquake of 1755: British Accounts* (Lisbon: British Historical Society of Portugal and Lisóptima, 1990)

Oeser, Erhard, 'Das Erdbeben von Lissabon im Spiegel der zeitgenössischen Philosophie', in F. Eybl, H. Heppner, and A. Kernbauer, eds., *Elementare Gewalt, Kulturelle Bewältigung: Aspekte der Naturkatastrophe im 18. Jahrhundert* (Vienna: WUV Universitätsverlag, 2000), pp. 185–95

Owen, W. J. B., 'The Perfect Image of a Mighty Mind', *The Wordsworth Circle*, 10.1 (1979), 3–16

Parker, Gabrielle, 'Michèle Perrein: The Parenthesis as Metaphor for the Female Condition', in Margaret Atack and Phil Powrie, eds., *Contemporary French Fiction by Women: Feminist Perspectives* (Manchester and New York: Manchester University Press, 1990), pp. 116–25

Parkes, M. B., *Pause and Effect: An Introduction to the History of Punctuation in the West* (Berkeley: University of California Press, 1993)

Parry, Jonathan, '*The Gift*, the Indian Gift and the "Indian Gift"', *Man*, 21.3 (1985), 453–73

Peck, Linda Levy, *Court Patronage and Corruption in Early Stuart England* (London: Unwin Hyman, 1990)

Pereira, Anthony, *A Narrative of the Earthquake and Fire of Lisbon of the Congregation of the Oratory, an Eyewitness thereof. Translated from the Latin* (London, 1756)

Perlina, Nina, *Varieties of Poetic Utterance: Quotation in 'The Brothers Karamazov'* (Lanham, MD: University Press of America, 1985)

Perry, 'An Account of the Earthquake felt in the Island of Sumatra, in the East-Indies, in November and December 1756. In a Letter from Mr. Perry to the Rev. Dr. Stukeley, dated at Fort Malborough, in the Island of Sumatra, Feb 20. 1757. Communicated by the Rev. Wm. Stukeley, M.D. F.R.S.', *Philosophical Transactions of the Royal Society of London*, 50 (1758), 491–2

Pétillon-Boucheron, Sabine, *Les détours de la langue: Etude sur la parenthèse et le tiret double* (Louvain and Dudley, MA: Éditions Peeters, 2002)

Poulet, Georges, *Études sur le temps humain*, 4 vols. (Edinburgh: Edinburgh University Press, 1949–68)

Preminger, Alex, and T. V. F. Brogan, eds., *The New Princeton Encyclopedia of Poetry and Poetics* (Princeton: Princeton University Press, 1993)

Pryor, Felix, ed., *The Faber Book of Letters* (London: Faber and Faber, 1988)

Quenet, Grégory, *Les tremblements de terre aux XVIIe et XVIIIe siècles: La naissance d'un risque* (Seyssel: Champ Vallon, 2005)

Rauber, D. F., 'The Fragment as Romantic Form', *Modern Language Quarterly*, 30 (1969), 212–21

Rauter, Herbert, *Die Sprachauffassung der englischen Frühromantik in ihrer Bedeutung für die Literaturkritik und Dichtungstheorie der Zeit* (Bad Homburg, Berlin, and Zurich: Gehlen, 1970)

Ray, Gene, 'Reading the Lisbon Earthquake: Adorno, Lyotard, and the Contemporary Sublime', *Yale Journal of Criticism*, 17.1 (2004), 1–18

    Terror and the Sublime in Art and Critical Theory: From Auschwitz to Hiroshima to September 11 (New York: Palgrave Macmillan, 2005)

Redfield, Marc, *Phantom Formations: Aesthetic Ideology and the Bildungsroman* (Ithaca: Cornell University Press, 1996)

Reflections physical and moral, upon the various and numerous uncommon phenomena in the air, water, or earth, which have happened from the earthquake at Lima, to the present time: In a series of familiar letters from a Member of Parliament in town to his friend in the country (London, 1756)

Ritter, Johann Wilhelm, *Fragmente aus dem Nachlasse eines jungen Physikers: Ein Taschenbuch für Freunde der Natur* (Leipzig and Weimar: Kiepenheuer, 1984)

Robertson, Revd Joseph A. M., *An Essay on Punctuation* (London, 1785)

Roe, Nicholas, ed., *Keats and History* (Cambridge: Cambridge University Press, 1995)

  John Keats and the Culture of Dissent (Oxford: Clarendon Press, 1997)

Rolleston, James L., 'The Politics of Quotation: Walter Benjamin's Arcades Project', *PMLA*, 104.1 (1984), 13–27

Rollins, Hyder Edward, ed., *The Keats Circle*, 2 vols. (Cambridge, MA: Harvard University Press, 1965)

Rothenberg, David, and Marta Ulvaeus, ed., *Writing on Water* (Cambridge, MA: MIT Press, 2001)

Rousseau, Jean-Jacques, 'Letter from Rousseau to Voltaire', trans. Roger Masters Judith Bush, Christopher Kelly, and Terence Marshall, in *The Collected Writings of Rousseau*, ed., Roger Masters and Christopher Kelly, 13 vols. (Hanover, NH and London: University Press of New England, 1990–), vol. 3 (1992), pp. 108–21

  'Essay on the Origin of Languages', trans. John T. Scott, in *Essay on the Origin of Languages and Writings related to Music, The Collected Writings of Rousseau*, ed., Roger Masters and Christopher Kelly, 13 vols. (Hanover, NH, and London: University Press of New England, 1990–), vol. 7 (1998), pp. 289–332

Royal Society, *Philosophical Transactions being an Appendix to those for the year 1750: Consisting of several Papers laid before the Royal Society, concerning several Earthquakes felt in England and some neighbouring countries in the year 1750* (London: The Royal Society, 1750)

Runge, Anita, and Lieselotte Steinbrügge, eds., *Die Frau im Dialog: Studien zur Theorie des Briefes* (Stuttgart: Metzler, 1991)

Russell, Bertrand, *A History of Western Philosophy* (New York: Simon and Schuster, 1945)

Russett, Margaret, *De Quincey's Romanticism: Canonical Minority and the Forms of Transmission* (Cambridge: Cambridge University Press, 1997)

Rzepka, Charles J., *Sacramental Commodities: Gift, Text, and the Sublime in De Quincey* (Amherst: University of Massachusetts Press, 1995)

  'Wordsworth between God and Mammon: The Early "Spots of Time" and the Sublime as Sacramental Commodity', in J. Robert Barth, ed., *The Fountain Light: Studies in Romanticism and Religion in Honor of John L. Mahoney* (New York: Fordham University Press, 2002), pp. 73–89

Saccheti, John Mendes, 'A Copy of Part of Two Letters, written by John Mendes Saccheti, M.D.F.R.S. to Dr. DeCastro, F.R.S. dated from the Fields of Lisbon, on the 7th of November, and the 1st of December, 1755', *Philosophical Transactions of the Royal Society of London*, 49 (1755), 409–11

Schlegel, A. W., *Vorlesungen über schöne Litteratur und Kunst* (Heilbronn: Henninger, 1884)

Schlegel, Friedrich von, *Kritische Friedrich-Schlegel-Ausgabe*, ed. Ernst Behler and others, 35 vols. (Paderborn, Munich, and Vienna: Schöningh, 1958–)

Schmidt, Andreas, *'Wolken krachen, Berge zittern, und die ganze Erde weint': Zur kulturellen Vermittlung von Naturkatastrophen in Deutschland 1755 bis 1855* (Münster: Waxmann, 1999)

Schmidt, Burghart, *Postmoderne – Strategien des Vergessens: Ein kritischer Bericht*, 4th edn (Frankfurt am Main: Suhrkamp, 1994)

Scholem, Gershom, *Zur Aktualität Walter Benjamins* (Frankfurt am Main: Suhrkamp, 1972)

Schwyzer, Eduard, *Die Parenthese im engeren und weiteren Sinne* (Berlin: Verlag der Akademie der Wissenschaften, 1939)

Seaford, Richard, *Money and the Early Greek Mind: Homer, Philosophy, Tragedy* (Cambridge: Cambridge University Press, 2004)

Severn, Joseph, *Joseph Severn: Letters and Memoirs*, ed. Grant F. Scott (Aldershot: Ashgate, 2005)

Shell, Marc, *The Economy of Literature* (Baltimore: Johns Hopkins University Press, 1978)

    Money, Language and Thought: Literary and Philosophical Economies from the Medieval to the Modern Era (Berkeley and London: University of California Press, 1982)

Siegert, Bernhard, *Relais: Geschichte der Literatur als Epoche der Post 1751–1913* (Berlin: Brinkmann and Bose, 1993)

Simpson, David, *Irony and Authority in Romantic Poetry* (London and Basingstoke: Macmillan, 1979)

    Romanticism, Nationalism, and the Revolt against Theory (Chicago: University of Chicago Press, 1993)

Siskin, Clifford, *The Historicity of Romantic Discourse* (New York: Oxford University Press, 1988)

    The Work of Writing: Literature and Change in Britain, 1700–1830 (Baltimore and London: Johns Hopkins University Press, 1998)

Sloane, Thomas O., ed., *Encyclopaedia of Rhetoric* (Oxford: Oxford University Press, 2001)

Smallfield, George, *The Principles of English Punctuation, Preceded by Brief Explanations of the Parts of Speech* (London, 1838)

Smyser, Jane Worthington, 'Wordsworth's Dream of Poetry and Science: "The Prelude", v', *PMLA*, 71.1 (1956), 269–75

Stam, James H., *Inquiries into the Origin of Language: The Fate of a Question* (New York: Harper and Row, 1976)

Stelzig, Eugene, 'Wordsworth's Bleeding Spots: Traumatic Memories of the Absent Father in "The Prelude"', *European Romantic Review*, 15.4 (2004), 533–45

Stevenson, S., 'Poetry Deleted, Parody Added, Watergate, Spark Style, and Bakhtin Stylistics', *Ariel*, 24.4 (1993), 71–85

Terada, Rei, *Feeling in Theory: Emotion after the 'Death of the Subject'* (Cambridge, MA: Harvard University Press, 2001)

'Seeing Is Reading', in Marc Redfield, ed., *Legacies of Paul de Man* (New York: Fandham University Press, 2007), pp. 162–77

Thomas, Jean-Jacques, 'Dada ne signifie rien, fermez la parenthèse', *L'Ésprit Créateur*, 20.2 (1980), 5–11

Thomas, Sophie, *Romanticism and Visuality: Fragments, History, Spectacle* (New York and London: Routledge, 2008)

Todd, Janet, *Mary Wollstonecraft: A Revolutionary Life* (London: Weidenfeld and Nicolson, 2000)

Tooke, John Horne, *Diversions of Purley*, reprint of 1829 edn, 2 vols. (London and Tokyo: Thoemmes Press Routledge, 1993)

Turley, Richard Marggraf, *The Politics of Language in Romantic Literature* (Basingstoke and New York: Palgrave Macmillan, 2002)

Turner, John, 'Wordsworth and the Psychogenesis of the Sublime', *Romanticism*, 6.1 (2000), 20–34

Ueding, Gert, and others, *Historisches Wörterbuch der Rhetorik* (Tübingen: Max Niemeyer, 1992)

Ulmer, William A., 'Rousseau's *Émile* and Wordsworth's Drowned Man of Esthwaite', *English Language Notes*, 33.1 (1995), 15–19

   'Wordsworth, the One Life, and *The Ruined Cottage*', *Studies in Philology*, 93.3 (1996), 304–31

Voigts, Manfred, '"Die Mater der Gerechtigkeit": Zur Kritik des Zitat-Begriffes bei Walter Benjamin', in Norbert W. Bolz and Richard Faber, ed., *Antike und Moderne: Zu Walter Benjamins 'Passagen'* (Würzburg: Königshausen and Neumann, 1986), pp. 97–115

   'Zitat', in *Benjamins Begriffe*, ed. Michael Opitz and Erdmut Wizisla, vol. 2 (Frankfurt am Main: Suhrkamp, 2000), pp. 826–50

Voltaire, 'Poem on the Destruction of Lisbon', in *The Works of M. de Voltaire*, vol. 20 (Dublin: Moncrieffe, 1772), pp. 219–30

   Candide and Other Stories, trans. Joan Spencer (London: Oxford University Press, 1966)

Warburton, William, *The Divine Legation of Moses* (London, 1738)

Waters, Lindsay, and Wlad Godzich, eds., *Reading de Man Reading* (Minneapolis: University of Minnesota Press, 1989)

Webb, Timothy, '"Cutting Figures": Rhetorical Strategies in Keats's *Letters*', in Michael O'Neill, ed., *Keats: Bicentenary Readings* (Edinburgh: Edinburgh University Press, 1997), pp. 144–69

Weinrich, Harald, 'Literaturgeschichte eines Weltereignisses: Das Erdbeben von Lissabon', in *Literatur für Leser: Essays und Aufsätze zur Literaturwissenschaft* (Stuttgart: Kohlhammer, 1971), pp. 64–76

Weiskel, Thomas, *The Romantic Sublime: Studies in the Structure and Psychology of Transcendence* (Baltimore: Johns Hopkins University Press, 1976)

Wells, John E., 'De Quincey and "The Prelude" in 1839', *Philological Quarterly*, 20 (1941), 1–24

Westbrook, Deeane, *Wordsworth's Biblical Ghosts* (New York and Basingstoke: Palgrave, 2001)

Wetzel, Michael, 'Liebesgaben: Streifzüge des literarischen Eros', in Michael Wetzel and Jean-Michel Rabaté, eds., *Ethik der Gabe: Denken nach Jacques Derrida* (Berlin: Akademie, 1993), pp. 223–47

Wheeler, Kathleen M., *Romanticism, Pragmatism, and Deconstruction* (Oxford: Blackwell, 1993)

Williams, Robert Grant, 'Reading the Parenthesis', *Substance*, 22.1 (1993), 53–66

Wolfson, Susan J., 'Keats the Letter-Writer: Epistolary Poetics', *Romanticism Past and Present*, 6.2 (1982), 43–61

    'The Illusion of Mastery: Wordsworth's Revisions of "The Drowned Man of Esthwaite," 1799, 1805, 1850', *PMLA*, 99.5 (1984), 917–35

    'Keats Enters History: Autopsy, *Adonais* and the Fame of Keats', in Nicholas Roe, ed., *Keats and History* (Cambridge and New York: Cambridge University Press, 1995), pp. 17–45

Wollstonecraft, Mary, *The Works of Mary Wollstonecraft*, ed. Janet Todd and Marilyn Butler, vol. 1 (London: William Pickering, 1989)

Wordsworth, Jonathan, *The Music of Humanity: A Critical Study of Wordsworth's 'Ruined Cottage', Incorporating Texts from a Manuscript of 1799–1800* (London: Nelson, 1969)

    'The Climbing of Snowdon', in Jonathan Wordsworth, ed., *Bicentenary Wordsworth Studies: In Memory of John Alban Finch* (Ithaca and London: Cornell University Press, 1970), pp. 449–74

Wordsworth, William, *Poems in Two Volumes* (London, 1807)

    The Prose Works of William Wordsworth, ed. W. J. B. Owen and Jane Worthington Smyser, 3 vols. (Oxford: Clarendon, 1974)

    The Prelude, 1798–1799, ed. Stephen Parrish (Ithaca: Cornell University Press, 1977)

    'The Ruined Cottage' and 'The Pedlar', ed. James Butler (Ithaca: Cornell University Press, 1979)

    'Poems, in Two Volumes', and Other Poems, 1800–1807, ed. Jared Curtis (Ithaca: Cornell University Press, 1983)

    The Manuscript of William Wordsworth's 'Poems, in Two Volumes', ed. W. H. Kelliher (London: British Library, 1984)

    The Fourteen-Book 'Prelude', ed. W. J. B. Owen (Ithaca: Cornell University Press, 1985)

    Shorter Poems, 1807–1820, ed. Carl H. Ketcham (Ithaca: Cornell University Press, 1989)

    The Thirteen-Book 'Prelude', ed. Mark L. Reed, 2 vols. (Ithaca: Cornell University Press, 1991)

    'Lyrical Ballads', and Other Poems, 1797–1800, ed. James Butler and Karen Green (Ithaca: Cornell University Press, 1992)

    The Five-Book Prelude, ed. Duncan Wu (Oxford and Malden, MA: Blackwell, 1997)

    Sonnet Series and Itinerary Poems, 1820–1845, ed. Geoffrey Jackson (Ithaca: Cornell University Press, 2004)

Wordsworth, William, and Dorothy Wordsworth, *The Letters of William and Dorothy Wordsworth*, ed. Ernest De Selincourt, and others, 2nd edn, 8 vols. (Oxford: Clarendon Press, 1967–93)

The Excursion, ed. Sally Bushell, James A. Butler, and Michael C. Jaye, with the assistance of David García (Ithaca: Cornell University Press, 2007)

Index

CAMBRIDGE STUDIES IN ROMANTICISM

General Editor
JAMES CHANDLER, *University of Chicago*